A **WESTERN HORSEMAN** BOOK

Ranch Horsemanship

*Traditional Cowboy Methods
for the Recreational Rider*

By Curt Pate
With Fran Devereux Smith

Photographs by Fran Devereux Smith

Illustrations by Ron Bonge

Ranch Horsemanship

Published by
WESTERN HORSEMAN® magazine
3850 North Nevada Ave.
Box 7980
Colorado Springs, CO 80933-7980

www.westernhorseman.com

Design, Typography, and Production
Western Horseman
Fort Worth, Texas

Cover photography by
Guy de Galard

Back cover photography by
Fran Devereux Smith

Printing
Branch Smith
Fort Worth, Texas

©*2004 by Western Horseman*
a registered trademark of
Morris Communications Corporation
725 Broad Street
Augusta, GA 30901

Second Printing: December 2004

ISBN 0-911647-65-1

DEDICATION

To my grandfathers, Ed Pate and Leonard Frank. I wish they were still here so I could learn some more from them.

ACKNOWLEDGEMENTS

I'd like to thank my wife, Tammy, for all the sacrifices she's made while I've pursued my cowboy lifestyle. To my children, Rial and Mesa, thanks for all the good miles on the backs of horses and going down the road with me. To all the horses I've ridden, good and bad, thanks for the lessons. To all my cowboy friends, thanks for sharing your skills and knowledge and to Buck Brannaman, thanks for helping me get things rolling. A special thank you to Sven Forsgren for making me think and to Darrell Burnett for believing in me and calling the public's attention to my work. To *Western Horseman*, especially Butch Morgan, for the confidence he gave me when I was in way over my head, and Fran Smith for putting my thoughts on paper.

—Curt Pate

INTRODUCTION

Ranch horsemanship and Curt Pate seem an obvious pairing. Curt's presentations as an equine clinician reflect much of his ranch experience. In either situation he works safely to achieve his riding goals and, as a result, usually enjoys his day's ride.

"And that's what riding is all about," Curt says, "having fun and being safe and, of course, getting your job done if that's how you make your living."

Most people soon realize that if they don't feel safe horseback, riding isn't much fun, and that's usually a goal in taking up any sport. Consequently, these uneasy riders often make changes — selling one horse and buying another, seeking professional assistance or sometimes even dropping the sport altogether.

Ranch Horses

Those who want a safe, well-broke mount often look to the ranching industry. While on the job, cowboys generally ride ranch horses often and for long periods of time, in cattle pens and cross-country on varied terrain. Ranch horses learn to maneuver up steep hills, through timber and down slick creek banks. They become accustomed to rain slickers flapping against their sides, ropes swinging overhead and hobbles.

In short, ranch horses are broke to accept a variety of experiences in a matter-of-fact way, and a lot of miles and wet saddle blankets ensure their lessons are well-learned. It's no surprise that ranch horses have become increasingly popular with recreational riders.

If you're like many recreational riders, you might not have a real desire or the requisite time to participate in a world show or start a colt. Yet you probably still want to improve your horsemanship and your horse's performance. That's where *Ranch Horsemanship* and Curt Pate can help your riding program.

A Cowboy Kind of Life

Curt grew up in Helena, Mont., and his mentors were his two grandfathers, both horse traders. One, who worked in the feed-lots, was "really good at conditioning a horse and training him to run barrels well," Curt says.

The other, also a cattle trader, "had a good eye for buying horses and making money at it. He'd buy problem horses, and we'd try to fix their problems. That was really a great thing for me because I got to ride a lot of different horses."

Curt's mother and stepfather had a ranch and cared for cattle at a nearby feed-lot, and Curt's father was in the auction business, so Curt became familiar with many aspects of the livestock industry. Growing up, he day-worked at area ranches and rodeoed, where he met wife Tammy, a native Texan who grew up in Montana.

"As kids we won all-around titles together at a rodeo one time," Curt grins. "She was in the junior division and I was in the senior. We've been married 13 years now and have two children, Mesa and Rial."

Although Curt rode bareback broncs and bulls for a long time, his 6-foot-plus height isn't ideal for such events. Nonetheless, he became known for his ability to ride rank bucking horses.

He later attended Bob Tallman and Bob Feist's school for rodeo announcers and worked with his dad in the auction business. Both experiences, he says, helped him become a better clinician. "They taught me how to speak to an audience and to express myself more clearly."

In his early 20s, however, Curt realized that neither announcing rodeo action nor calling bids at a livestock auction was his heart's desire. Curt then began working for another ranch, building its cow herd and riding young horses for the public, which he thinks helped to improve his horsemanship as much as anything. He better learned how to evaluate his mounts, picking the right colt for a particular ranch job, so that he could complete his ranch work more efficiently and more effectively train a horse at the same time.

Eventually Curt and Tammy purchased a small place, where they could run their own cattle and train horses, and Curt began coaching other riders through problems with their horses.

PHOTO BY DAVID STOECKLEIN

The Pate family, left to right, Rial, Mesa, Tammy and Curt.

That's when friend and mentor Buck Brannaman asked Curt to join him as a technical adviser on the set of *The Horse Whisperer*. "I expected to learn great things there, being around Buck so much. But I learned that working horses isn't about great things — just the basics," Curt points out.

After completing the film, Curt returned home to care for his cattle and train horses. Shortly thereafter, he attended a stockman's meeting with his father. There the director of the Midwest Horse Fair in Madison, Wis., invited him to attend and make several horsemanship presentations.

That experience opened doors throughout the industry for Curt to work as a clinician, and he now schedules clinics, seminars and demonstrations nationwide for 9 to 10 months each year. The remainder of the time, he and Tammy run stocker cattle and train horses on their Montana ranch, where the photographs for this book were taken.

With the Pates, what you see is what you get — ranch horses, cow dogs, cattle, kids and great scenery, and one is seldom found without the others nearby. In addition to commercial cattle, the Pates have a few prized Longhorns, and their cow dogs make every step the kids, cattle and horses do. "These aren't show horses, but ranch horses," Curt says, "and we use them as such, so they're pretty broke." Add the inviting Montana scenery to the mix, and the Pate place naturally appeals to young people who like to ride. They know they'll have fun horseback and get positive encouragement in their riding, just as the adults attending Curt's clinics do.

Authenticity and Balance

Curt's found success as an equine clinician for several reasons.

He's the real deal. He doesn't just look the part of an American icon, the cowboy; he is one. His authenticity is obvious. By the same token, he doesn't want his reality to mislead anyone about another cowboy's world or his work.

"My experiences might not be the same as those of a cowboy in another part of the country, riding in different terrain or handling a different breed of cattle or horse. So I've included what I call 'cowboy generalities,'" he says, "not specifically what every cowboy in every region does, but what many of them do much of the time."

Curt knows what constitutes a dependable, well-broke horse — and from the perspective of a man who's ridden the range. How broke a horse is can determine if a cowboy makes it back to the bunkhouse in one piece.

Recognizing a broke horse is one thing; knowing how and why he became that way takes horsemanship to the next level. Curt uses a keenly analytical mind — his own — to understand the "why" of any horse, so that he knows how to better achieve the desired response with his mount.

Likewise, Curt's analyzed the ranch experiences that help make a solid ranch horse and adapts them for use by the recreational rider. Although he might not be on the ranch, Curt shows any rider how to ride as if he is.

"Finding the balance," as Curt describes it, is a cornerstone to good horsemanship and more. He lives the principle in his personal life and his professional one. It's no surprise that he's able to strike a balance between the sometimes vastly different worlds of the working ranch cowboy and the recreational rider.

An Overview

The first section of *Ranch Horsemanship,* "Ranch Horses and Their Work," provides an overview of ranch-horse life and, thus, a better understanding of the training information that's to follow and how it contributes to making a well-broke, seasoned mount.

In Part Two, "Cowboy Horsemanship," Curt describes how the rider can best use his body to work with his mount and the six transitions that ranch cowboys master with their horses, both afoot and from the saddle, for more precise control and maneuverability. Used in combination, the transitions create more advanced maneuvers, such as the side-pass, considered appropriate not only for the show arena, but also for ranch and recreational applications.

The book's third section, "Practical Applications," relates how Curt uses the six transitions in practical ways, maneuvering through both natural and manmade obstacles, such as timber and steep hillsides or gates and alleyways.

Knowledge of working a horse afoot plays an important role in Part Four, "Rope- and Cattle-Handling Basics." Curt explains how to transfer that experience to cattle work. He discusses the basics of roping, too, but not necessarily because the average rider wants to become a world-class ranch hand or roper. These chapters are included because basic rope-handling and cattle-working skills are useful tools in developing a more well-rounded and bomb-proofed horse.

The book's final section, "Ranch Kids and Competitive Cowboys," addresses two more aspects of ranch horsemanship — how using these techniques can help children become safer, more confident riders and how cowboys use similar methods in ranch-horse competitions.

Throughout the book, Curt explains how to adapt and apply ranch-horsemanship skills to any riding program. His step-by-step, building-block methods offer a hands-on, do-it-yourself and in-your-own-time approach to making your horse a better mount and you a better horseman.

"My riding goal is to do my job and not ruin my horse's day, so he'll be better for me to work with the next day," Curt says. "I try to be respectful of my horse because he's doing way more for me than I'm doing for him. If I treat my horse right, he'll look forward to being with me."

And that's what *Ranch Horsemanship* with Curt Pate is all about — riding like the cowboys do and enjoying the experience.

—Fran Devereux Smith

CONTENTS

PART 1

RANCH HORSES AND THEIR WORK

Ranch horses aren't just for cowboys and ranchers anymore, but also now have a strong following among recreational riders. That's because the weekend rider wants nothing more than a well-broke horse, one that's experienced different situations and approaches them matter-of-factly. That's why a good working ranch horse fits the bill. Riding such a horse means ranch cowboy or pleasure rider alike can feel confident that he'll enjoy his ride and feel secure that he'll come through the experience in one piece.

The average recreational rider seldom has the time, inclination or ability to start his own horse under saddle; nor can he devote the hours necessary to develop a truly broke and trained horse. However, during the course of his work, a ranch cowboy usually rides often, consistently and for long periods of time, and his horses benefit as a result.

While packing a cowboy around to do his work, a ranch horse learns to deal with most anything. He might start his day with a group of horses as the cowboy helps sweep a pasture clean of cattle, then trail behind the herd as it's driven to another graze. Or the ranch horse might work all day with only his rider for company, checking fence or cows that are calving or need doctoring. Another day, the horse might be in a branding pen around a lot of horses, people and cattle.

Because his work is so varied, the ranch horse learns how to handle himself in all kinds of terrain, and he's probably crossed a few bridges and creeks. He's agile and quick enough to sort a cow from the herd, yet knows how to be quiet, calm and still if that's what it takes to hold the herd. And he's usually rope-broke, too. All these experiences make him a suitable mount for the average pleasure rider, who might ride alone one day, trail ride with a group one weekend or help his neighbor gather cattle the next.

Even though the desired end result — a solid, well-broke mount — might be similar for both the ranch cowboy and pleasure rider, obviously the ranch horse's lifestyle differs from that of a horse raised or kept on a 5- or 10-acre place. That's not to say either way is right or wrong; they're just different.

This first section of *Ranch Horsemanship* provides an overview of ranch-horse life and how it differs from that of the average recreational riding horse's life. I also discuss some of the gear and equipment that ranch cowboys use and that I prefer. All this gives a better understanding of the training information that follows and how that contributes to making a well-broke, well-seasoned mount. This book section isn't meant to be a ranch-colt-starting essay or one on ranch-horse health-care for that matter. But some differences in how a ranch horse is handled and introduced to riding ultimately affect how broke the horse becomes and how well he rides.

The good thing is that anyone can adapt some of the cowboy's methods and ideas to his own riding program. He can learn what cowboys consider important in their strings of horses and how to better evaluate a horse to see if he makes the cut. Obviously not everyone has everyday access to hundreds of acres and miles of trail as ranch cowboys do; 5 to 10 acres probably is closer to the mark. Nonetheless, in many cases a pleasure rider can apply what works for the cowboy on the ranch's many acres to his riding situation, whatever it might be.

Moving cattle over varied terrain is part of a ranch horse's job, as is handling cattle for someone who's as comfortable roping left-handed as he is roping right-handed, which Curt is.

THE RANCH-HORSE LIFESTYLE

The ranch horse's lifestyle differs somewhat from that of many recreational-riding horses. Yet those very differences give the ranch horse the well-seasoned experience that many riders want in their mounts and for which they often pay a premium.

To better understand how the ranch horse gains that experience from the life he leads, you must understand the working ranch cowboy's approach to this most important tool of his trade and what he considers assets in the horse he rides. The overviews in this chapter and the next aren't meant to be colt-starting or horse-care instructions. My comments simply describe the big picture for a ranch horse.

Knowing that big picture provides you a point of reference when you consider purchasing a ranch horse for pleasure riding or using ranch-cowboy methods to work with a horse you already have. With this greater understanding, you can more easily adapt ranch horsemanship techniques to your own riding program and expect reasonable success in helping your horse deliver a more solid, reliable performance from one day to the next.

Mares and Geldings

Some ranches still hold to traditional thinking as far as mares and geldings are concerned. Ranch geldings are started under saddle, then go to work as part of a cowboy's string of horses. Although a cowboy might not ride the same gelding every day, ranch work is every gelding's job. Ranch mares, on the other hand, might be started under saddle but, for the most part, a mare's job traditionally has been to raise babies, keeping ranch hands well-stocked with horses to ride.

Nowadays that approach isn't as hard and fast a rule as it once was. As ranch-horse competitions and sales have grown in popularity, more ranch mares are being ridden longer to earn their credentials both on the job and in the show arena. This, in turn, makes their produce potentially more valuable to the working rancher and recreational rider alike.

Many ranchers understand that, generally, when riding mares and geldings are kept together, they bicker, kick and fuss a lot among themselves, which can result in an injured horse. Sometimes particular geldings and mares grow strongly attached, then nicker and carry on continually when they're separated during the day. Many ranches try to run geldings separately from mares so cowboys don't have to deal with those problems in their everyday work. Although not every horse owner has the acreage to maintain separate pastures for mares and geldings, that's usually a good idea if space is available.

Pasture Etiquette

Ranch cowboys usually prefer to turn horses out to pasture, rather than stall them constantly, and not only because turning out a horse seems to help maintain his good attitude. Most cowboys also do that because an old boss horse in the herd teaches the other

Ranch horses are accustomed to pasture-living in a herd.

horses to respect his or her space, which really can work to a cowboy's advantage and help make his horse-handling job easier.

When I trained horses for the public, the first week a stall-raised horse came to my place, I always turned him out to pasture, and the other horses taught him some manners. A horse learns more from a week of that kind of pasture-mannering than I can teach him in a month by bumping on a halter lead. The same thing happens when young ranch horses are turned out with the herd of riding horses. Plus, the pasture-mannering better fits the horse's natural ways, and I don't have to be the bad guy as far as the horse is concerned — the boss horse fills that role.

When a boss mare or older gelding teaches the newcomer to respect another horse's space, the new horse might be kicked at first. Although the boss mare, for example, might've pinned her ears and threatened the newcomer right off the bat, he probably didn't even see it at the time. But the next time — after the mare has kicked him — when she twitches an ear or wiggles her tail, a horse new to the herd figures he'd better give her some room and travels way around her.

The important thing to realize is that the boss mare starts working that new horse and signaling him way ahead of time, long before he ever gets close to her. She heads him away

from her territory before he becomes a problem, which is just what we need to do when handling horses — head off problems before they start.

When the horse is turned out, his attitude improves because he learns to make his own decision about crowding the boss horse. Even if, for example, a young horse's decision is wrong, and he's run off by one horse or has to ask another horse's permission to come back to the group, it's the young horse's choice, and he learns from it how to get along in the herd hierarchy. This holds true no matter if a colt being started under saddle is turned out with the riding horses, or if a mature newcomer is turned out with the herd.

For many ranchers, another general consideration about turning horses out to pasture is that a horse then has to graze to make his living. That means he has something to do and a reason to stay busy during the day, which also helps improve his general attitude.

Going Places

To ranch cowboys, perhaps the most important reason for turning out a young horse is that it teaches him to go places. On a ranch, the waterhole might be a couple hundred yards or a mile away, so a young horse learns to pick up his head, look where he

It takes a broke mount to wrangle horses.

wants to go and go there. And he goes there straight — in his body and his path of travel.

A horse kept in a corral or small stall never learns how to go to something because everything — feed, hay and water — is brought to him. When he's first ridden, it seems much harder to get him to travel straight, compared to a colt that's learned to travel on his own to his water or feed. The stalled horse just doesn't know how to do that. So that's a big difference with ranch-raised colts — they learn how to travel to get somewhere.

As a result, when he's ridden, a ranch-raised horse usually goes in the direction he's pointed. That's because going somewhere has become his idea; he's already learned that on his own in the pasture. And once a horse's mind goes somewhere — to water, the gate or a herd of cattle — it's much easier to get his body to follow.

DO IT YOURSELF

If you have only 5 or 10 acres, put your salt block in one corner of the pasture, your feed tub in another corner, and your water trough in a third corner. Then your horse has to learn to go somewhere and teach himself how to go straight from place to place.

Cowboy Feed Code

Everyone knows the old cowboy code: Feed your horse before you feed yourself. People nowadays criticize the old-time cowboys for being so tough in the way they handled horses, but their livestock was their priority, and they took care of their horses before taking care of themselves. Horses provided their transportation. Fueling them was a priority, and often the closest feed was only the graze available wherever a cowboy might be. Nonetheless, he always made sure his horse had a meal to carry him through the next day's work.

A big problem for horses today: Feed rations now are so strong and so potent, and horses don't have to work most of the day to get their rations as the old-time horses did. It's good that knowledge and technology are available, but the horse actually is designed to spend his day grazing, instead of being put in a pen or stall, where we throw him a flake of hay and give him grain twice a day. It takes maybe a half-hour's time for him to eat each feeding, and that's only about an hour's work altogether out of his 24-hour day.

For example, consider the mustang that spends his whole day walking, eating and looking around. He's probably more fit than many stalled, well-fed, too-fat horses. That mustang's lifestyle is similar to that

DO IT YOURSELF

A horse outside, even in a 10-acre pasture, is always moving. He grazes and checks his territory continually. Even if you have only a few acres, try to allow your horse turnout time every day. You might have to alternate, turning out one horse during the day and keeping the other one outside overnight. If you can, turn out your horse all the time. That's even better since it allows him the opportunity to do what a horse does naturally.

If you must keep your horse stalled or penned, try to figure out a way to extend his eating time, to keep him busier more often during the day. Try feeding your horse three times a day, just for the simple reason that it helps keep him occupied while he's confined.

of range-run western-style horses of yesterday and to that of ranch horses today.

In any case, a turned-out horse might travel 15 or 20 miles a day grazing, even on a small acreage, which develops his muscles and bones. But when a horse is stalled and fed more than he's ridden, he's so out of shape that it takes 2 months' time and work just to get him fit enough to ride. Plus, his attitude often seems less pleasant than that of a turned-out horse.

The Cowboy's String

A ranch cowboy's string, the mounts he uses for his everyday work, includes a variety of horses. On the really big ranching out-

fits, the average string probably is seven or eight head of horses. When a cowboy finds out what his day's work will be each morning, he then catches whatever horse he needs from his string.

His circle horse, for example, usually can cover a lot of country in a consistent fast walk or a ground-eating long-trot, and he might be a younger horse with lots of go. I think of a circle horse as a more Thoroughbred-type horse — big, long-shouldered and long-strided to cover the distance.

There are probably more circle horses than corral horses in a cowboy's string, especially on large ranches, because circling the pastures is strenuous work. When a ranch cowboy rides a big pasture in a day's time, he might cover as many as 50 miles in some parts of the country. If he has to "pedal," or kick his horse, all the way, it makes for a mighty long day. So he wants his circle horse to really step out freely, even to the point that the cowboy might have to hold the horse back a little. Even though a good circle horse wants to go somewhere and covers a lot of ground, he does it mostly at a walk or trot, without much loping.

A corral horse, on the other hand, might not be quite as large as a circle horse; he doesn't have to be because he doesn't log as many miles cross-country in a day. Instead, a

These three horses are similar to those found in most cowboys' strings.

With his ground-covering stride, this tall Thoroughbred-cross horse can make a big circle.

A medium-build horse with excellent conformation can make a good circle horse or work in the corral.

DO IT YOURSELF

When you select a horse for pleasure riding, take a look at how the ranch cowboy chooses his horse to match the job. If you like to trail ride a lot, you probably want a horse that can travel easily cross-country, one more like a circle horse. If you want to attend the local team-penning practice each week, you might choose more a corral-type horse, one a little more compactly built and handy on his feet. Either way, you want a horse that can physically do the job you want him to do, just as the ranch cowboy does.

A small horse with a big heart works great in the cattle corrals.

ranch cowboy gets on his corral horse after the circle has been made and the cattle are gathered. He works cattle in the pen, where the corral horse's smaller size usually works to his advantage.

A corral horse isn't necessarily small like a competitive cutting horse because a ranch cowboy doesn't always have the luxury of picking exactly what he'd like to ride. But whatever the corral horse's size, he must be an athlete that can stay gathered up and ready to move. He also needs a lot of cow savvy, and he should have smooth lateral movement so he can sweep his front end around to head a cow.

More than anything, a corral horse should be calm, willing to relax and settle down quickly. The more excited a horse gets when he works cattle, the more stirred up the cattle become. So a corral horse must be able to make that really quick, really big lateral move to head the cow, and then relax again without jigging or dancing around. When he does that, there's still plenty of horse left at the end of the day's work.

Many ranch cowboys also have young horses in their strings, colts that have just been started under saddle. The important consideration for the cowboy is that he doesn't overload a colt with more job than he's prepared to handle. That's why a cowboy waits until the outfit's cow boss tells him what his day's work will be before selecting the horse he rides. If the job is a little simpler or less taxing that day, it might be a good opportunity for a cowboy to introduce his young horse to a new experience or add to his seasoning without overstressing him.

Most cowboys know which horse to take to the branding, for instance, and which one to leave at home, and most times, they're fairly accurate in their decisions. A cowboy won't, for example, take a second-ride colt to the branding, where he might blow up and buck through the cow herd. That can ruin the whole day's work or get somebody hurt.

And that's horsemanship — knowing what overloads a horse and his abilities. A cowboy might take a young horse to a branding, but won't use him there, and just lets him take in the new experience. Or maybe the cowboy rides the colt during the gather, but not in the branding pen because the colt can't handle that yet. The next day, if it's a low-key, quiet branding crew, a cowboy might even use his young horse to drag three or four calves to the fire, but that would be enough. Mistakes happen, of course, but most cowboys use common sense to avoid them, especially with their young horses.

What's important to a working cowboy, as much as anything, is the ranch horse's overall attitude — how willing he is to work and how pleasant he is to handle and ride. Granted, when a ranch cowboy is given a string of horses to ride, he doesn't always get exactly what he wants. He has to do his job with the horses available. So most cowboys try to handle and ride each horse in a way that he becomes a little bit better at his job from one day to the next.

A Big Advantage

The big advantage for the recreational rider who doesn't plan to show or compete: There are many great riding horses that somebody's probably overlooked because the horse wasn't absolutely show-ring pretty or maybe was the wrong color to suit somebody else. Nobody should pass up the opportunity to ride a good horse that fits his bill and riding program — no matter the horse's color.

For most cowboys, the color and sometimes even the breed aren't that important — how well the horse does his job is the main thing. About the only critical thing is size. A tall, large-framed guy like me really *needs* a larger horse because I can overpower a smaller horse, but that certainly doesn't mean everybody should choose a big horse.

However, some people get so wrapped up in finding a horse with the perfect color or pedigree that they sometimes miss a wonderful opportunity to have a really great horse they can enjoy riding. Many ranch horses — really good ones — might not be quite so attractive or have eye-catching color, but they're available for the recreational rider to purchase. Better yet, those horses don't always cost as much as a show horse, and can offer the rider just as much entertainment and fun as any horse. A ranch horse often can be a good bargain because he's affordable and, more important, has that quiet mind, which most pleasure riders really want and need.

Any and every job on the ranch can help create a broke horse.

A good, willing mind is bred into some horses, just as it seems that certain lines of horses are broncier and snortier than others. Of course, the way a horse is raised and handled affects him, too. For the average backyard rider, though, it's good nowadays that

A hobble-broke horse should always be there when his rider returns.

ranch horses are being handled more when they're young. Particularly in the past, ranch horses weren't always handled a lot until they were started under saddle at 4 or 5 years old. Anyone who considers buying a horse like that better be a good hand when he throws on his saddle — if he can get the saddle on the horse's back.

A key point any recreational rider should know and realize: Riding is a good time; it's recreation. Maybe a solid, old ranch horse is just what's needed to enjoy the ride, instead of a horse with built-in problems that require a lot of time to fix.

Conformation

Good, healthy feet, straight legs and well-formed withers are conformational aspects that are important for a horse to last a long time, whatever his job. A cowboy, of course, can't do his job unless his horses stay sound and their backs don't hurt, and for most cowboys, nothing is as important as getting the job done. They don't seem to worry so much about a lot of other things as long as the horses in their strings can hold up to the daily work. And, of course, cowboys are like anybody else: If they find a horse with prominent withers, good feet and legs, *and* he's nice-looking, that's all the better.

The first thing to look for in a prospective mount is sound feet and legs. Look at a

A wise purchaser notices scars when he horse-shops.

horse from the ground up — no crooked legs allowed. His feet should be large enough to support his body size, and the column of bones in each leg should line up reasonably straight. A ranch cowboy won't make a trade-off here, no matter how good-looking the horse might be, because a horse with poor feet and leg structure always has problems somewhere down the line.

Another thing I watch for, too, when looking at a horse's legs, is wire cuts. If a horse has a lot of scars from wire cuts, he might require doctoring more often just because he gets into wrecks around fences. Although I might not pass up a horse just on that basis, it's something I always consider.

Prominent withers support the saddle without allowing it to hurt the horse's back; they make a place for the saddle to sit so the rider doesn't have to cinch the horse so tightly. Also, good withers are important when riding in the mountains or roping, for example, because the withers help keep the saddle in place on the horse's back, no matter what the rider does.

Another concern with any horse: His withers should be at least level with or higher than his hindquarters. That helps him stay balanced as he moves, and he's more comfortable to ride because the rider doesn't feel like he's going downhill all day. A horse with good withers holds up to his work better simply because a long day's ride is less apt to hurt his back.

Another general consideration: When a horse is less prone to back or leg problems of any kind, he's less apt to have a sour attitude. That's important, too.

In recent years saddle fit has become a big issue, and there are good, well-built saddles and poorly made saddles as well. But, bottom line, saddle fit always comes back to the horse's build. If his withers and back are well-made, many saddles should fit him reasonably well. Not everyone can have custom saddles made to fit every horse. The budget just won't stretch to that, and it shouldn't have to.

A top ranch horse works well in the pens and outside in the pasture, too.

A broke ranch horse helps a young rider become a better hand.

Try and Willingness

More than anything, ranch cowboys value a horse with a lot of "try," a willingness to go somewhere and do something — and keep doing it. A horse with try can make a long day's ride seem much shorter. His rider doesn't have to pedal him across the country; he's always moving toward something. Granted, some horses are born with more try than others, but most cowboys work to develop and direct that willingness to their advantage.

That's why an older ranch horse might offer a lot to the recreational rider, who perhaps rides only two or three times a week. The older ranch horse already has that good attitude built-in, and he's been through a variety of experiences. A dragging rope or slicker shouldn't bother him, and he's probably hobble-broke and has been picketed. Odds are, he won't blow up or buck when

somebody gets on him, and he knows where to put his feet in rough terrain. In short, he takes care of his rider.

In recent years high-dollar, good-looking horses have brought premium prices at ranch-horse sales. But any cowboy at the sale might have another horse for sale at home — a 12- or 14-year-old horse a bit past his prime as a working ranch horse. Maybe the horse can't take a 40-mile circle on the ranch every day, but he can still easily handle a weekend trail ride or evening rides after work. A job like that is almost semiretirement to a hard-working ranch horse. Plus, the recreational rider offers a comfortable lifestyle for a good horse that's served the ranch well. It's a great deal for everyone.

Personalities

The same try that a ranch cowboy prizes as an asset in a horse's attitude also is some-

When a horse's and his rider's personalities fit, challenging obstacles, such as a teeter-totter, aren't so difficult to master.

DO IT YOURSELF

If you're a go-go-go-type person, and you buy an old, deadheaded horse without much try, you'll always be pushing him to speed up and probably won't be happy with him at all. But if you're never in a hurry, that quieter horse might be perfect for you.

If you tend to get angry or easily upset, you don't want a horse that becomes antsy and jigs the minute he turns toward home; otherwise, the two of you will fuss much of the time. However, if you have a cool head, are patient and control your emotions well, you can probably deal with that jigging horse and might even help him become better about it.

Whatever your riding program, try to match your personality to the horse's; then the two of you complement each other instead of fussing with each other every time you ride.

thing a recreational rider should consider when buying a horse. Some pleasure riders can handle more try in their mounts than others. A horse that really wants to go and needs to stay busy might suit one person's personality just fine, but not his neighbor, who has a more laid-back attitude.

When a recreational rider tries a prospect, it's best that he be honest about his personality and that of the horse. He should consider both in the purchasing decision to increase the odds that both he and the horse will enjoy one another's company during each ride.

Fixing Problems

As for a horse's attitude, I think a rider can change that somewhat, but not a lot. I say that simply because I've noticed that most people's horses eventually start acting pretty much the same after a period of time. More often than not, that's probably because the horse learns to fit in with his crowd — both his people and his other horses.

But I don't count on changing a horse's attitude a lot, especially if fixing a major problem in a horse might compromise my safety. I've tried to fix problem horses for years. Even though I might've changed some horses a little bit, I don't know that it's ever been worth the time and effort for me or the horse. Some horses are just the way they are, no matter what I do or don't do. Granted, I've learned a lot while fixing problems, but if I'd just bought a nice horse from the start, one more willing to learn, I'd have had many more solid rides than I could count.

Most folks shouldn't plan to try and fix too many problems on horses they buy. For one thing, problem-solving usually takes more time than many people have to give,

Creek crossings are a big part of ranch life.

and the results might not really be worth the effort. That's especially true when considering that the time spent solving a problem could've been spent having a nice ride on another, more pleasant horse.

Riding a problem horse requires the rider to concentrate; he can't relax and visit with friends, but must keep things right and be correct as much as possible to help solve the problem. That probably explains why so many horsemen don't say much — they're concentrating more on what they're doing. They think and ride, and work to make the horse better, and when they stop riding and take a break, they might be able to laugh and have a good time then.

That approach usually works fine for a professional horse trainer or a ranch cowboy because it's important to his job. But that approach is tough for the recreational rider, who doesn't want to spend a half-day training, nor has time to do that. Think about how much training time and how much entertainment you want from your horse. If you want more entertainment and less training, an older, seasoned ranch horse might be the way to go.

It's hard to pin down a horse's development to certain ages. Generally, until a horse is more than 5 years old, he's still in the green stage and learning a lot about life. Five to 10 years old is about middle-aged for

Today's ranch horse must become accustomed to many distractions.

When horses are treated well, they like to be around people and are easy to catch.

Ranch horses are experienced at trailer-loading and being hauled to other pastures.

a horse; he can be pretty solid in his responses then, but still continue to make a lot of changes in the way he does things. But if a horse is spooky at 10 or older, he'll probably be spooky at 20. If he's broncy at 10, he'll be pretty broncy when he's 20. Few horses change much after they're 10 or 12 years old.

Ways and Means

When considering a horse to buy, take a good look at the way he handles everything that comes his way, from the time he's caught until after a rider's in the saddle. That's what a ranch cowboy must do in order to evaluate and get along with the horses in his string.

When I buy a horse, for instance, I want to know how easy he is to catch. Some horses are really sour about being caught, and if one has any age on him at all, I probably won't be able to change that much, no matter how hard I try.

I'm careful about buying a hard-to-catch horse or allowing him to be with my young horses simply because I don't want them to pick up his bad habits. It's the same with a cribber or wood-chewer. I won't turn a horse with a bad vice out with mine. Not many horses with a bad habit or vice really are worth putting up with, or at least not for pleasure riding. A truly outstanding performance horse might be a different story, but I'd still worry that my other horses might pick up his bad habits.

When I buy a horse, I try to make sure the owner doesn't work the horse right before I arrive, but that's sometimes hard to do. Often a horse is worked until right before somebody comes to see him, and is then turned back out to pasture. That isn't always the case, but I'm always wary. The fresher the horse is, the more I can learn about his attitude.

When looking at a prospect, it's best to first stand back and watch. Then I can see how the horse acts with other horses in the pasture. I can watch the owner catch the horse to see how hard a chore it is and the horse's attitude about being caught. Does

he pin his ears at the other horses? Does he threaten to kick? Does he leave when the owner goes into the catch pen, or does the horse come toward the owner?

I might even ask the owner to feed the horses because a lot can be learned about a horse at feeding time, things that might not show up elsewhere. When I feed, my horses don't fight and bicker. I put a stop to that, whatever it takes. When I feed after dark, if I don't know what's going on with the horses behind me, I might get in trouble. And it's never the horse right behind me that causes the problem. It's the one behind him, who bites the closer horse and runs him over me.

I just don't allow that type bickering at my barn, and I'm particular about that because I don't want my kids run over or my wife stepped on. I do whatever it takes to change a horse's attitude, so he's more worried about running into me than running into another horse. I watch for that kind of thing when I horse-shop, too. Then I know before I buy what I might need to work on if I take the horse home.

I also watch while the owner saddles the horse. How does the horse respond? Is he cranky when he's cinched? Does he pin his ears and switch his tail? What does the person handling the horse do to prepare the horse to be saddled and ridden? How much time does the person take? The handler

"Any buyer must make sure the owner does things at the buyer's level of horsemanship... ."

might cause some of the horse's crankiness. Or the person might handle the horse well enough, and the horse is just cranky. Either way, I watch closely, again, for a better evaluation of what might become a problem should I take the horse home.

If I wasn't really good at working a horse in the round pen or really capable of getting a strange horse ready to ride, I'd ask the owner to step on and ride right then — without taking the horse to the round pen, if that's possible. Any buyer must make sure the owner does things at the buyer's level of horsemanship and that the horse can handle it.

Later, before I commit to buy, I'll probably saddle and ride the horse, to see how he and I get along, but I often first stand back and watch. The horse's attitude will show, and his ears can tell me a lot. I really like to see his ears forward, even if a horse is a little bothered when I get on his back. If he pins his ears and cranks his tail, that's not necessarily a deal-breaker, but I consider it when making my decision. Can I change that problem? Maybe, maybe not, but probably not if the horse is 15 or 16 years old.

After riding the horse where he's comfortable, it's also a good idea to ride a prospect away from his home surroundings, if at all possible. Although a seller might not be willing for a prospective buyer to haul his horse elsewhere, he might be willing to meet a purchaser at a local saddle club arena or even bring the horse to the buyer's home for another test ride. Either way a potential purchaser can get a little better feel for how broke the horse is.

A Broke Horse

The terms *breaking* a horse and *broke* horse sometimes can be confusing to people. Breaking a horse is simply a term sometimes used to describe the training process when starting a young horse under saddle. Although it doesn't mean literally breaking a horse's spirit, the term seems to misrepresent the real situation as often as the word *training* does. Most people are quick to say that they don't train horses, yet we all train our horses every time we ride, whether we realize it or not.

Likewise, a broke horse is not a dull, lifeless horse that's lost his willingness and try. When cowboys speak of a well-broke horse, they're actually complimenting the horse and whoever's responsible for the horse being that way. A broke horse is a responsive mount that takes a matter-of-fact approach to his work and whatever he might encounter along the way — even the unexpected. Ranch cowboys prize broke horses because they're a pleasure to ride and they're safe rides, too.

Safety is the first thing to consider and expect of a broke horse I plan to buy. And safety doesn't always mean the horse is a gentle dog. A broke horse is one I can saddle and lope without him blowing up and bucking.

A seasoned, quiet horse is essential for roping.

But I also want a broke horse to be lively enough that, when an old bull gets on the prod and comes at us, my horse moves out of the bull's way. If my horse won't move then, that's not safe either.

To me, a broke horse might be able to perform a lot of maneuvers, yet when they're done, he's still calm. That's the important thing. For example, I might be holding a bunch of cattle, and my horse might look half-asleep. But when a cow breaks from the herd, my horse jumps out, stops the cow and then goes back to sleep without stirring up the other cattle. He does his job, and I still have horse left at the end of the day. To me, that's a broke horse.

The important thing: A broke, safe horse always comes back to me for help and guidance when he's uneasy, instead of trying to leave when something bothers him. If he pays attention to me then, together the two of us can handle whatever the problem is, without creating more problems, because the horse believes in me. He knows I won't normally put him in a bad situation. Then, once in a while, if we do get into one, the horse trusts me to help him through it.

An Honest Evaluation

The main thing anyone must do when purchasing a horse is to think and evaluate. How sound are his feet, legs and withers? Does he have a nice attitude? Is he as respectful of his handler as his handler is of him?

The buyer must evaluate not just the horse, but his own ability, too, and be honest about it. Is he horseman enough to really enjoy this horse at his level of training?

To me, a beginning rider has to really think about staying on a horse, where to be in the saddle and how to hold the reins. Nothing's second-nature to him yet. The intermediate rider doesn't really have to think about things, but he hasn't yet had all the experiences of a totally advanced horseman. The advanced rider can handle absolutely any situation at any time without panicking through it. He can find the middle of his horse without consciously thinking about it, and those are good goals to have.

A broke horse accepts the feel and the noise of a clipper.

Handling a horse's feet shouldn't be a problem, but an everyday fact of life.

It's best to approach a horse that's ready to be caught, as this colt's relaxed attentiveness indicates, with the halter ready for use in the left hand.

HANDLING RANCH HORSES

2

Although this isn't a colt-starting book, some understanding of the ranch horse's start should help you better apply the cowboy's methods to develop a broke, well-seasoned horse. Because the job — ranch work — takes priority, many ranch cowboys have learned to make the most of their limited horse-training time. They use it effectively to create good results and sometimes fairly quickly. Almost anyone can benefit from applying the cowboy's time-management techniques for more efficient horse-handling. Many ranch training ideas and methods, discussed briefly here and in the next two chapters, are explained in more detail later in this book.

First Contact

The first thing I do when handling or riding a colt is choose something that I can do, or use, to help settle the horse. It's usually something really small — lowering my hand to the horse's neck or lifting on the halter lead or a rein a little bit. Whatever it is, it helps reassure the horse. It becomes the cue the horse learns that tells him everything's all right, and it's what I can use to get the horse to relax when I need him to be calm.

The response I usually look for when I lift the lead or touch my horse's neck is for the horse to work his jaw a little, and maybe even lick his lips. That tells me the horse has relaxed. Getting a horse to relax is the most important thing, no matter if I do it by rubbing his neck from the ground or by picking up on a rein from the saddle. When a horse

Establishing contact with the hand on a horse's neck helps the horse feel more secure.

works his mouth, I know the horse will be soft from head to tail, without any resistance. Over time it becomes a habit for him to respond quickly to the cue that encourages him to relax, and that's a good tool for me to use with any horse.

Leading the Way

Generally, I do most of my ground-work from the time I catch my horse until I get him to the barn. Back when I was cowboying, I usually had little to no time to spend in the round pen before my day's work started, but I didn't just throw a halter on a colt and take off walking.

When I halter a horse, I do it in a way to soften or relax the horse. I take the time to rub the colt's neck or lift the lead until I see the colt respond and relax. That's the first contact between the horse and me, and by the

A horse's reluctance to go through the gate is an opportunity to help the horse learn to be more responsive to the halter rope or lead.

This colt responds to a soft feel on the halter rope and comes through the gate.

Sending the horse through the gate is an easy way for him to learn to move his hindquarters.

DO IT YOURSELF

No matter your horse's age, if you have barn chores to do, why not first catch your horse and then let him be with you as you do your chores? Lead him around, back him or step him across as you do your work. If he becomes tight and tense, take a minute right then to encourage him to relax. You can accomplish so much doing this with your horse because he learns how to be with you, yet stay out of your way.

Remember: You must be sharp about thinking ahead of your horse when you do this — you might get freight-trained if you aren't paying attention. But this experience gets both you and your horse in the habit of being more aware of one another and teaches each of you so much about the partner at the other end of the lead. It's a similar approach to that of the cowboy, who's always mindful of the horse from the moment he catches him. Cowboys can build such a good rapport so quickly with a horse and get a lot done even with green colts because they pay such close attention to their horses.

time I lead him to the barn, the colt's already learning to respond.

As I walk to the barn, I pay attention to how the colt responds — if he comes willingly or if he's tense. I notice how the colt goes through a gate. If the horse is jumpy there, I take a moment and use my signal, whatever it is, to relax the colt. Then I might move the colt's hindquarters across or back him a step or two and reassure him again. Whatever I do, I always make sure the colt relaxes right at the gate, where the problem is.

I want a colt to become responsive enough to the halter lead that he can move his hindquarters around or bring his front end across, if that's what I need the horse to do, to work through a tight place. I want my horse to move because I asked him to, not because he's scared, tense or dodging me — then he's only reacting, and that isn't really thinking about the maneuver.

I also look for places to relax a colt. If I have a choice between going through a 12-foot gate and a 6-foot gate with a snorty colt, I take the

6-foot gate every time. That way, when the colt becomes bothered in the smaller gate, I can use that opportunity to help the horse relax. With the 12-foot gate, there's no pressure; he walks through and it's no big deal. But with the 6-foot gate, I have to think and plan ahead so that my colt doesn't get scared.

Grooming and Saddling

When grooming a colt to saddle or picking his feet clean, I usually take the time to be sure the horse is comfortable then, too, just as I do when leading the colt. I want to actually see the colt visibly relaxed when he's being brushed, and if the colt becomes bothered by having his feet handled, I take a few minutes to help the horse relax then, too. Investing a few minutes in a colt at this stage of the game usually pays big dividends for years to come because a potentially troublesome experience becomes old-hat to the colt.

Like most cowboys, I won't spend all day grooming a horse because I'd rather ride than groom any day. When I have only an hour or so to ride, I clean where the saddle sits, and then ride. And like most cowboys, if I plan to go to a rodeo or an event, I might want to groom my horse longer, but I concentrate on riding him as much as I can at home.

When I groom and saddle a horse, I expect him to stand untied while I work. If a horse won't stand still for saddling, he probably won't stand still when I'm on him, and that's a safety issue. So saddling also becomes an opportunity that I can use to advantage for preparing a horse to be ridden safely.

It's harder, sometimes a challenge at first, to saddle an untied horse, but in the long run, I really believe it helps me become a better horseman and helps him become a better horse, too. This is another opportunity for the two of us to learn things about each other and how to read one other.

I usually drape the lead over my left arm as I saddle. Then every time the horse shifts his weight — before he steps off to leave — I can head off that problem before it happens. That's because, as the horse shifts his weight to walk, his head naturally moves to one side

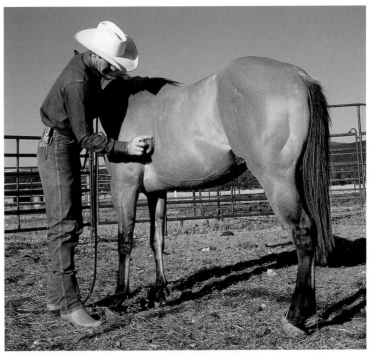

Grooming a horse when he's untied helps prepare him to accept things touching his body.

When the handler stands on the halter rope, which is over the right arm in this case, he can lift his arm and establish contact with the horse without stopping the grooming.

When picking up a front foot, the handler can use one hand at the horse's withers to maintain contact with the horse, reassure the horse by his touch and unweight the foot to more easily pick it up.

After successfully picking up a front foot, the handler should let a horse relax before gently setting down his foot.

DO IT YOURSELF

One of the best things you can do with your horse, especially one you've just bought, is saddle without tying him. It's one of the fastest ways to improve your horsemanship because you learn to practice preventive horsemanship and see a possible problem coming. You start thinking in terms of vitamin-C horsemanship instead of taking the penicillin approach and trying to cure a problem after it's developed. Quit tying your horse to groom and saddle him, and you must learn to think ahead to get the job done.

Be sure to saddle any horse for the first time, no matter if it's a colt, an old horse or a broke horse that's new to you, in a safe place that has a durable fence. If something goes wrong and the horse becomes scared and tries to buck with the saddle, he won't be totally loose. But when a horse bucks and breaks through a weak fence, he can get really scared, and then he'll go through more fences and over people at that point.

Another safety consideration: If something scares a tied horse, or the cinch pinches him as you tighten it, he might jump backward. When he's tied, he really has nowhere to go, so he lunges forward. He might land right on top of you. You might not have a place to dodge and move out of his way because the barn wall, fence or side of the trailer is there. However, if your horse is untied and something scares him, you can go wherever you need to go, no matter the problem.

or the other, and I can feel that change through the lead over my arm.

Another benefit of not tying a horse: He learns to focus on me. If I tie or crosstie a horse for saddling, before long his mind's on one thing, and my mind's on another because neither of us really has to focus to see if the other is paying attention. But when the halter rope is loose and over my arm, I'm constantly aware of where my horse is both physically and mentally. If his mind goes to a horse in the pasture, his body soon follows. Just by lifting the lead, I can bring his mind back on me. So he soon learns to become more aware of me, just as I learn to pay attention to him.

The handler should position one hand high on the horse's hip to push his weight over and off his hind foot, making it easier for him to pick it up on his own.

It's important for the handler to move in closely under a horse's hind leg, rather than pulling and extending it too far to the rear, so that the horse remains comfortable while his foot is being cleaned.

Some ranch cowboys clip the mane at the withers to prevent a horse from getting sore under the saddle pad. As part of old-time traditional horsemanship, doing so also indicates that the horse is a snaffle-bit or hackamore horse.

A cowboy might clip a small bridlepath, but never trims his horse's ears or muzzle because doing so interferes with his sensory perception.

The blanket should be centered on the horse's back and placed a little forward of where it'll be under the saddle, so that it slides back into place without ruffling the hair.

Balancing the saddle on the hip leaves one hand free to control the horse if necessary, and saddling from the right saves steps.

Set the saddle softly on the horse's back.

It's best to lift the pad or blanket into the saddle gullet to ensure there's no pressure on the withers.

Throwing the saddle on from the horse's right side is an effective time-saver because it's easy to drop the cinches.

By reaching for the cinch with the right hand, the handler's left hand is free to control the horse.

Taking one wrap with the latigo and then fastening the cinch-buckle minimizes bulk under the rider's leg. A tight cinch isn't necessary on a good-withered horse.

Always fasten the back cinch after the front cinch, and the cinch hobble between the two should be checked regularly for wear. Should the hobble break, the rear cinch could work back into the horse's flank.

Properly position the headstall before putting the bit in the horse's mouth.

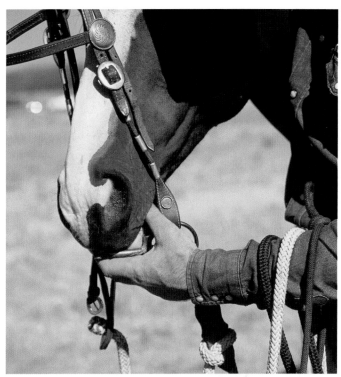

Open the horse's mouth and guide the bit into it with the left hand while the right hand lifts the headstall.

When the bit's in the horse's mouth, put the right ear forward and slide the headstall over it, and then the left.

A browband headstall allows a snaffle bit to hang evenly in a horse's mouth.

It's essential to properly adjust the throatlatch so that the horse can flex freely at the poll but is unable to rub off the headstall.

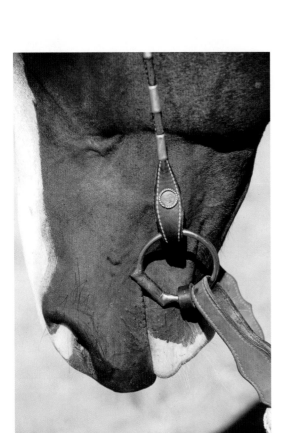

A snaffle bit should fit snugly in the corners of the horse's mouth without causing wrinkles, and the bit hobble is fastened below the reins.

The loop rein is the last thing to go over a green horse's head.

What's the Rush?

Any rider can learn to do all the things a cowboy does as he catches, leads, grooms and saddles his horse. That's horse training. A cowboy constantly looks for little signs that his horse is relaxed or that he's uneasy. Because the cowboy responds when he notices those signs, by the time his colt is saddled, often there already are many good things working between the two of them.

Recreational riders might not always think and evaluate horses like that as they prepare to ride, but they should. Unfortunately, most folks think they have to hurry to the round pen to train a horse, but by the time they get there, the horse can be so tense and tight, just from the way he was caught and saddled. Maybe he got scared and jumped through the pen gate, and his handler didn't even see that at the time because he was too busy thinking about being a trainer in the pen.

A ranch cowboy can't allow that kind of thing to happen because he'd then have to spend additional time in the pen to relax his colt again, and the cow boss is waiting on him to start the day's work. So unless a cowboy's a pretty good bronc rider, he pays attention from the moment he catches a colt and does the little things that help get his horse in a willing mindset.

When a person thinks about those little things only after he gets to the round pen, he might've already undone some good things he had going with his horse before they got to the pen. Anytime someone hurries to halter his horse or rushes through a gate to saddle quickly, his horse naturally figures he needs to be in a hurry, too — which might not be what the rider wants at all when he gets on his horse.

So many things can happen from the moment a horse is caught, and it's important for the handler to notice and respond to them. That's why anyone who rides should become good at doing all those preliminary things that happen before he mounts — catching, leading, grooming, saddling and bridling his horse. A horse knows it'll be an

After a colt's been worked, turn him loose in a calm, relaxed frame of mind.

easy day when a person can't get him caught easily or put on the bridle correctly. Most any horse quickly picks up on those things that determine how good a hand the person is. As a result, the horse figures out he can "buffalo" his rider all day long — before the person ever gets in the saddle. That's why developing these basic skills is important.

To a ranch cowboy, what happens in the round pen is all about what will happen when he rides a colt outside.

THE PEN'S PURPOSE

3

Obviously, the big difference in how a ranch cowboy starts a colt is that he's learned to be more efficient with his time. That also holds true when he takes a colt to the round pen. Ranch work simply doesn't allow the time to spend months working a colt in the pen. Instead, a cowboy must work effectively so he can ride the colt out of the pen as soon as possible and into the pasture to gather cattle. Basically many ranch cowboys use the round pen only long enough to get a horse to understand what's expected of him — as quickly as possible.

That's the same approach I take. When working a horse in the round pen, I always think about what I can do right then that will benefit me when I ride the colt outside the pen. Again, it's thinking ahead to be safe. That's how ranch cowboys get by with so little round-pen work on colts, then ride them outside and get ranch jobs done early in the game.

Another thing I consider, as I think most cowboys do: If I have to do more of whatever I'm doing in the pen each day, then that isn't the thing to do. The idea is to make sure that it takes less time in the pen every day instead of more. That's important to think about when working or riding a horse.

Many people work a horse in the pen 15 minutes one day, 20 the next and so forth until the horse really becomes fit and in good shape. Soon the person feels he has to work the horse longer and longer each day to feel safe when he finally mounts to ride.

That person is stuck in the round pen and might not even realize it and doesn't seem to know how to get out of it. He's probably stuck because the pen seems the easiest and safest place for him to work his horse. The pen creates almost a false sense of safety, but the only thing that situation really reveals is that the person doesn't have a good understanding of what it takes to make a horse safe to ride.

Perhaps the person hasn't realized that the little things he notices, or fails to notice, when he catches and saddles his horse can be important to his own riding safety. Maybe he hasn't developed that touch on the horse's neck or lift on the lead that reassures his horse everything's okay, and hasn't watched long enough to see when his horse really is relaxed and comfortable. The person probably hasn't developed that sixth sense, thinking and looking ahead to see a potential wreck, and heading it off before it happens by calming his horse.

But most ranch cowboys do all those things, and I think most cowboys probably are a lot like me. I *think* I can ride anything in the round pen, so I don't worry about that. To me, what happens in the pen is all about what will happen when I ride outside. That's why I pay attention to little things. That's why I handle a colt in a way that encourages him to relax, so that he softens and comes back to me, instead of getting on the muscle when his buddies go the other way or something else happens. Anytime I can get a colt to relax, it gives me the confidence that I'll have the control I need when I ride the colt outside.

A colt can learn to wait at the end of the halter rope until he's asked to move.

Here, I've lost the colt's attention and shake the halter to get his mind back on me.

When the horse's attention returns to me, I release the pressure momentarily before resuming work.

Balanced Ground-Work

To me, the idea of hooking a horse on to his handler is overused and really for the horse who isn't yet halter-broke. If he's halter-broke, I can use the lead anytime to refocus the horse's attention on me and do it fast. Each time I ask the horse to come forward and he does, and I release him, it's the same thing as getting him hooked on to me.

But what I can't do with a horse on the lead is teach him to move out freely because he knows that I can always physically bring him back. That's where a lot of people run into problems when they work afoot with horses.

When a horse is too hooked-on, the handler has made it all the more difficult for the horse to move freely in the pen and later outside the pen. It almost becomes a bad thing for the horse to go forward; the hooking-on part tells him that the good, safe place is beside the person. So, before long, the horse is so close that he steps on his handler, who can't shove him away. And the horse is afraid to go away because the person has made him think that "out there" in the pen is a bad deal. Just think how much

Stepping forward and away from the horse …

… is another way to draw his attention back to me.

To drive a horse forward, I must step behind the breaking point at the horse's withers.

After stepping ahead of the breaking point to stop the horse, I can step to my right to shift his weight back and move his forehand across to the inside.

tense and scared. His flight-or-fight response kicks in, and he feels he really has to leave. As a result, when he finally does move, he moves way too fast.

Working afoot in the pen with a ranch colt, I'd rather take a more balanced approach. It's okay to bring the horse to me in the pen, but I also want to be sure that I can stop my horse at any point and send him away from me. By taking that balanced approach, I can teach a colt that although it's good to be near me, or any person, it's also just as good to be somewhere else or moving forward.

That balance is also my main goal when making upward and downward transitions in the round pen. All the emphasis on hooking a horse on mentally has nothing to do with him running away. But the balance between upward and downward transitions does, so I concentrate most on that when I work a horse in the pen.

worse "out there" will be outside the pen.

This situation also creates a problem when a person mounts and asks the horse to move forward — by then, he's even become suspicious of forward motion. The horse isn't comfortable enough to move forward freely when he's worked afoot, so why should it be any different when a person's on his back? That's when a horse becomes

When I work a colt afoot and want to slow his walk, I slow my pace as I walk around the pen, just as I would if I was on my horse's back. If the horse is loping, to bring him to walk, I must really slow my body and make the change obvious. Most horses pick up on that and fairly quickly. Before long, I don't have to be so obvious with my body language because my horse

After I step forward to direct the colt, I maintain just enough pressure on the colt that he turns smoothly to the right.

In a downward transition from a trot to a walk, I step forward, ahead of the breaking point, but not so far ahead that the colt turns back.

soon learns to respond differently to the various ways I handle and move my body. Soon I can change my body position when I'm completely across the pen, and my horse responds. Although sometimes people want to think that's some big, mystical deal, it's simply that the horse has become more aware of my movement.

As for gait changes, any downward transition should require no more energy than the corresponding upward transition. In other words, it should require no more of my energy to transition a horse from a lope to a walk than it takes for him to make a walk-to-lope transition. I always try to strike that balance. If the horse won't slow down when I work him afoot in the pen, he probably won't rate back outside. In fact, if I must step in front of my horse to totally block his forward motion and stop him, I won't have that downward transition to a stop outside, and I'd better have a stampede string on my hat, because I'll need it.

A Trial Run

Here's how I might work afoot with a colt in the pen. First, I might have the colt walk out fast all the way around the outer edge of the pen — without him trying to come to the center — out on the rail. Then in my mind, I pick a spot on the edge of the circle. When my horse gets there, I move my whole body a little faster and with more energy to see if I can get the colt to break into a trot. I might trot the colt three full rounds, then pick another spot and ask him to lope there, or to come back to the walk for another two revolutions. If the horse won't travel steadily around the pen, whatever the gait, or won't trot at a specific point when asked, why would he do those things with me on him outside?

The same thing holds true when asking a horse to change direction and sending him away to move forward again. That's when a colt often bucks because his reverse path looks like a whole new world to him. After stepping in front of a horse to

DO IT YOURSELF

Instead of thinking of ground-work as round-penning your horse, imagine yourself on the horse's back. Walk as if you're riding. If you want a lively walk from your horse, you must walk lively, just as you'd have lively movement on his back when riding him. If he's trotting, you should move more in a trotting manner around the pen. And if your horse travels so fast in the pen that, if you really were riding, you might fall off, slow down. Better yet, imagine that a small child is on the horse you're working from the ground. Your job is to keep that horse this side of trouble so that imaginary child won't fall off.

DO IT YOURSELF

When you work your horse afoot, have a specific plan in mind. For example, walk your horse two rounds, then ask him to trot as he passes the gate, and directly opposite the gate, ask him to reverse and lope three circles or whatever you want. Continue making transitions until you're satisfied with his responses.

If your horse doesn't travel forward freely, don't turn him back in the other direction a lot because he'll lose even more forward motion. On the other hand, if your horse really wants to go fast, turn him back the other way more often to help control his speed. In any case, be careful and pay attention so your horse doesn't run over you. You'll soon learn to step ahead of his withers to turn him smoothly and then behind them to drive him forward in the other direction without making a production of it.

Remember: Whatever problem your horse has in making transitions in the round pen, he'll probably have when you ride him outside. If it takes 2 pounds of pressure to get him to trot, it better take that same 2 pounds of pressure to get him to stop. If he transitions smoothly in the pen, he'll better make those same changes outside, and that's important for your safety. Always think about what your pen work contributes to your coming ride outside, and you can help your horse become more responsive more quickly.

turn him back, I pay attention. If the colt bucks or looks tense, I usually keep moving him forward until he becomes visibly comfortable going in the other direction. Then I might change the colt's direction again several times, being sure each time that he's comfortable with the change. In the process I watch and learn what that horse does to slow down, how he shifts his weight and handles his body, so I can better evaluate the horse's comfort level with what's being asked of him.

It's important when riding outside to know that the horse can change direction and move forward again without it being a big deal. But what I really want to see is the horse become relaxed in his work. Then, I've not only learned how to change the horse's direction, I've also learned how to change his mind. When that happens, the colt has learned to do his job without a lot of ear-pinning and tail-switching.

Preserve the Try

Sometimes when a person rides a colt in the pen, he continually bends the colt to slow or stop him. That horse might be bent around so much or have his reins pulled on so hard in the pen that he no longer wants to go forward anymore. So often a person bends and stops a colt too much because the rider's afraid that the horse might buck; he can't bring himself to let the horse move forward freely. When that happens, the rider takes away all his horse's motivation, just as working him too hard physically can.

So that's one school of thought — to bend a horse a lot to have that control — but that's not from the ranch cowboy's school. Sometimes, when I first get on a colt, I know he's going to buck. If he throws me off, that's his right. But like most ranch cowboys, I refuse to work and work a colt in the pen and terrorize him until he can't do anything or won't.

But that's what happens when a person's not a good-enough hand to get along mentally with a colt — he usually takes the try right out of the horse. Then later, when somebody rides that horse in a tough spot or has a lot of miles to cover, the horse quits making any effort, and the rider must pedal all day, continually bumping the horse with his legs, to keep him moving steadily.

I don't want to pedal a horse. I want him to move out freely, and I don't think I'm much different from other cowboys in that respect. A ranch colt eventually must work long days outside the pen, so I don't want to take away any of that colt's willingness to work when he's inside the pen. If a colt moves forward easily and there's any problem, he probably won't buck too much or too hard anyway.

At least that's the way most cowboys see it: The horse that really moves out is the safer ride. Granted, that approach isn't for everybody, but maybe it should be. Then people might really learn to evaluate and work with their horses, instead of bending and stopping the horses so much that they lose the entire try.

Overbending can cause a horse to run through his shoulder; in other words, he moves left, leading with his left shoulder, although he's bent to the right.

Too much bending can hinder a horse's desire to go forward, but many people do that because they're afraid the horse might buck.

To the cowboy's way of thinking, not everybody in the outfit is a colt-starter. Traditionally, a ranch colt-starter had to be a pretty salty bronc rider for that very reason — that he wouldn't take the try from the horses. To keep from doing that, he sometimes had to ride a bucking horse, but he didn't bend and double the horse every few feet; he just let him go forward and rode him through the problem. Then, when the old-time cowboy rode the colt outside, the horse knew how to go somewhere and, by the time he was broke enough for someone else to ride, he still had the try. Nobody had taken that from him.

Some showmen call that try "sting," and some horses always will have it. Recognizing and using that sting to advantage is why some people win consistently.

Those who don't understand try or sting need to own one of those special horses who can tolerate a lot of rider mistakes. That's why I think, when someone who doesn't ride that well starts a colt, he could well take some great potential away from the horse by not fully developing his try. Of course, I realize that some people want to start their own horses, and if they take that asset from the horse, that's their right.

But for a cowboy, it isn't the right thing to do. The old-time cowboy thought the worst thing somebody could do to a horse was eliminate his try. That was kind of a cowboy code that all comes back to the amount of time a cowboy spends in the saddle, which helps him better read and evaluate horses more quickly than many people.

Since the horse is slightly braced, I use the reins to ask him to relax his jaw and make a downward transition.

When the horse relaxes his jaw, he also relaxes his body for a smooth downward transition.

A Round-Pen Ride

When riding a horse in a round pen, I want enough room for the horse to walk, trot and lope in a pretty natural way — at least a 50- or 60-foot pen; 70 feet is even better. The larger the pen, the less a horse must bend his body as he travels around it and the more room there is for him to make transitions without getting into trouble.

In a 30-foot round pen, it's really hard for a horse to freely move forward, which means it's harder for him to buck there, too. A lot of people prefer to use a 40-foot pen for those same reasons. But for me and most ranch cowboys, the bigger the pen, the better.

When I get on a colt in the pen, I want the horse to move, and let him go. Once a colt moves forward freely, I can work on upward and downward transitions to rate his speed by shifting my balance forward and back in the saddle. Again, that prepares the horse to be ridden outside so he'll be comfortable making those changes there, too.

In the pen I don't ask for big changes at first. I just shift my weight forward a little and test the colt's responsiveness. If I want the colt to go faster, I pick up my energy and shift my upper-body position a little more forward. If I want my horse to slow, I melt back in my saddle, just like I'd slow down to sit back in a chair.

I also take that balanced approach to riding previously discussed in the ground-work section. Each time I ask for an upward transition in speed, I also ask for a downward one; then the colt learns to be as comfortable slowing down as he is with speeding up. Again, I work for balance so that the downward transitions require no more effort than the upward ones.

When first riding a colt in the pen, I don't want to give the colt a reason to brace against me. Usually with a direct pull on the reins, a colt at first pulls right back and locks his jaw.

Instead of a hard direct pull, the way I soften a colt's response to the rein is by almost leading him from his back. I take one hand way out to the side, really wide, and tip the lower end of the colt's head in the direction I want him to go, just as if I was leading him, or as if the colt was tied to the highline. Then the colt doesn't brace because it's something he understands, and there's no stiffness from his withers to his ears. As soon as the colt gives to my pressure, I move my hand back where I'd normally have it and complete the turn.

"If I ask for big changes in a hurry, a colt might feel as though he needs to buck."

The main thing about those first rides in the pen: If I ask for big changes in a hurry, a colt might feel as though he needs to buck. But by asking for little changes gradually, a colt might never really have that need for flight or fight, so he goes from walk to trot to lope without bucking. But I have to pay attention to be sure the colt relaxes following each change. As soon as a colt's fairly relaxed while making changes on a big circle around the pen, I'm ready to ride outside and leave the pen behind.

DO IT YOURSELF

If your pen is square-cornered, and you work or ride your horse there, he might get "stuck" in the corner and feel as though he has to hurry out of it. To remedy that reaction, fasten a portable panel diagonally across each corner of the pen to eliminate the problem. When there are no corners, he can move steadily and confidently around the pen.

This thumb-up emergency stop is a safe way to shut down a horse and keep his body straight, and it's easy to practice before it's needed.

RIDING OUTSIDE

4

ost anybody who cowboys for a living wants to ride a young horse outside the round pen as quickly as possible. Giving a colt a place to go outside the pen keeps him from becoming really dull to everything around him, including the rider on his back. Besides that, a cowboy can't spend a lot of time in the pen with a young horse and still get his work done. And, although it's good that he has a lot of country to ride with a colt, a cowboy must pick and choose which ranch jobs he can do on a young horse, being careful not to overtire a colt or work him too hard.

Depending on the horse, a lot of ranch cowboys ride a colt outside the pen the first day he's ridden — the good hands, that is. To them, as I've said, the worst thing a cowboy can have is a horse that doesn't want to go. For somebody who really can't ride, that might be the best thing to have happen with his horse.

But for a cowboy who can ride, it's the worst. When the try is gone, the same thing basically happens with the colt that often happens with a stalled horse — neither has a focus. There's no direction to go, nothing for the horse to look forward to and no place to put his mind out ahead of his body.

However, a horse putting his mind ahead of his body is exactly what keeps many ranch cowboys safe. As I've said, most cowboys think they can ride and handle anything as long as a horse keeps moving forward. Most cowboys get very good at being safe on horses; if they don't, they lose their livelihood.

Thinking Outside

Because the ranch cowboy also wants to survive, he learns to look and think ahead when he rides outside and recognizes anything that might cause him trouble with a

DO IT YOURSELF

As you ride into different situations, practice looking ahead to see how you can keep yourself safe, and make that a habit. When you see anything that might create a problem, be prepared to circle your horse, rub his neck or do whatever's necessary to keep the two of you safe. Then you already have a plan in place before your horse overreacts.

It's so important for all riders to look ahead. So often, though, one rider is visiting with other riders, and suddenly a tractor-trailer rig comes from behind and spooks his horse.

Then the rider's mad at his horse or wants to whip the truck driver.

But the rider didn't think ahead. If he's near a road, he should realize that traffic might be there, too, and prepare for it. A trail rider knows that a bear might be in the trees at the park, or that he might meet a llama on the trail. So be a good horseman and prepare yourself to deal with something that might startle your horse. That's what good colt riders on ranches do because they know it's important to having a safe, successful ride.

colt. But many people work a horse in the round pen for months and never, ever learn to think ahead of the horse. That's why they're so uncomfortable riding outside.

Outside, if a kid rides up on a bike, the cowboy sees him coming because he looks ahead. He doesn't wait until the kid is near enough to scare his colt, but takes care of that problem the minute he realizes it might exist by making sure the colt has seen the kid and his bike. If the colt becomes really scared, the cowboy usually puts him to work, even if it's only circling in a trot. That lets the colt move his feet and gives him a place to go, which satisfies his flight-or-fight need, but still brings his mind back to his rider. Deer, cattle,

hikers or anything might startle a horse in a similar way. A good colt or outside rider is like a watchful airplane pilot, always looking ahead to see where he can go and what he can do in case something goes wrong.

Riding Outside

Obviously because of the hours he spends in the saddle, it's easier for a ranch cowboy, or anybody who rides a lot regularly, to take a colt outside the round pen successfully. Doing so probably seems easier for people like that because they don't have to constantly worry about being in balance with the horse. That good balance is second-nature, so the rider subconsciously uses his body to advantage, and can really concentrate on giving a colt a good start as a riding horse.

Someone who doesn't have that kind of balance probably shouldn't try to put the first outside ride on a colt. It's far too easy for the person to lose his balance and, in the process, scare the colt unnecessarily or run into more problems than he's capable of handling.

Even more important: A colt needs to learn to look to his rider for help. If it's provided when the colt first becomes uneasy, that builds confidence between horse and rider. But if the rider doesn't see or feel the need to reassure the colt, or do it in a timely way, the colt can become so tense or scared that his body is totally stiff and braced.

There's an old-time saying that if a horse is confident in his rider, that person can ride him down a gopher hole or up a telephone pole. The horse knows his rider will help him through those situations.

That's why it's so important to help a horse whenever he tenses, no matter if he's being caught or saddled, or ridden inside or outside the pen. When a person can help him feel more at ease, his horse believes in him.

Saving Yourself

Nobody likes to think about a horse running away with them, but it happens, and some horses will try to do just that. If a

DO IT YOURSELF

When you make the first outside ride on a horse, try to have somebody with a fairly gentle horse ride with you, so your friend can lead the way. The important thing is to get your horse outside and then go somewhere on him. That's easier to do when your horse feeds off what another horse is doing. If that horse trots, you probably won't even have to ask your horse to trot, but just urge him into it. That means you don't have to force and fix your horse, and that makes a nice first outside ride for the colt.

You might ride your colt to a pond or waterhole that he's familiar with. He knows it's there, and probably lines out to travel straight to it. Or ride to a pasture where other horses are kept. Their presence usually draws the colt and makes it easier to get him to go. Riding a colt through cattle is good, too, because as you and your colt ride to them, you must look ahead. You might have to ride a

half-mile to get to that particular spot where the cattle are, but as you do, you're working on the colt's straightness without him even knowing it.

I don't think horses really understand or relate to drills and exercises with no purpose. But when you ride through sagebrush or cedars, and the horse has to turn around a tree, he understands the reason he must bend his body — a physical object is in his way. That makes it much easier for him to understand what you want and for you to teach him with minimal correction.

Remember: When you don't force and fix him, it's a nice ride for the horse. In a pen or arena, there's seldom much for a horse to see or look forward to, so he takes more fixing there. But outside, when a horse sees the cattle or a gate, his ears go forward, and that's when you can quit fixing him. The ears tell you his mind has gone there, and his body soon follows.

Instead of pulling on the colt's head, which can cause him to run through his shoulder, I hold my hand out wide to lead him from his back.

As he responds and gives his head, I bring my hand in closer toward his neck.

I complete the maneuver where my hand should be for a finished bridle horse.

DO IT YOURSELF

Check out what your horse's response might be if the need ever arises to lead him into a circle from the saddle, and practice until you'll know you can handle the situation. With your horse standing still, move one hand out to the side and wiggle your fingers. If he gives the response you want by following the feel of your fingers, give back and release him immediately. Then try the same thing as he walks and trots, always releasing him immediately when he responds.

You now know that your horse will respond if you must lead him into a circle to be safe when you ride. But don't overuse your horse's good, soft response. Then when you do need it, you'll have it, and your horse won't have learned to brace against you. Use this maneuver only in a real emergency.

horse tries to run, instead of pulling on his head, I might first try to lead him from his back, just like he's a colt being ridden for the first time. But instead of pulling his head around close to my knee, I move my hand out really wide and try to lead the horse, basically just guide his nose around. That way I don't cause the horse to brace harder, and I can use the horse's momentum to advantage by directing it around in a circle, rather than fighting to pull him to a stop. Once I can circle the horse, I have the control I need.

Emergency Stops

A lot of people might wonder about using a one-rein stop in a runaway situation. In this stop, one rein is shortened to bring the horse's neck and head around to one side and, at the same time, disengage the horse's hindquarters. Ideally the one-rein stop should be a fluid, balanced movement.

A one-rein stop isn't about turning; it's about stopping the horse's forward motion — and it could save your life. And I believe

in that, although I think the traditional one-rein stops are overused, especially in clinics.

Too many people get hurt practicing a one-rein stop because they tip their horses so far off-balance that the horse falls. Anyone who can't keep his body plumb-bob straight and balanced over his horse's withers, so that the horse can more easily maintain his balance, probably isn't ready to ask a horse for a one-rein stop.

A one-rein stop can be dangerous, and it shouldn't be used lightly. To me, it's for an emergency only. I haven't made a one-rein stop in 2 or 3 years. It's there on my horse if I need it, but I try to think far enough ahead of a horse that I don't have to use it.

Instead of bending a horse into a one-rein stop when he gets scared and wants to run, I've learned how to put his spine in a bind where I don't have to bend him so much, but can still shut him down. I've heard this is an old cavalry trick used because the officers had to quickly teach troops who weren't experienced horsemen to perform fairly high-level maneuvers. This is one of the more effective methods

DO IT YOURSELF

Unlike the one-rein stop, during which you might throw down your horse, you can practice this thumb-up maneuver without endangering yourself. Practice the hand position when your horse is standing still. Then try the maneuver at a walk and later at a trot.

Just lift on one rein, and be sure to keep your horse's neck straight with the other rein. As soon as your horse shuts down, release him. By knowing how to perform this speed check, you can let your horse move out, even if he's fresh or young, and still feel in control. You won't have to pull on the reins constantly because you're afraid the horse will take off. That makes for a wonderful ride because you can let your horse travel forward freely and still feel safe.

the officers devised for less-experienced people to use in practical situations.

To slow a horse or stop him from running, I use my right hand on the rein to keep my horse's neck straight, and keep it locked in position. Then, like a bronc rider, I lift up my left hand and turn out my thumb. That puts my horse's spine in just enough of a bind that he has to slow down. I've worked with that thumb deal a lot, and I can use it to stop a horse from bucking or running. It's as easy to do as a one-rein stop and much safer.

Seasoning and Experience

Although a mature ranch horse is controllable, his try isn't gone. He's been well-seasoned by a variety of experiences and had all those experiences with a hand good enough to help him through the new and different things he might've encountered on the ranch. The main factors in making a broke horse are the rider's confidence, the horse's confidence and, of course, the time factor. The older a horse gets, the more exposure he's had to many different things and the more broke he often becomes.

DO IT YOURSELF

Even if you don't have a big ranch, act as though you do and set up some situations to help season your horse. Give him an opportunity to do and learn some things in your pasture. That's what makes a really broke horse.

Set up some ground poles in your pasture, for example, or some cones or jumps — something your horse can really see. You might even use a row of hay bales. Let your horse look them over really well until he becomes relaxed about them. Then give him a job to do — going through the poles, between the cones or over the bales and jumps.

That's why the ranch horse has become popular with recreational riders in recent years. An even better deal is that now the cowboys and ranchers, who do such good things with horses, are getting paid well for all their time and effort. And for the ranch cowboy, that's what makes his effort so real and so gratifying — people are willing to pay for his expertise.

But even an average pleasure rider can cultivate that experience and get his horse more ranch-broke, if he puts a little time and effort into it. As the cowboys say, "It's a case of more mileage, less silage."

However, a pleasure rider must make the seasoning time real to his horse; it can't always be arena time. Even though I ride in an arena, too, anytime I can, I ride outside. That's the place to be because it's so much more pleasant for me and my horse to go outside and see things.

For instance, our Montana neighbors have a big sage-brush pasture that's the perfect place to ride colts. When I leave my place, I have to go uphill and down, and cross a creek. At first, a colt usually doesn't want too leave the other horses but, pretty soon, he sees the culvert up ahead that he has to cross — and his ears go up. To some people, that culvert might seem a potential obstacle, but it always takes my colt's mind off the barn and gives him another focus. As long as I keep up his energy, by keeping up mine, the colt usually will go straight there, or anywhere. But if I relax, before long my colt loses his drive and direction and wants to go back to the other horses.

To season a colt or even a grown horse, I can't sit on my horse and do nothing. I must be willing to work to pick up the energy and life in my own body in order to keep my horse's life and energy moving forward. I must recognize that when my horse's ears go forward, he's focused on the place I want to go — and I must let him go there.

On the way to my neighbors, there are railroad tracks for me to cross and a gate to work. I often get off my colt to work the

"When things don't go as planned and a horse is ready to buck, I prefer to ride him through it with help of my night latch and rope strap."

This horse shows tension throughout his body. His head's elevated, his neck is stiff and his tail isn't relaxed.

Using a night latch with my left hand is one way to ride through a rough spot.

gate because then he has to relax and stand still for me to get back on. Then we have a steep climb up to the meadow, and trees, where I can lope the colt. It's a beautiful place to ride. There also are buffalo, cattle and deer, so my colt sees a lot and, before long, he becomes relaxed with what we were doing.

I've been figuring out things like that to do with my colts since I really don't have a ranch job now, and spend so much time on the road. But because I've had those ranch jobs, I know how to create similar situations to help season a colt.

The main thing: Any average pleasure rider can take some of these cowboy ways to the barn and have a better ride today than he had yesterday. Anyone can learn to think and make the most effective use of his time with his horse. He can become more aware of his horse as he leads and saddles him, and create jobs for his horse so the two of them can learn to work together. And when there's a problem with his horse, he should try to fix it or get help from someone who can.

Remember the overriding thing about a cowboy and his ranch horse: They're always going somewhere to do something; they have a purpose. That's how things should work. Even when a person has only 5 or 10 acres, he should aim for something every time he rides across his place, just to give his horse a sense of purpose and direction.

Holding my rope strap on the right helps me stay in the saddle.

I've ridden the horse through the problem, and he's ready to go to work with no hard feelings on either side.

The *bosalillo*, or *bosalito*, can be a stylish piece of gear for a California cowboy.

COWBOY TRAPPINGS

5

When discussing ranch horses and their work, it's helpful to know something about the gear and equipment cowboys typically use. In most cases a ranch cowboy prefers a specific type of gear because that's usually what works best in his particular terrain and climate, on that particular cattle operation and with that ranch's remuda, or string of horses. Such factors affect a cowboy's choice of rope, saddle, headgear and even his apparel, and each cowboy's personal preferences, from among the many styles and decorative options available in today's market, make his gear unique.

Stand two horseback cowboys from different areas of the country side by side, and their appearances can vary greatly.

One might follow the vaquero or California tradition and use a full bridle with reins, romal and a spade bit on his horse. A spade-bit rider won't lead his horse with the reins because that affects how the bit hangs inside the horse's mouth, which has been protected through a slow, traditional bitting process. Instead, a vaquero-style cowboy leads his horse with a "get-down" rope tied around the horse's neck. The vaquero-influenced cowboy also is particular about how he hangs up his reins and romal; if they fall down and get broken, they're very expensive to replace.

That tradition, of course, came down through the years with the Spanish land grants in California, where the vaquero's horsemanship skills were highly prized; he was expected only to ride his horse and work cattle. He had the time to make a really broke horse, keep him well-groomed and even make pretty gear that often had silver mountings.

On the other hand, the traditional Texas-style cowboy came along after the Civil War — hard times, no money — and he caught wild cattle. His heavy gear was practical for work in that region. His saddle wasn't shiny or pretty, but a serviceable swell-fork. He used a grazing-type bit and while working usually dropped his big, thick split reins, which were easier to pull out of the brush, to let his horse graze. The Texas cowboy's clothing also was durable rather than fancy; he wore thick chaps while the California guys used *armitas*, or short chaps much like chinks.

Texas cattle country was different, too — brush country — so the cowboy's method of working was different. He had to get a loop on a wild cow quickly and used a short rope tied hard and fast to his saddle; when he caught something, he didn't want to lose it. His overall lifestyle was a little rougher and coarser than the Californian's because of the rougher country and livestock.

The list of differences goes on and on. For more than 150 years various styles of cowboy gear have developed, some more popular than others. My preferences, for the most part, are included below.

Halter and Lead

I prefer using a rope halter and tied-on lead instead of nylon or leather halters with snap-on leads. The rope halter works best

I prefer using a well-fitted rope halter with a tied-on lead.

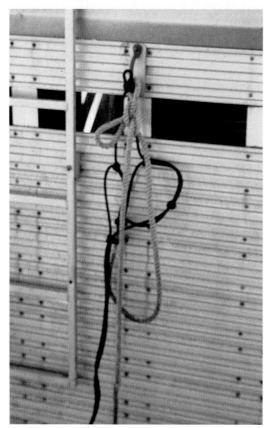

This is a safe way to leave a halter hanging on the trailer.

when I handle a horse afoot because it applies pressure where I want it.

Properly adjusted, a rope halter takes hold of the horse under his jaw — not over his poll. When the initial contact is across the poll, more often than not, a horse sets back first when being led, before he moves forward. So a poorly fitting halter soon teaches him to become resistant. I don't want that to happen with my horse. When the first contact is underneath his jaw, he won't develop the habit of setting back initially when I lead him.

There's one place I'm particular about halters and leads, and that's around my trailer. When somebody bridles a horse tied to my trailer, I don't want his halter left hanging down to the ground. That can be a hazard when any rider comes back to the trailer because his horse might put a leg through the halter.

Blankets and Pads

I usually put a felt pad, with a Navajo blanket on top, underneath my saddle. That much padding isn't a problem with a good-withered horse, but does make it even harder to keep a saddle in position on a round-backed, mutton-withered horse. It's better to use a thinner pad on any horse with less prominent withers.

There are many types of blankets and pads available nowadays, some cut well to really fit a horse's back and made of both natural fibers and synthetics. For example, one combination pad I like has sheepskin underneath, a Navajo blanket as the top layer and a wool pad in between.

More often than not, ranch cowboys usually stick to the old-time, traditional basics — a plain wool pad with a Navajo blanket on top. And it's not that they're necessarily against any of the newer technology; it's simply that for more than 100 years, these old standards have worked well for people who spend hours in the saddle.

I'm a big guy, so the less additional weight I put on my horse's back, the better, and that's something every rider should consider.

Some traditional and some not-so-traditional cowboy gear.

I pay more attention to my gear's weight now and try to lighten my horse's load as much as I can, and that even includes the weight of my blankets and pads.

The average recreational rider needs only a pad that really fits his horse — and it doesn't have to cost a lot of money. In most cases, a lightweight pad or blanket is fine because a pleasure rider seldom spends the long hours horseback a working cowboy does.

The Saddle

I prefer a saddle built on a Wade tree because of the way it fits a horse. The tree is shaped so that it fans out in front, which, in my experience, fits a greater variety of horses. I've used mine on everything from Clydesdales to Arabians.

The saddle's a slick-fork, built with the big horn I like to use as part of the tree, which has the wide front base to support the horn. The front of a Wade sits low and close on the horse's withers, so when I must rope and hold a cow for a long time, there's less torque on my horse's back. In fact, I don't need to use a rear cinch much of the time, usually only when I step off to tie

down a cow. Otherwise, my weight keeps the back of my saddle down just fine.

A swell-forked saddle is fine, too, but I really like the way the Wade rides and the comfort of it. And, because the Wade also has a narrow build through the seat, that helps me sit straighter and stay in balance with my horse.

This is a flat-plate rigging in the three-quarter position.

I prefer using an Oregon crossover rope strap on my saddle because it keeps my rope where I want it.

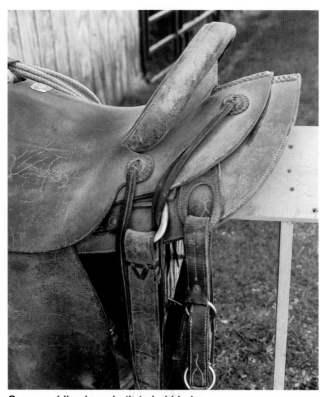

Some saddles have built-in hobble-hangers.

This night latch is simply a dog collar run through the saddle gullet.

Many saddles have built-in cinch-hangers.

Too, the Wade is lighter. I've quit using saddles built with so much heavy, bulky leather, and I have the skirts made as small as I can to lighten the load, just out of respect for my horse. I want a solid, well-built saddle, of course, but not one so heavy that it hinders my horse's movement.

The most important thing on a saddle is the rigging position. I prefer mine to have a seven-eighths to three-quarter rigging because that position sets my saddle farther ahead toward the horse's withers. The farther back my cinch rigging is toward the middle of the saddle, the more forward on the horse my saddle sits, which places me closer to his balance point, or center of gravity. Having my balance right over his center allows me to help balance the horse for the different jobs we do, such as roping and holding a big bull. Because the pull when holding cattle is farther back, more from the center of the saddle, the weight also dissipates more evenly on my horse's back.

With a full-rigged saddle, the weight usually puts pressure right on the edge of the tree, and the saddle horn puts all its pressure at the front of the tree bars, right down on the horse's withers. Then a wide back cinch is necessary to prevent the saddle's back end from rising up from the horse's back, which creates a fulcrum that applies even more pressure on the withers.

My saddle's plain, rough-out leather, so I don't worry much about scratching it. I ride wide-based stirrups; some are Monels with flares at the bottom. Although I have stirrups 3, 4 and 5 inches wide, I like the 4-inch stirrups best. They have a good base for the whole ball of my foot, so I have a lot of balance. Although that type stirrup is a little more expensive, it won't crush my foot if a horse falls with me.

Stirrup safety is important. Too many recreational riders make do with too-big stirrups, and make their kids make do, as well. That's just looking for a wreck. A stirrup should be small enough that the rider's foot can't go through it. It's worth it to swap saddles, ride bareback or keep feet out of the stirrups altogether when the stirrups don't fit.

When a kid rides an adult saddle, even though the child's feet don't reach the stirrups, he can get hung up in another place — the rope tied on the saddle. If something goes wrong, and the child comes off or the horse falls, the child's foot can go right through the coils. It's always a good idea to take the rope off a saddle before letting a child ride.

My saddle has an Oregon crossover rope strap, which holds my rope close against my leg. Also, I can use the strap as a handhold if a horse bucks or jumps a ditch. It makes a nice handle and keeps my rope where I need it for easy access, without allowing it to flop over or under my leg.

Another handhold on my saddle is my night latch, a strap that buckles through the gullet. The night latch is discussed in more detail in Chapter 7. People who don't carry a rope on one side of the saddle might want to use two night latches, one on either side of the horn, so they can use either hand to hold on when necessary.

Headgear

Headgear for horses is a huge subject; an entire book can be written on that alone. When I was a kid, I rode with whatever I had, and I survived. I've since learned that, to a good horseman, it doesn't matter so much what's in the horse's mouth, because a good horseman's savvy enough to get along with the horse anyway.

When bitting horses I've come to like the old, slower vaquero way, which had been more of a regional thing until recent years. Most of the tradition came from states such as California, Oregon, Idaho, western Montana, and Nevada. Western Montana has a strong California influence although eastern Montana, Nebraska, Wyoming, Colorado and New Mexico have more Texas influence among their cowboys. The Continental Divide roughly splits the spheres of influence.

Nowadays this slower, vaquero-style bitting method is becoming popular all over the country. Perhaps that's because horsemanship clinics also have become so well-accepted in

Properly cared for, traditional cowboy headgear will last for years.

The old-timers, of course, used the bosal during the time a colt shed his teeth, to minimize training problems when the colt was naturally fussy about his mouth. In fact, some of the older guys never used the snaffle bit at all; they just started colts in the hackamore.

When a horse works well with a hackamore, he's ready to go to the two-rein, which includes a bosal and bit used together with two sets of reins, one pair on the bosal, and one pair on the bit. The two-rein rig gives me the opportunity to acquaint a horse with a half-breed or spade bit very slowly.

At first I use the bit very little, only as my horse travels along straight, and I fall back on the hackamore for faster cattle work because the horse is so comfortable with it. When the work might require quicker action, I don't want my horse to learn to brace his jaw against the bit. Over time, however, I gradually use the bosal less and the bit more to direct my horse and ultimately develop a highly responsive, full-bridle horse.

the past 10 or 15 years, and have helped popularize the tradition.

People now take time to refine their bridle work with horses; that's great and a good tradition to continue. The vaquero gear is really fancy, but the one concern I have is that it seems some people just buy the pretty silver bit and fancy headstall, reins and romal — without taking the time to truly make a bridle horse in the old-time, traditional way. I now see a lot of horses that aren't full-bridle horses, but do have that gear hanging on their heads and in their mouths.

Following the tradition, I start a colt in the snaffle bit first, and later switch to a hackamore, using a 5/8-inch one initially, until a colt is soft and responsive and really understands how to operate in the hackamore. When he does, I switch to the next size, riding with a 1/2-inch leather bosal that's really supple, and I finally use a pencil bosal that's about the size of a little finger.

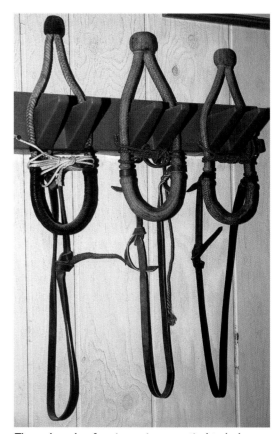

These bosals of various sizes are tied to help shape them to fit a horse's head.

I always use a browband bridle on the snaffle bit, to ensure that my contact with the bit creates a balanced pull. The more worn the browband, the more freely the crownpiece leather can work through it. Then there's no excess pressure around my horse's ears. Some browbands on the market have D-rings to hold the throatlatch in place, but I don't use that style browband because the rings often hit the horse's ears and put pressure there any time the reins are pulled.

With the half-breed bit, which has a lower mouthpiece attachment, it's fine to use a one-ear headstall, but with the spade bit a browband is critical to balance the bit and keep it hanging straight in the horse's mouth.

I also use a leather curb on my full bridle, which is proper when bitting a horse in the vaquero tradition. Outside of that tradition, a curb chain is most often used on shanked, leverage bits.

McCarty, Reins or Romal

Most often I use a McCarty, as we call it in my part of the country. That's a common term among cowboys, and is an Americanization of the Spanish term *mecate*, which still is used in some regions of the country to describe a loop rein with the tail serving as a get-down rope.

With a McCarty it's easy to lead a horse, and I can use the tail like a dressage whip if I need it. I also like using a McCarty because it's handy for roping. I can drop, grab or get shorter on the closed rein when I need to, and then step down and use the tail to lead my horse or help him work the rope when I'm afoot.

When I bridle a snaffle-bit horse, I keep the loop rein of the McCarty over my arm until the headstall is on. The loop is the last thing to go over the horse's head. That's just part of the old-time bitting tradition.

Adjusting the length of the loop rein is a personal thing, and I sometimes change the size of my loop. When riding a small horse, I might shorten the loop, but lengthen it on a

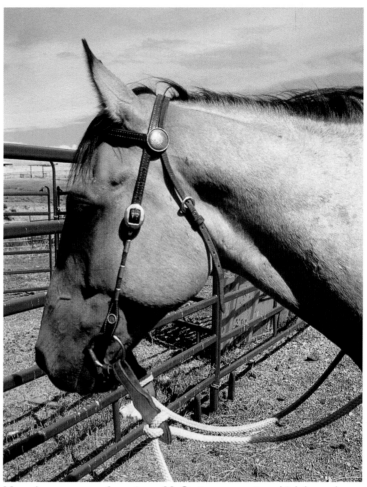

Many horsemen prefer using a McCarty, or mecate, which has a loop rein and tail, when they ride with a snaffle bit.

large horse. It's easy to adjust the loop size where the rein ties to the slobber strap, just by pulling the necessary length through the strap, which, in turn, affects the length of the get-down part of the McCarty.

Typically I set my loop rein just long enough that I can cross it and hang it over the horn, when I step off, without the loop putting any pressure on my horse's mouth. When I mount, I make a small coil in the loop rein and hold it in one hand, and as I ride, I use that small coil to adjust my rein length even more. The more slack I give my horse — in other words, the longer the loop rein — the smaller the coil in my hand.

A really nice McCarty might be made of horsehair, but for everyday use, many cowboys prefer one made of inexpensive parachute cord.

However, when using the hackamore, I really like horsehair reins. The horsehair provides a nice, soft feel, especially when used with the pencil bosal, and I like offering that sensitivity to my horse.

When a horse is in the full bridle, I generally use rawhide reins and a romal, which are easier to work with when I rope. In this instance, I put the reins over my horse's head first, before I bridle him because, for one thing, he should be broke enough for me to do that. The second reason: Should there be a problem, the reins will be ruined — not my horse's mouth. Putting the reins over a bridle-horse's neck first is traditional, just as they're put over a snaffle-bit horse's neck last.

Although a lot of show people nowadays don't use rein chains on a full bridle, I do because they allow me to give even more signal to my horse. When he feels the rein chains move, he can prepare to make a move. And, because the chains offer such subtle signals, they help maintain the softness in my horse's mouth. Without the chains, when a rider picks up on the reins, the action becomes more of a quick hit on the horse's mouth, rather than a subtle cue.

One thing I'm particular about, as far as headgear is concerned: When I haul saddled horses, I want the headgear over the saddle horn and tied with the saddle strings. Then a horse can't pull a bridle off the horn, and his headgear wind up on the trailer floor.

DO IT YOURSELF

Adjust the loop rein on your McCarty by working it through the slobber strap as shown in photo 1. The loop rein is just long enough to cross over your saddle horn, as shown in photo 2. Photo 3 shows how to carry the small loop, or coil, in hand, which you also can use to adjust your rein length.

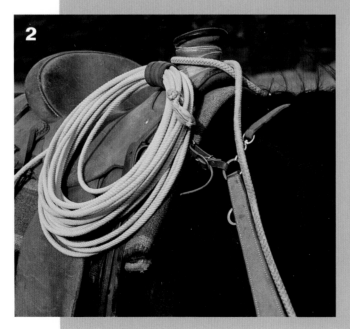

DO IT YOURSELF

I never tie a horse with a bridle rein, and that's one advantage of the McCarty — I don't have to. Instead, I tie the loop portion around my horse's throatlatch and use the McCarty tail to tie my horse without hurting his mouth or breaking my outfit.

There are several ways to tie a horse with a McCarty, but this is the way I like to do it.

With the loop rein over my horse's neck, I hold the loop rein at the end of the left slobber strap in my left hand. With my right hand, I pull the remaining portion of the loop over my horse's poll from the left side to the right. As I do, I also grasp a portion of the loop rein just above the right-hand slobber strap, as shown in photo 1. (That's the McCarty tail in the crook of my left elbow in the photograph.) I bring the now-doubled rein portion close under the horse's neck and up to my left hand.

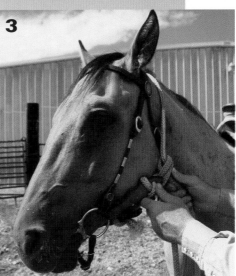

To secure the loop rein so I can tie my horse with the McCarty tail, I take the doubled rein over the single portion over the horse's poll and around his neck, from front to back. I then bring the doubled rein underneath the single rein from back to front, as shown in photos 2 and 3, and then put the doubled rein underneath itself to create a half-hitch near the end of the left slobber strap, as shown in photo 3. Now the tail of the McCarty and the doubled loop rein both hang underneath the horse's neck (photo 4).

(Continued on next page)

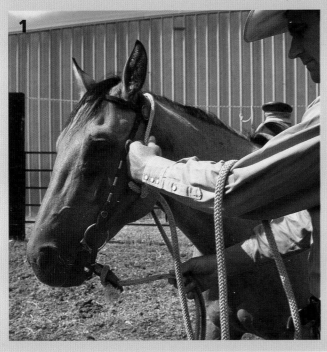

DO IT YOURSELF

(Continued from previous page)

Photo 5 shows the loop I make in the McCarty tail, and in photo 6 I've pulled the doubled loop rein through the smaller tail loop to start tying the bowline knot shown in photo 7. After pulling the bowline snug, I simply use the doubled portion to make a couple of half-hitches around the tail, as shown in photo 8.

Now I can use the tail of my McCarty to tie my horse (photo 9). Even if he sets back, it won't hurt his mouth, and the loop rein is secured under his neck, so there's no danger he'll get a foot through it.

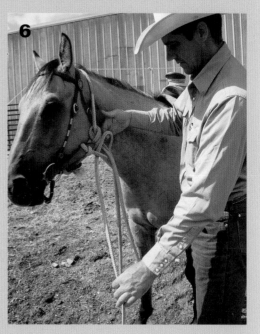

DO IT YOURSELF

Here's the way I prefer to tie a horse. It's commonly called a bank-robber's knot because it's quick to get loose. Ideally, it's best to tie your horse to something that's above his withers so if he does pull back against the lead, he's less likely to injure his neck. He's also less likely to get a foot over the lead rope when he's tied high.

First, double the halter rope where you want to tie the knot in it, and slip the loop from left to right behind a solid object suitable for tying a horse, in this case, the trailer ring (photo 1). Next, pull the lead rope, not the tail, but the end tied to the halter, through the loop from left to right (photo 2). This forms a second loop. Now pull the tail of the lead through the second loop from left to right (photo 3). This forms a quick-release chain (photo 4), which is just like a daisy chain crocheted from yarn. To secure the knot, make a half-hitch with the halter-side of the lead rope over the final loop (photo 5), and snug it down as shown in photo 6.

You might need to practice this knot a few times to adjust the length of your lead so that your horse stays safe, but can stand comfortably. It should be short enough that he can't get a foot over it.

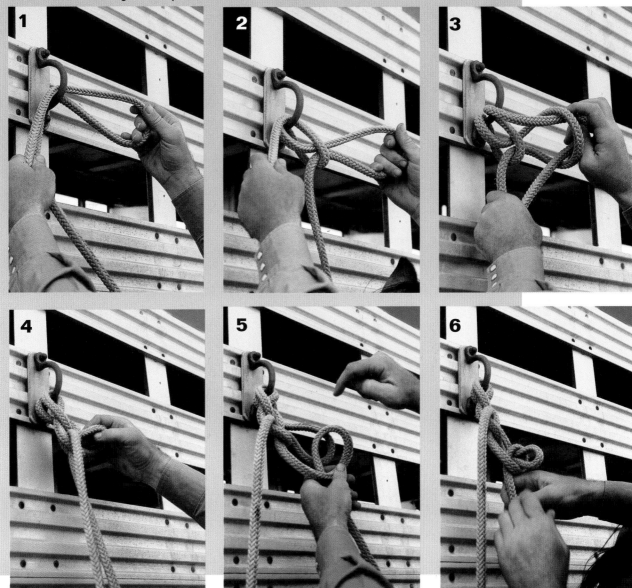

A clove hitch can fasten the get-down rope to the saddle.

Another way to fasten the get-down rope is to coil it and tie it using a quick-release knot.

DO IT YOURSELF

When using a McCarty, you can coil the tail and use a clove hitch to tie it to your horn, or you can use your front saddle strings to tie the McCarty tail. You also can tuck the tail under the belt on your chinks or chaps. However, it's important to tuck the tail under your belt properly; otherwise, doing that is dangerous.

First, make a loop in the tail of your McCarty, then bring the loop over the top of your chap or chink belt, down and under the leather. Don't bring the loop underneath the belt and out over the top; if you do and you're thrown from your horse, the tail binds more and is less likely to come out from under the belt.

The most common, but also the most dangerous way to carry a get-down rope is to tuck it under the belt on a pair of leggin's or chinks.

Bits

I start my horses in a snaffle bit because it's much easier to get a horse to relax his jaw in a snaffle than with a hackamore, halter or shanked bit. Once he understands how to relax and give to the bit, then it's okay to use a shanked bit. With a shanked bit, a horse tends to lock his jaw if he doesn't understand what I want. With a halter or bosal, there's no manipulation of the horse's mouth, so I can't work his jaw to help the horse relax.

Because the snaffle gives a more direct feel for the horse's mouth than other bits, I can better tell when his jaw relaxes. The snaffle bit also makes it easier for a horse to understand what I want as I work slowly to help him find his balance during different maneuvers. The easiest place to balance a horse is at the end of the nose, so the closer my contact there, the better I can position my horse's head for balance. It's much like a dog using his tail to help balance his body.

With the snaffle bit I can develop that good balance and a relaxed horse at the same time. Using the bit correctly, with a light, milking motion, actually encourages the horse to relax his jaw, which, in turn, helps his entire body to relax. Everything's tied together — when a horse's mouth works, he relaxes inside.

However, used improperly, a snaffle bit can be harsh because the rider ends up pulling on the horse's mouth all the time. Soon the horse becomes unresponsive, dull and heavy in hand.

How long should a horse be in the snaffle? If a person uses it properly, he can ride his horse in a snaffle bit forever. But roping, for instance, is much easier with the reins in one hand, and the snaffle is a two-hander. I want to be able to ride my horse with one hand, so I can get my cattle work done. That's why the old spade-bit guys took so much time bitting their horses — to allow the horse time to learn to balance himself with the rider. The end result: The vaquero could then ride one-handed without the horse slinging his head or being unresponsive.

Another reason I'm all for advancing to a full bridle: Doing so means I've become a better horseman. It's easy for me to keep riding my horse in the snaffle, but to create real subtlety in my horsemanship, it's important for me to advance beyond riding with two hands on a snaffle bit.

As I've said, once a colt works well in the snaffle bit, I switch to a hackamore, starting with a 5/8-inch bosal and working my way down to pencil-size bosal. Especially when first starting a horse in a hackamore, I use my hands wide apart, just as if I'm leading him from his back and just like I lead a colt from his back when I first ride him with a snaffle. I don't pull, but lead the horse in the direction I want him to go. When he gives and responds to my hands, over time I move them closer toward the horn, and work with the horse to achieve a soft response. Ultimately, I want the horse finished and responsive to a soft touch from my fingers. Then, when I switch to a smaller-diameter bosal, the horse should know how to give to the feel of the hackamore, and there shouldn't be any problem with using the smaller bosal.

When a horse responds well to the pencil bosal, I put him in a two-rein rig so I can continue to use the bosal and also introduce the full bridle with a shanked bit to the horse. Some folks really devote a lot of thought to different bits for different horses, and that can become quite a science. But, I'm not that much of a scientist. To me, simple is better,

This buckaroo-style outfit includes a tooled slick-fork saddle, full bridle with reins and romal, a get-down rope and a 60-foot rope tied, in this case, on the left, because I sometimes rope left-handed.

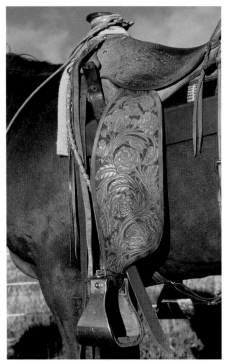

After dismounting, a buckaroo uses his get-down rope and sometimes tucks the romal under his stirrup leather to protect his horse's mouth and his gear.

and bitting a horse is just a feeling, that soft responsive feel a horse gives no matter if he's in a snaffle, a hackamore or a full bridle.

I start a horse in a full bridle by using a spade or half-breed bit with my hackamore and pencil bosal outfit. Which of the two bits I use basically depends on the horse's conformation.

Most of the time I use a spade bit on a thin-necked horse because he's usually fine through the throatlatch and naturally bridles up well. A horse built like that can pack a spade bit correctly because he can more easily keep his face on the vertical than a thick-necked horse can. With a spade, when a horse runs out his nose, the spoon touches the top or roof of his mouth. When it does, he should respond by dropping his chin and flexing a little more at the poll, which allows his face to become more perpendicular to the ground, where it should be to best balance a spade bit.

For a thicker-necked horse I use a half-breed, or even a Salinas bit with the copper hood, because those bits are a little more tolerant when a horse's face isn't absolutely vertical. The horse doesn't have to worry so much about the bit's balance or about holding his head vertically right over one of these bits as he does with a spade. When a horse's head is out of alignment with a spade, the bit weighs heavily on him; his face must remain vertical for the bit to feel balanced. But it's physically harder and less comfortable for a thick-necked horse to flex at the poll and become as vertical as he should be to pack a spade. With a half-breed bit, he can carry his nose a little ahead of the vertical and isn't punished for it.

The main thing about using two sets of reins is to be sure they're even. Then when a correction's necessary or something startles the horse, the rider doesn't inadvertently pull on his mouth or head.

When learning to use a two-rein rig, it's best for a person to do slow dry work until his muscle memory for handling two sets of reins becomes second-nature. Only then should he try faster-moving cattle work with his two-rein rig.

But until that time, it's best to put the two-rein rig on a horse and ride down a dirt road or trail. Then the rider can get comfortable with the feel of two sets of reins in hand without having to manage them so much at first. He should learn to direct his horse on a straight path of travel initially. Only after he's mastered that should he gradually learn to turn his horse in a two-rein rig. Then horse and rider must do each maneuver enough times over a period of time that they develop the necessary muscle memory to work effectively together with the two-rein rig.

Breast Collars, Martingales and Tie-Downs

Because my horses have good withers, I seldom use a breast collar, which only adds more weight for my horse to carry. Occasionally I might use a breast collar when riding outside or in the mountains, but I don't use one at all when working in an arena.

Although I don't use a martingale on my horse, it wouldn't bother me much to use one now. That's because I pay more attention to straightness and balance than I once did. Generally, using a running martingale seems to restrict my hands too much. I can't get them out wide, far enough to the sides of my horse's neck, if I need to lead him from his back to stay out of trouble. There's no way to do that with a running martingale. Instead, it forces me to pull more steadily on the horse, which creates more brace and unbalances him.

A traditional three-piece breast collar fastens to D-rings set in the saddle.

A martingale works on the same principle as a workhorse collar.

As for the tie-down, it just keeps a horse's nose in; it doesn't keep his head down. Even with his chin tucked, a horse still can raise his head. So this piece of gear isn't really about tying down a horse's head; it's about keeping him from locking his jaw, which, in turn, keeps the horse balanced. Remember: When he's not braced in his jaw, he won't brace his body either.

A word of caution: A tie-down is dangerous when crossing a river with a horse. It restricts his head so he can't get his nose up and out, which he must be able to do so he won't drown.

Miscellaneous Gear

It's fairly standard for most ranch cowboys to have a set of hobbles hanging on their saddles. I use leather two-ring hobbles. Knowing how to use hobbles makes them a valuable tool for any rider, and I discuss that more in a later chapter on handling ropes.

When I work cattle, I usually pack a medicine bag on my horse although

DO IT YOURSELF

To have a supply of cool water for an all-day ride, freeze water in a plastic jug the night before. The ice melts during the day to provide you a cool drink. Use whatever size plastic jug or bottle you prefer, but don't overload your horse with several huge bottles of ice water.

Carrying a Leatherman multipurpose tool in a belt pouch provides easy access.

The Leatherman Wave is the model I prefer because it opens with one hand.

occasionally I carry a small set of saddle-bags. I'm not a big saddlebag fan because I don't like packing a lot of bulky items on a horse. Instead, I sometimes use a cantle pack for frozen water in a plastic jug and a sandwich.

Cowboy Apparel

When it comes to clothing and apparel, cowboys take a lot of pride in their footwear. Many prefer custom boots simply for their comfort; after all, cowboys work in their boots many hours each day. Too, custom boots offer another way for cowboys to express their individuality, often with ranch brands and bright colors on the high tops.

The main reason for the cowboy's boots, however, is safety. Boot heels, of course, should be high enough that the rider's foot won't slip through the stirrup.

Soles also are a consideration. When riding outside, where a horse might go down on a hillside or slick bedding grounds, it's important to have slick leather or synthetic soles, not crepe soles that can bind in the stirrups. A slick sole allows the foot to come out of the stirrup much easier. Even though a crepe sole or packer-type boot might come out of the stirrup after a few jumps, if the rider's thrown, that few seconds of delay before he's clear might be just long enough to put him right at his horse's feet, where he can be stepped on or kicked.

There are tall-top boots or short ones, whatever a person prefers, but most cowboys ride with a taller boot-top, just for calf protection. Most wear a really tough, work-type boot. Personally, I prefer pull-on boots to lace-ups, mainly for the convenience and because I also want my boot to slip off if I get hung up somewhere.

Spurs are fine if the rider is disciplined to use them correctly, and many cowboys are. Spurs also offer a way of making a fashion statement, which is one thing when a top hand wears them, and something altogether different when someone

who doesn't know how to use spurs straps on a pair. (For more on how to use spurs, see Chapter 8.)

As for spur styles, again, the two main influences come from the vaqueros and the Texans. The California vaqueros and their neighbors, the Nevada buckaroos, want a lot of "gaud," fancy spurs with big rowels and lots of silver. A working cowboy in another part of the country — Wyoming, Montana or Texas, for example — often seems satisfied with something more practical.

The ongoing deal with spurs, and a great subject for debate, is whether real cowboys buckle the straps to the outside or the inside of the foot. That varies from one region to the next. I buckle mine to the outside, which probably comes from my rodeo days and riding bucking horses. I always buckled to the outside because the spurs were angled in toward the horse. Sometimes I believe a cowboy's buckles are on the inside just to show off the spur straps. Most Texans wear their buckles to the outside, it seems, and it also seems that most Californians wear them to the inside, which might just be more of a buckaroo thing.

Then there are chaps and chinks to consider. Chaps are full-length leggin's, and chinks are shorter, usually ending about boot-top high, with long fringe across the bottom. Sometimes the fringe flopping on a pair of chinks can spook a colt, so I prefer the leggin's, or chaps. They're also warmer, which is nice here in Montana in the winter, but in the summertime chinks are a little cooler. However, chaps also offer more protection and help keep the calf of my leg from being rubbed and keep my jeans cleaner, too.

I don't wear batwing chaps like cutting horse riders wear to emphasize the action in the show arena. Mine are shotgun leggin's that fit close the entire length of my leg. I don't want leggin's made of really thick leather, but I do have a heavier pair that I wear when it's cold or I'm riding in really brushy country. I typically prefer a medium-weight pair and don't feel comfortable riding without them, and that's true of most anybody who's become used to riding with a pair of leggin's.

The main safety consideration about a pair of chaps is the strap across the front. It's an old-time, safety consideration among cowboys, who don't want a heavy strap that won't break if it hangs on the saddle horn. For the same reason, cowboys generally don't use big buckles across the front of their chaps. Instead, they use a lightweight piece of leather or string that'll break loose if there's a problem.

It's important for any rider to carry a knife when he's horseback, and have the knife where he can get to it, so he can cut a rope, if necessary, should any problem arise when roping cattle or with a horse setting back on the lead, for example. I carry a knife I can open with one hand if I have to, and the cutting edge on the knife should work on nylon as well as leather.

A multipurpose Leatherman Wave tool, which folds up, actually has all the small tools built-in that I need to repair a piece of broken gear. I carry my Leatherman Wave in a pouch on my belt. It's a tool I can open with the thumb of one hand—and that's sometimes important. Some people carry a knife or Leatherman, thinking that they'll have to cut a horse loose eventually. I carry mine on my belt so I can get to it in case things get really bad.

As for jeans, there's the longtime saying that a cowboy's pants are snug for a purpose — to keep them from wrinkling underneath his legs. For the most part, a cowboy's jeans are designed for practicality, just as much of his apparel is.

Most cowboys also are particular about wearing long sleeves, even in the South when it's so hot. They do so because long sleeves offer more protection from scratches, scrapes and the sun.

Cowboys sometimes wear silk scarves around their necks, also called wild rags. Neck scarves are nice when the wind blows and it's cold because silk is such a warm fabric. Silk also dries quickly when it's wet. But, in all honesty, I get a kick out of seeing a guy wearing a vest and silk scarf when it's 100 degrees — and most cowboys get a kick out of that, too.

When the weather's cold, I know people who ride in coveralls, and do so comfortably. I don't, mainly because I don't think I ride as well in coveralls. And I seldom wear one big, heavy coat. Instead I layer on clothes — longjohns, wool pants, chaps, vests and coats. That way I can take off a layer and tie the clothing to my saddle as the weather changes, and I'm still comfortable.

Ranch cowboys almost always wear hats— felt or straw, depending on the region. In the summer a straw or palm-leaf hat can be nice because it's cooler, but I prefer a felt hat, and I don't get that hot wearing it. In fact, I see a lot of people even in the South and Southwest wear black felts year-round.

A hat offers protection from limbs as I ride through timber; when a limb hits a felt hat brim, it bends down to protect my eyes. I can't say a cowboy hat's better than a helmet, but I know I'll be wearing my hat when I leave the house and won't take it off until I go in at night.

The important thing about a hat is to buy one that fits snugly. Then it won't blow off and scare somebody's horse or spook a colt. And you don't have to chase your hat every time the wind blows. Put a stampede string on your hat, if you must, so you can keep your hat on your head.

DO IT YOURSELF

Stampede strings are inexpensive to purchase and easy to attach to your hat, or you can make your own. The string attaches to the hat in one of two ways: with a thin clip that hooks inside the hatband or through a hole punched in the hat brim. Some western stores will even punch the holes and attach eyelets so the hat material doesn't fray from the string sliding through the brim. An inexpensive string might be made from natural or synthetic fibers, or you can purchase a more expensive, braided horsehair string.

PART 2

COWBOY HORSEMANSHIP

Good horsemanship is about doing less instead of more to get good results. Some people seem to think that the more obvious and complicated the cues, the better their horsemanship. Nothing's further from the truth.

A good horseman is like any top athlete — he makes doing whatever he does look easy. In this case, horse and rider move fluidly together because each is so well-balanced individually. Each one's movements complement the other's motion, rather than counteracting it.

That's why good position in the saddle and understanding how the rider's balance affects the horse's straightness, balance and movement play large roles in a sound horsemanship program. Using a light touch on the reins to develop a soft response, instead of resistance, is equally important. All these qualities directly affect how well horse and rider perform any maneuver, from a simple walk down the trail to a more complex flying lead change in the competitive arena.

Improved horsemanship is within anybody's grasp. The bottom line: Anything a person can do horseback comes down to riding a horse through one or more of six basic transitions. That's because any advanced riding maneuver can be broken down into six basic transitions, which, in turn, can be broken down step by step.

1 and 2: Upward and downward transitions. These changes deal with a horse's pace or speed of travel, and how smoothly he makes the change from one pace to another.

3 and 4: Hindquarter transitions left and right. These address how easily a horse moves his back end from left to right, or vice versa.

5 and 6: Forehand transitions left and right. In the final two transitions a horse moves his forehand laterally, from left to right and vice versa.

Although a flying change or a side-pass initially might seem impossible, they aren't out of reach for most riders. The key: Master a few steps that make up each transition, then combine the transitions to create more difficult maneuvers.

The real challenge comes in finding the ideal balance to precisely perform each step in the necessary transitions. Only then can smooth, fluid changes be made. For an accomplished horseman, those little things are, in fact, the big things on which he bases his success.

That's what this second section is about, all the little things that individually might not seem so big in an overall riding program. Yet collectively, they give any rider the tools he needs to improve his skills and his horse's response. As those improve, horse and rider become more secure, confident and comfortable with the other. And that's when riding not only looks easy, it is.

A basketball player's stance with heels, hips and shoulders aligned is the balanced position for riding.

POSITION AND BALANCE

6

Dressage books describe the ideal riding posture and classical seat in the saddle. When I look at the way many ranch cowboys ride, most use the classical seat if the saddles they're riding will allow it. They've learned to use the classical seat and ride properly because they spend so many hours in the saddle that they must find that ideal position to be comfortable.

That's why I always recommend that anyone who wants to become a better horseman should spend a lot of time riding outside the pen. That's how he can best learn to find and use a good seat in the saddle. This is especially true for someone learning to ride, once he feels safe and comfortable horseback in the round pen or arena. Going for a 5- or 6-hour ride is the best thing anyone can do to improve his horsemanship.

At first his body says, "I feel all wrong in the saddle." But before long his body says, "I've got to get this right, or this is going to kill me."

That's when he subconsciously starts realigning his body to find the best place when he's horseback. That's when he finds his balance in the saddle.

The better balanced a rider is, the better balanced his horse can be, and the easier his movement. When it's easier for the horse to perform, there's less resistance, so both horse and rider enjoy a far more comfortable and relaxing ride.

Balanced Stance

The perfect stance for riding is probably much like that a basketball player uses for a free throw. Everything in his body is aligned so that it's easy for him to move quickly. He's in correct position for the throw because he's balanced and easily can step backward, forward or side to side. He doesn't stand flat-footed on his heels or up on tiptoes, but balances on the balls of his feet.

To me, using that same balanced stance with my feet in the stirrups provides the best, most secure base for horseback riding. I used to ride in oxbow stirrups a lot, but now I really prefer stirrups with a broad base and flat tread because I can better balance on the balls of my feet — just as if I'm shooting a free throw.

The Classic Position

With the balls of my feet balanced lightly on my stirrup treads, my legs hang straight underneath my torso, and my ears, shoulders, hips and heels are aligned. It's the classic riding position described in all 4-H and horsemanship books. Anybody who has proper posture horseback rides in that position.

When I'm horseback, I really see myself as if I'm a plumb-bob hanging from above. Imagining that helps me keep my body aligned the way it should be from ear to shoulder to hip and to heel.

To ride well and work best with my horse, it's important that I sit up straight, with my pelvic bones open and my legs hanging right underneath my hips and torso. If, instead, I close my pelvis and rock back on my seat, that puts me out of

Don't get too long on the reins and lock the knees, which forces a rider out of position in the saddle.

Do ride in a balanced position to work most effectively with a horse.

balance and behind my horse's action; then I'm always trying to catch up with my horse. That's why barrel racers starting a run, jockeys beginning a race and ropers coming out of the box raise up and move forward in their saddles — to get their bodies balanced right over the action as their horses accelerate.

That's another reason why I don't ride with oxbow stirrups as much as I once did. Doing so pushed me a little farther back in my saddle, and that sometimes left me a little out of position and behind my horse's action. Now whenever I work a cow or teach a horse a maneuver, I make sure I'm up and off the back of my saddle, toward the horn as far as I can be and still maintain proper body alignment. Then it's much easier for me to stay in balance with my horse.

Feeling Secure

To feel more secure and competent when riding, I've learned to spread my feet wide for balance. That doesn't mean pushing them stiff-legged out in front of me. That only rocks me farther back on my seat, behind my horse's action. Instead, I just move my feet slightly out from the horse's sides to achieve a wider stance for better balance.

Riding is like skiing; when a slalom skier going through the turns thinks he's about to fall, he takes a wider stance to find his balance. That's important for any rider to remember, especially when he travels over steep terrain or into a situation where his horse might spook, so that he feels more secure in the saddle.

I used to tell people to put a lot of weight in their stirrups, but my thinking on that has changed over time. Although doing that might help me feel a little more secure when riding, too much weight in the stirrups really makes me late in using my legs to support my horse in whatever I ask him to do.

The reason: When I press down hard

to put weight in the stirrups, my muscles tighten, pushing my legs away from my horse's sides. To use a leg cue, I must first relax my leg muscles, and contract them again to bring them in and around my horse's sides to cue him. Doing all that delays my timing, which is so important when communicating with a horse.

The same holds true if I lock my knees as I ride. Locked knees usually make me weight my stirrups even more and push my feet forward too much. That, in turn, sets me out of position, on my back pockets in the saddle, with my legs held stiffly away from my horse's sides. If I'm a knee-locked rider, again, I also must first relax my legs, then again contract my leg muscles to help my horse. That momentary delay also affects my timing when I cue my horse.

Instead of weighting my stirrups or locking my knees, I sit relaxed in the saddle. I let my legs hang softly around my horse's sides. I use just light pressure in the stirrups, without actually pushing against them. That way, my feet stay closer to my horse's sides, and my leg-cue timing can be much better. I can use my legs all the quicker because they're already close to my horse. Because my timing's better, I can better support my horse in any maneuver, from a canter departure to a turnaround.

The Fear Factor

Fearful riders tend to curl into the fetal position — even when horseback. They bring up their knees, lean forward and wrap themselves around the saddle horn, which usually causes the horse to drive forward even faster. That's the worst thing for anyone who wants to feel more secure on a horse to do.

When a frightened rider grabs hold of the saddle horn, he usually stiffens his arm, especially if he reaches over the top of the horn. If his horse jumps forward, the motion could fling the rider right over the saddle horn and out of the saddle.

DON'T

Don't go into the fetal position, which contributes to poor balance when riding.

DO

Do sit up straight to feel most secure and balanced.

DO IT YOURSELF

It's easy to make a night latch for your saddle. Just run a leather strap or a piece of rope through the gullet of your saddle. The length depends on how the saddle is made and the size of your hand. Then place the back of your hand against the gullet, under the strap, to measure your night latch's

length before you fasten it securely with a buckle or tie it. Even an old dog collar buckled through your saddle gullet works as a night latch if you're sure the leather is sound. Obviously, having your night latch break right when you really need it is the last thing you want to happen.

A strong piece of leather, like a dog collar, makes a good night latch.

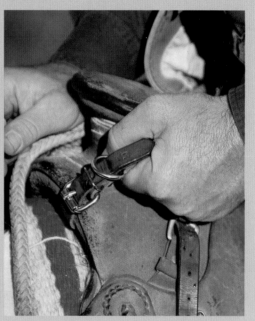

Here's how to use a night latch when riding gets rough.

That's where a night latch, which many ranch cowboys use, comes in handy. Cowboys who don't use a night latch often call it a chicken-strap. A night latch is simply a rope, leather strap or dog collar fastened through the saddle gullet and around the pommel. The night-latch strap is loose enough that the rider can slide his hand, thumb-up, between the strap and the saddle and close his fingers around the strap. The big difference: Holding on that way curls the rider into the saddle, rather than bouncing him out and over the horse's front end as the overhand horn grab does.

When I grab my night latch with one hand, set my feet wide in my stirrups, and grab the back of my saddle with my other hand, I don't think there's a horse alive that can buck me off. I'm sure one can — but I don't think so. I have that kind of confidence, and that's why I'll step on almost any colt, but anyone who doesn't feel that confidence should use caution — even with a night latch on his saddle.

The Rider's Balance

My main job as a rider is to not affect my horse's balance while he does his job. I have a working partnership with my horse, and good partners don't get in each other's way while they work. When one does, it usually puts the other out of sorts.

Perhaps that's why so many horses switch their tails and pin their ears as people struggle to ride. Often the horse is out of balance because what his rider does — or doesn't do — gets in the horse's way of doing his job, for example, making a lead change. Turn out that same cranky horse, and he makes flying lead changes across the pasture — no problem. But when the rider's in the saddle, he can't get the job done.

That's because the slightest shift in the rider's weight affects the horse's balance so much. So often a horse can't take the correct lead because an unbalanced rider has made him an unbalanced horse. Even though a rider might lean only slightly to one side, and not even realize he's doing that, when he does, his horse must brace with that side of his body to compensate for the unbalanced weight on his back.

It's important that I stay plumb — really straight up and down — in my saddle. Then I don't affect my horse's balance to the point he must stiffen and brace somewhere in his body to support my weight. When that happens, I must first reposition myself to overcome that brace, or stiffness, before the horse and I can work well together to perform the next maneuver.

Balance also is why it's important for a top rider to start a colt. A colt's really uncomfortable at first, trying to learn how to balance a rider's weight, and any good colt-starter knows that. Because he's ridden so much, it's easy for him to feel when the colt first gets off-balance and help the

DO IT YOURSELF

To better understand how quickly and how much your balance affects your horse, try this exercise. First, sit in a balanced position on your horse when he's standing still. Then see how far you must lean one way or another before your horse has to rebalance himself by moving a foot. It doesn't take nearly as much leaning as you might think to affect your horse's balance.

colt recover by staying as balanced as possible in the saddle. That's so important in helping any colt more quickly become comfortable carrying a rider.

But, if the colt-starter doesn't find his balance quickly and stays out of position, that might scare a broncy-type horse to the point that he bucks. And if the rider remains out of position too long, a colt inexperienced in packing a rider's weight might even fall. That's why it isn't safe for someone who isn't well-balanced in the saddle to start a colt; if he can't maintain his own balance, he can't quickly help the young horse find his.

Although that's not such a big deal for small riders, balance is especially important when a big guy like me rides a colt. At 200 pounds, I can make a colt fall if I don't maintain proper position in the saddle — and I won't have to be far off-balance to do it.

The same thing holds true when riding a horse on poor footing: I won't have to be extremely off-balance to have a problem. As all ranch cowboys have, I've worked a lot of cattle on slick ground, where my balance needed to be right or my horse and I were in trouble. Even when I'm not working cattle, I always remember how easy it is for a horse to go down on poor footing. That's especially true when his rider isn't well-positioned in the saddle, and it's his safety at stake.

The Horse's Balance

I think of my horse standing on a level teeter-totter with his weight equally balanced on either side. His balance point, or center of gravity, over the center of the teeter-totter is right behind his withers, where his weight is most evenly distributed from his front end to his hindquarters, and that's the strongest part of his body that can best support my body weight. When I ride or even sit still on my horse, I want to be as close to that point on my horse as possible.

Whatever I do with a horse, once any maneuver is complete, I always quickly reposition myself over his balance point. For example, as soon as my horse completes his stop, I sit up straight and realign my body right over my horse's point of balance. If I'm out of position, riding the back of my saddle when he stops, I must work even harder to regain my position, which puts more strain on my horse, making it difficult for him to find his balance. So anytime I complete a maneuver, I always return to that basic position in the saddle and as soon

"...I don't make my outside riding a structured drill. Nobody should have to do that."

as possible. The more I'm out of that balanced position, and the longer, the more my horse must compensate by bracing his body to balance himself beneath me.

Even when I relax horseback, I never just sit flat on my saddle. If I want to relax and let my horse relax, I might loosen my stomach muscles and allow my shoulders to droop a little, but that's as close to just sitting flat on a horse as I get. As with most ranch cowboys, when I relax on a horse, I won't cock one leg over the saddle. Most of us think that's disrespectful to the horse, but many people do it. If I'm tired, I get off and sit down so my horse can relax, too. If I cock a leg around my saddle horn, my shifting weight throws off my horse's balance. Then he can't relax, but must brace to support me or even reposition himself.

In addition, cocking a leg around the horn is a good way to get hurt, should something startle the horse. It might look great in a Will James' picture, but I don't think too much of it.

Finding Your Balance

It's so hard for some riders to find their balance horseback, and other riders don't care or just don't realize how their sloppy riding affects their horses. Although these people read all about excellent balance in

the books and understand it when they watch the videos, the only thing that can really put them in a balanced position on the horse is their muscle memory. And the only way to develop that muscle memory is by riding.

That's why it's so important for novice riders to get outside the arena as soon as they feel it's safely possible. Only then can they go up- and downhill, cross creeks and "side-hill" or zigzag their way to the top of a steep slope. That's when green riders best learn how to adjust and compensate as their horses move over varied terrain, and still maintain a comfortable balance.

If the only riding available is an arena or stable situation, that's fine. Performing horseback exercises in the round pen while somebody longes the horse is another way to develop riding balance. But I've never done that. Why should I when I can ride outside, see all nature has to offer and find my balance in beautiful surroundings? I can learn so much easier while riding outside, and with far less bother for my horse, because it's more interesting to both of us than going around in circles in a pen.

Whenever I can, I enjoy a trail ride or just ride through my pasture, stepping over downed timber or tracking a cow. Sometimes I play in my pasture, first circling this tree and then another. I always work to make my riding more precise, but I don't make my outside riding a structured drill.

Nobody should have to do that. Even riding with a friend and playing follow-the-leader through timber helps a novice rider learn how to better balance his body with his horse's body. Better yet, he doesn't consciously think about his body position because he's too busy thinking about the timber or following his friend, but his subconscious mind fixes his body position anyway.

Riding in a fun, relaxed way helps anyone learn and maintain proper saddle posture because the body naturally does what

DO IT YOURSELF

If you do nothing else to change your routine, ride down the driveway to get your mail every day. You and your horse can learn a lot just by doing that. So what if it takes 5 minutes to saddle your horse and only 5 or 10 minutes to ride to the mailbox and a few minutes longer to maneuver your horse close to the box and retrieve your mail? In the meantime, you've ridden your horse outside the pen and picked up the mail. You and your horse probably learned something about each other, too. Part three covers more ways you can prepare your horse for safer outside riding, and Chapter 12 discusses the side-pass, which is helpful when retrieving the mail.

it must for the rider to feel balanced. When a rider spends all day in the saddle, his subconscious will take over that balancing job — and he should let it. Seeing ranch cowboys ride proves that approach works. A lot of them have never seen or heard anything about classical riding, but most sit a horse almost perfectly as far as a classical seat is concerned.

Balance and Movement

When I want my horse to perform a maneuver, there are two ways I can go about it. I can let him find his balance to make the movement, or I can have him make the movement to find his balance.

For example, if I want to move my horse's front end to the left, I might first balance him just like he'd balance himself naturally before I ask him to turn. I make sure he's relaxed and elevate his head slightly to engage his hindquarters. Then I shift his weight back and off his left front foot, so it's easy for him to step his forehand across to the left. In this approach my horse finds his balance first, and then makes his move.

But I could, for example, first ride my horse forward in smaller and smaller circles until his front end just literally falls across the circle as he finally steps one foreleg across the other one before I release him. In that case, my horse moves first, then actually falls into the balanced position after he's in motion, rather than finding his balance before he moves.

Before I really thought about balance and movement, trying to understand them more, I sometimes worked a horse while his body was bent until he fell into a maneuver. That worked, but my horse always seemed cranky because he found his balance after he moved instead of before he moved.

After I began to figure out what my horse really did with his body, I learned to better set him up to perform a maneuver by first balancing his body. Because my horse feels more secure and comfortable, he no longer becomes cranky about performing maneuvers, such as turnarounds or lead changes.

This idea of letting my horse find his balance before performing a maneuver also seems to speed the bitting process, especially when I follow the old-time vaquero horsemanship tradition. That's when the rider develops a horse from the snaffle bit to the hackamore, then to a two-rein rig using both bosal and bit and, ultimately, into the full bridle. It's a thorough, but time-consuming method of bitting a horse. However, when I take that balance-then-movement approach in my riding, it's much easier to ride my horse in the snaffle or hackamore just as I would in a full bridle. Because I don't have to do all that bending with my horse, he often learns to work better in the bridle all the faster. And that's a real, valid reason for balancing my horse before I ask him to perform.

Chapters 9, 10 and 11 explain more in detail how I use my body posture and the reins to better balance my horse before opening the door for his movement.

Quiet hands keep a horse relaxed and balanced in his work.

STRAIGHTNESS AND SOFTNESS

7

In Chapter 6 I mentioned that when I'm off-balance, my horse must brace or stiffen somewhere in his body as a counterbalance. I've also learned that anytime I pull steadily on the reins, for instance, or push on a horse steadily with my legs, he braces and stiffens against that, too.

That thinking kind of shoots the normal hand and leg cue things we're all accustomed to using right out of the water because we must pull and push on a horse to teach those cues. To my way of thinking, we

Heavy-handed overbending causes the rider to get out of position and the horse to lose his balance.

actually teach horses to brace against us when doing those things. So I've really changed my mind about conventional approaches, even though some people might think it's a little controversial.

I believe now that, more than anything, a horse most wants his head and body

By using only my little fingers on the reins, I can quickly signal my horse for a release.

straight because, when they are, he's in his most balanced state. And when he's balanced, he shows the least resistance or brace. By moving one part of his body only a little, he can become unbalanced and, as a result, must stiffen or brace somewhere in his body.

That's why I now try — and I'm getting much better at it — not to pull much on my horses. The more I pull on a horse's head to bend his neck here, it seems, the more out of balance he becomes and must brace with his body over there, and sometimes must even tightly contract his muscles to keep from falling down completely. If I continue pulling on the reins when he's off-balance, before long a horse develops the habit of bracing against my pull.

Granted, in some cases pulling a horse's head around to the side might be a great thing that could save my life. By doing that, I can keep him off-balance just enough that he can't buck me off or run away.

But, if at all possible, instead of pulling and

bending my horse, I'd rather keep his spine straight so there's less brace in his body and, obviously, less resistance.

Straightness

I believe most horses want their bodies and necks straight because that's the way they feel most balanced. A horse in the pasture might turn his head when another horse approaches, but straightens his neck almost immediately as soon as he realizes the other horse isn't a threat. A horse often bends to reach a fly on his side, but straightens himself as soon as the fly's gone. When a horse dozes under a shade tree, he doesn't stand with his body bent and twisted — it's straight.

A cutting horse doesn't really bend his neck to make a move unless he's overplayed the cow and must turn to face it; once he does, the horse becomes straight again. He normally shifts his weight back, to lighten his front feet so he can make those big, long reaches as the cow moves, but his body's basically straight. He pivots off his rear end like it's an axis and balances himself well. But if the rider bends and pulls on him, the cutting horse gets out of balance, his work becomes harder and his turns become heavy. In fact, I was watching cutting horses when I first realized that I don't need to bend my horses so much, but keep their spines straighter instead.

Most people have seen a horse that "runs off" through his shoulder. The rider might have the horse's nose pulled to his knee, but the horse steadily moves in the wrong direction, leading with his opposite shoulder. This sometimes happens when a barrel horse runs down the fence, rather than turning the first barrel; his head usually is pulled to the right, but he travels to the left and leads the way with his left shoulder. That happens because the horse's spine is bent too much, rather than straight. But, with a straight spine, he can engage his hindquarters and use them as an axis, just like the cutting horse. And he won't drop and run through the shoulder; his shoulders stay even and level because his spine is straight.

In similar situations I've noticed that when a horse drops his left shoulder, for example, and pushes through it in that direction, his head and neck change position to help him maintain his balance. As they do, his left ear, when he's traveling to the left, becomes lower than his right ear. That's another indication that his spine isn't straight.

I also believe that pulling on a horse to bend him causes him to drop one ear, which, in turn, means his shoulder has dropped out of proper position. That chain reaction is another reason I try not to pull and shape my horse's body as much as I once did.

In this case, watching my horse's ears isn't really about his ears at all, but about his spine; his ears are a good, visible guideline that I easily can watch. I pay attention to how level my horse's ears are. Noticing that is important because it tips me off about his spine's straightness.

When my horse's ears are level, it's almost physically impossible for him to drop a shoulder; his straight spine won't allow it. So to ensure that my horse doesn't drop his shoulder in a left turn, for example, the first thing I do is pick up on the left rein to keep his ears level through the turn. Then, obviously, one ear can't drop lower, which would indicate that his spine is bent, making it easy for him to drop the opposite shoulder.

Here's another way I think about straightness and my horse's spine. I consider how differently he travels as I leave the barn. I sometimes must help keep him going, and I compare that with how he feels when he's headed

DO IT YOURSELF

It's important to learn to look where you're going and not down at your horse's ears. Focus on whatever you're riding toward — the gate, the cattle or just some spot you've chosen. But, as you ride there, practice using "soft eyes," which allow you to see your horse's ears in your peripheral vision. As you ride, focus on the place where you're headed, but really be aware of your horse's ears at the edge of your vision. Learn to watch for his ear movement. When his ears go forward, you can almost feel your horse get straight; it's like somebody pulls him with a string, straightens his body and takes him where you want to go.

back to the barn after a day's ride. His body lines out as he hits a good, steady pace going to the barn.

That tells me that straightness also is as much a mental thing to a horse as it is a physical thing. Everybody talks about getting a horse to go straight in the physical sense. But when I turn him around to head back to the barn, his straightness becomes a mental thing, too, because his mind focuses on where he's headed — the barn, and that mental focus makes it much easier to ride him there. That's another reason I pay attention to my horse's ears. They tell me when his mind goes where I want him to go, which means his body will travel there straighter and more fluidly. When his ears go forward, I leave my horse alone and try to be at one with him because I know his mind has already gone where I want him to be.

I even used to recommend that people rub a horse when his ears went forward, but not anymore because doing that only brings my horse's mind back to my hand, and takes it off the place I want him to go. So now his reward is that I don't do anything to distract him; I just go with his motion and try not to throw off his balance.

If my horse then becomes off-course, I offer some guidance, but I try to be subtle and fix him with my fingertips, without using a lot of rein or leg pressure. Using heavy leg pressure also makes my horse's mind come back to my legs, away from our destination, and if my leg pressure is steady enough, he also braces against it.

So when I try to control and straighten a horse's spine, I do it softly with light pressure on the reins. Once my horse understands that I won't pull, bend and fix him all the time, he learns to find that straightness, mainly because that's where he finds the release from all pressure.

Straightness in a horse's body is such a primary thing because, when I have that, any maneuver becomes so much easier for him to perform. My horse really understands how to be comfortable with his body and does whatever I ask of him so much more willingly.

Soft Hands and Jaws

Before ever using the reins to ask a horse to do anything, the rider first needs to understand that a horse doesn't have a collar bone; simply put, his back end hangs inside his front end and is connected by soft tissue. Many people don't know that and think that when a horse raises his head, he automatically hollows his back. But that's not true unless the horse elevates his head and pushes it up and out with his jaw locked, which will hollow his back. However, when a horse raises his head with a relaxed jaw, it actually engages his hindquarters.

How he elevates his head is the important thing. A good horseman knows that, thinks ahead while riding, and learns to handle his reins in a way that encourages the horse to relax his jaw in a softer response, which is described later in this section.

Another real benefit: If his horse gets a little scared, and a rider develops this skill before he really needs it, he probably can ride his horse through whatever situation is bothering him, just by softening and relaxing his horse's jaw with his fingertips on the reins. Like the cowboy who touches a colt on the neck in reassurance, a top hand milks his reins with a slight touch and sets his horse at ease by relaxing his jaw.

"Whenever a horse braces his body, his resistance usually starts in his jaw... ."

Whenever a horse braces his body, his resistance usually starts in his jaw, and that's often the first thing most any horse learns when somebody pulls on a rein — to lock the jaw. Think about chewing gum. When you get mad, you usually quit chewing, grit your teeth and lock your jaw. As your jaw locks, your whole body begins to stiffen, too. I think the same thing happens with the horse: Once his jaw locks, his entire body tenses.

In traditional training the rider typically bends his horse a lot through his neck to help

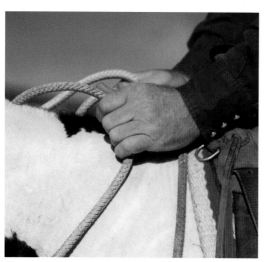 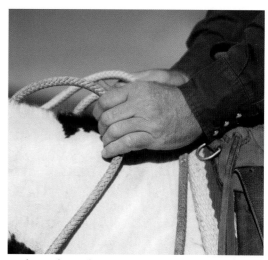

The cue to signal a horse should be so subtle...   ... that only my fingers move slightly, not my hand.

relax his jaw, so that his body won't stiffen and lock up. I'm not saying that bending the horse through the neck is wrong, but I wonder if there aren't other ways to gain that same softness in the jaw and decrease resistance. Maybe it puts the cart before the horse to pull on him first, which also tends to kill his forward motion, another by-product that's also undesirable in riding horses.

That's why it's important for me to pay attention to how I use my hands on the bridle reins. I don't want to pull on them in a way that causes my horse to brace.

There's a difference in two common motions I can make with my arms and hands. When I open a pasture gate, for example, I grab it with my hand. Should the wind blow it, I can stop the gate's motion or go forward with the gate's flow in a back-and-forth, sawing motion.

The other common motion is using my arms and hands as I would when milking a cow. My back's nice and straight as I reach underneath the cow, then squeeze gently with my thumbs and forefingers, working them up and down. It's not a back-and-forth motion like that used at the gate, but an up-and-down milking one. I don't pull hard because that old cow kicks, and I must keep my thumbs up and my elbows close to my body so I can direct the milk to hit the can.

That's the same way I should use my hands on the bridle reins when I ride two-handed,

with the reins coming up, through the bottoms of my hands and out over the top of my closed fists. When a horse braces against me, he tightens his jaw to push his nose out in resistance in that back-and-forth sawing motion. But I can't out-pull a horse when he does that, so I don't even try.

Instead, I keep light contact with the reins and work them in a milking motion, with my fingers and thumbs moving softly up and down, until the horse softens his jaw instead of bracing against me. I've learned to be so subtle with my hands that people seldom see what I'm doing with my fingers, and yet a horse can respond to that light touch.

So instead of trying to pull and drag a horse around wherever I want him to go, I condition him with my fingers to soften and become elastic in his jaw by relaxing it. I don't pull hard because I want that softness; I use a light feel instead, as if I milk that softness out of my horse. He eventually learns to relax his jaw and be soft in hand, and my hand motion is so subtle that it becomes almost invisible.

As my horse softens and bends his jaw, I can guide him more easily in whatever direction I want to go. Even though his head is elevated, because his jaw's relaxed, his body's still straight. He can shift his weight easily, engage his hindquarters and, for example, cross one front foot over the other, side-pass to or from an obstacle, whatever I want. The horse's spine still remains straight, just as it'd be naturally, so he's comfortable and secure in his balance. Being able to relax his jaw ultimately makes it far easier for me to help him through a problem.

The Highline

Some people leave a horse tied for hours, but that's not good to do because the horse learns to give up. A horse tied against a fence or the trailer has nowhere to go. He can't move his feet much, and that's usually when one starts to paw, pull back or rear, which gives some people a reason to hobble-break him.

Any scared, uneasy horse needs to move his feet; that's part of his flight-or-fight nature. In the same way, when a tied horse becomes bothered and uncomfortable, he needs room to move his feet, too. Ranch cowboys understand that, which is why some of them like using a highline, much like the old Californians did when they tied their horses to high tree limbs.

A highline is a chain stretched between two upright poles that are well-anchored in the ground. A swivel is attached to the chain, and a lead rope and snap are attached to hang down from the swivel. A cowboy snaps the rope to his horse's halter to tie him to the

This highline is stout enough to hold several horses, or to attach a tire for dallying practice.

A young horse can learn to stand tied and to relax his jaw at the highline.

highline. The great thing about a highline is that nothing's in front of the horse, so he can move his feet and even turn around completely, but he can't get tangled or hurt because the highline swivels overhead.

Using a highline is an effective way to teach a horse about standing tied, and the highline also softens a horse's jaw so that he won't be resistant when a person picks up the lead or even a bridle rein. When a horse tied to a highline moves around and reaches the end of the lead, he has a choice. He can continue to feel pressure from the lead, or he can bend at the jaw, moving the lower part of his head to find relief. When he does the latter, the pressure is released, and because his feet can move, the horse can then straighten his spine completely.

A horse never stands with his body crooked. He might reach back to get a fly, but his body straightens immediately afterward because that's more comfortable to him. That's the reason some horsemen prefer using a highline, rather than tying a horse's head around to the stirrup to teach him to give to pressure. Tying to the stirrup, even though the horse learns to bend his neck and arc his body to put slack into the rein, never allows him the complete straightness he needs to feel comfortable, which is what a good release should offer.

DO IT YOURSELF

Using a highline helps soften your horse's jaw, making him more responsive when you direct him with the lead rope or bridle rein. Setting up a highline isn't difficult, although you might need some help to set the upright poles and anchor posts.

You'll need two 12-foot uprights, two anchor posts, chain or cable (how much depends on the distance between the uprights), a swivel to attach to the chain or cable and a lead rope with snap to tie to the swivel.

I used two railroad-switch ties for my highline uprights. Before setting them in the ground, I drilled a hole in one end of each, just large enough for my chain. The chain overhead shouldn't be so low that a horse can get over it or that a saddle horn can catch on it. The rope with snap should be just long enough that, when fastened to the halter, the horse flexes his lower jaw from side to side as he moves around.

About 8 feet of each upright is above-ground, which seems safe for most horses to freely move under, yet leaves the snap low enough for most people to reach. With my height I have no problem snapping a highline rope to a horse's halter, but it's hard for my kids to do.

The uprights should be at least 12 feet apart, which allows a horse ample room to completely rotate his body underneath the highline. However, my highline is wider and has more than one rope attached. That's because I used the gateposts supporting two 12-foot gates into my round pen as my highline uprights. I just open the gates whenever I use the highline.

My anchor posts, one for each upright, are made from cross-ties and set in the ground with only a foot or so exposed. Again, I drilled the exposed end of each anchor just large enough to accommodate the chain.

With the uprights and anchors set, I fastened the chain through the hole in one anchor, ran it up and through the hole in the first upright, across to the second upright, through the hole in it, then down to the second anchor and fastened the chain securely. I then attached the swivel to the overhead chain before fastening the lead rope and snap to the swivel.

Use a link and a swivel to fasten a lead rope to the highline so it doesn't get kinks when a horse is tied to it.

Use a turnbuckle to keep the highline chain, anchored to the ground, tight.

Handling the Reins

Many people ride with too-long reins, and I even do that when I'm out on the trail. But when a cow's in front of my horse, I crawl my reins to the point that all I must do, for my horse to know I'm there, is close my fingers an eighth of an inch. I avoid flexing my arm muscles when I make contact with my horse's mouth, but tighten only my fingertips.

That way I have the contact I need without pulling continually on my reins.

However, many people haven't ridden enough with split reins to feel comfortable using them, let alone shortening them for quicker contact with a horse. In fact, that's why many western riders have horse-handling problems — they aren't good at shortening their reins.

But, instead of practicing that enough to become really good at it, many riders often pull the reins up high, to their shoulders, or completely back, behind their waists. They rush to do one or the other probably because they don't think they have enough time to shorten their reins before trying to fix the horse's problem. As a result, the rider's hands get way out of position, which allows the horse to continue doing something wrong. Even worse, the horse learns he can get by his rider without ever giving a good response.

I've realized that I can throw my horse out of balance by moving my body only slightly. That's what happens when I pull on too-long reins; I lose my good position in the saddle. When that happens, again, my horse must brace against me to feel balanced and secure. So I take that half-second necessary to shorten my reins enough to work with my horse when there's a problem. Then he learns to take and make a correction and do it well.

So what if it takes more than 3 days to learn how to shorten my reins? And so what if it takes longer than that for my horse to feel my fingers wiggle on the reins and respond to them? If my riding program doesn't include specific show-entry deadlines, then I'm always on time no matter how long it takes when I work my horse.

If my reins are just long enough that I can rest my hands on the saddle horn or pommel without putting pressure on the bit, I still can ride my horse with a lot of feel, but without pulling back on him all the time. I'm able to close my fingers slightly, and my horse can feel that and learn to respond to it.

Less is better when using the reins. I always try to see how little it takes to get my horse to listen to me. That subtle, quiet style of horsemanship develops a horse that

The horse is balanced, soft, relaxed and prepared to move in any direction.

By slightly elevating my hands, and shifting my weight I don't have to pull on my horse for a back-up, which would cause him to brace and stiffen. My elevated hands also prevent the horse from overflexing and getting behind the bit.

DO IT YOURSELF

Some people pull too tightly on the reins simply because they became scared when they first started riding, and they've never corrected the habit. If you keep a death-grip on your reins and find it hard to give your horse some slack, use a cracker, a cookie or even a dirt clod to help relax your grip. Ride with a cracker or cookie in each hand as you hold the reins. Don't crush your cookies! Holding the cookie helps you remember to soften your grip. You'll soon learn to be comfortable with the reins in your hands — without the death-grip — and your horse will follow suit and become more relaxed.

DO IT YOURSELF

People often forget to keep their thumbs up when they ride two-handed, and that's important in giving a horse clear signals. If you have that problem, break a couple of twigs, 6 or 8 inches long, off a tree and put one in each hand with your reins. The twigs sticking out of your fists make obvious what's happening with your hands — if your wrists are too bent or your thumbs are turned down. Even if your thumbs are up, but your elbows flap when you ride, that also becomes obvious. The twigs call attention to what your hands actually do, which helps you become more conscious of developing that soft, quiet feel for your horse's mouth by riding with soft, quiet hands.

always tries to figure out what I want without it becoming a contest between the two of us.

That's why the ranch cowboy's deal is so nice. He often has time, as he rides to and from his pasture work, to weave through the sagebrush or trees, just to see how little rein pressure it takes to get his horse to respond well. And the minute his horse responds, the cowboy always remembers to release his horse quickly. Soon it's hard for anybody to really see what the cowboy does with his hands and, before long, he can ride his horse effectively with only one hand.

That's the big goal here: to ride and feel safe with only one hand on the reins, especially for anyone planning to rope or work cattle. Ranch cowboy or pleasure rider, everyone ultimately wants that light response to one hand on the reins.

The 0-to-1 Effort

One thing most people miss when handling a horse is getting him to operate on the scale at 0 to 1. I think about measuring my effort to get a horse to perform a particular way on a scale of 0 to 10. If my horse's mind is on the other horses across the pasture, and I have to crank his head around and really thump on him to get him moving the right direction, that's a 10 on my part, and it usually makes his mind go toward the horses even more.

I want an effort somewhere between 0 and 1 on the scale. That's when the most

important thing is my thought becoming my horse's thought without a lot of cranking and thumping. If I want a horse to go a particular place, 0-to-1 means once I think about it and get my horse's attention on it, his ears quickly go there. I know he's thinking about what I want, and the maneuver is easy when I give him time to balance his body before we move.

But until that happens, I'm trying to force a 1,000-pound animal to do something, and it's always harder to get the performance I want. However, once my horse decides to do something on his own, and tells me he has with his ears, any maneuver is much easier — upward and downward transitions, lead changes, stops.

To develop that 0-to-1 effort, I first maintain straightness in my horse's body, and direct his attention to what I want. When I do those things and his ears go forward, I simply need to go with him when he moves. I especially pay attention and release my horse to move when his ears are forward because that means he's decided to perform on his own, and it'll be a much prettier, natural, flowing maneuver.

"Eartitude"

I've previously discussed some things about a horse pinning his ears and switching his tail. Many horses learn that by behaving that way, they get a physical release from the rider's pressure.

We all want a good attitude in our horses. And we all think that a horse learns from the release of physical pressure. That's kind of standard thought in the industry. I think a horse learns not only from the physical release of pressure but, more importantly, from the mental release of pressure.

I've already mentioned that when a horse's ears go forward, he's made up his mind to go wherever I want or do whatever I ask. In this case, his ears indicate that he's come around to my way of thinking, and is no longer mentally resistant to my idea. That's why, once his ears go forward, it's smart for me to just go there with him, without pulling or prodding. It gives my horse a release from the mental pressure he feels.

If a horse pins his ears when I cinch him, and I stop cinching when they're back, he thinks I stopped because he's cranky. Doing so teaches him to have a bad attitude. Instead, I can watch his attitude and quit working the cinch when his attitude is better and his ears are up. That's a mental release because my horse's attitude, his mental outlook, has changed.

If I'm a thoughtful rider, I can teach my horse to have a good attitude about many things, and I can change my horse's expectation that cranky behavior has its rewards, too, just by timing my release when a cranky horse's ears are forward. He soon learns to hunt that release by being more pleasant and minimizes his crabby responses.

Here's another example of how timing that release works in a common situation I often see with horses that are stalled most of the time. Nearly every time a person walks by a horse's stall, the horse pins his ears. In his mind, he's run off that person. That can become a real problem at riding stables, and some horses even bare their teeth like they want to bite off somebody's arm.

Instead of continuing down the barn aisle, I hang around the stall until the horse changes his attitude. I might rattle his stall door a little or move my hat around until his ears come forward. I always try to get that little change of attitude before I leave his stall. Then that horse doesn't learn how to be cranky. Waiting at the stall is such a subtle thing, but it means something in the horse's little world, and in my little world, I want to see his attitude change.

I don't consider that dominating a horse. I'm not much into that kind of thinking because I believe a horse and human can have a far different relationship than a horse and a mountain lion or two horses. The traditional herd pecking-order ideas are fine, and people seem to love that approach. But I think there's a higher level where horse and human can have a completely different view of each other simply because the human is able to think and reason through these problems.

With the stall situation, I'm not a predator trying to make the horse my meal, or a thief trying to steal his food; after all, I'm the one feeding him. And, at first, he might think of me as another horse. But when I don't leave as another horse would, our relationship changes. And when I don't try to make a meal of him, the relationship changes more. All I want is his good attitude, and I can help him deliver it.

To me, that kind of thinking is what's so great about being around ranch cowboys. They're always figuring out better ways to work around a horse and how to make things better. A lot of ranch cowboys haven't seen many clinicians or many show-horse hands, but so many ranch cowboys do many of the same things with their horses, and often without realizing it. Ranch cowboys watch their horses closely and consistently, so they learn well how to really evaluate a horse's responses to many different things.

DO IT YOURSELF

To become more aware of and in tune with your horse, develop the habit of closely watching his ears — and not only when you ride. It's good, of course, to notice his ears when riding because that helps you learn how straight your horse's spine is, if he's dropped a shoulder, for example, or when he's best balanced to perform.

However, be careful that you don't reward your horse's cranky behavior when you work him afoot. Don't take your hands off the cinch until his ears are forward. Don't keep tightening the cinch, just act as if you're cinching until your horse's expression is more pleasant.

Also watch your horse's response as you walk down your barn aisle, and especially when you feed him or clean his stall. Does his expression remain pleasant, as if he's looking forward to seeing you? Or does he wear a get-out-of-my-stall expression? Always use good judgment as you wait for your horse's expression to change, but don't let him run you off. Each small act of crankiness, left unchecked, might grow into a larger problem.

Wrangling horses is a ranch job that keeps a horse moving out freely.

MOVEMENT 8

A horse really searches to find comfort, it seems, no matter what I do with him. If I let him, he learns to match my movements, rather than making me match my body movements to his, because that's the most comfortable thing for him to do.

Even when the poorest rider bounces around on a horse's back, one of two things happens: The horse comes out from under the rider to get comfortable or rates his speed to that of the rider's bounce, so that the rider doesn't cause more discomfort by pounding so hard in the saddle.

Many people try to make something mystical out of horse and rider matching their movements. But there's nothing mystical about it — horses are sensitive, plain and simple.

A good horseman can match a horse's motion whether he's afoot or on his back because he's constantly aware of his horse. A novice rider might wave to his neighbor and scare the heck out of his horse, without even noticing that the motion scares him. An old cowboy horseback might only wink or nod his head. That old cowboy has spent so much time in the saddle, he's learned how sensitive a horse can be.

Everything a rider does in the saddle affects his horse. Some horses become dull simply because they must tolerate their riders flopping around in the saddle. That's the only way a horse in that situation knows to survive the experience.

On the other hand, I want my horse to become sharper and more responsive every time I work with him, so I evaluate how much life I put into my body, whether I work my horse on the ground or under saddle. That's the only way to develop those really sharp responses in him. My life force, even when I'm afoot, is something a horse easily can relate to even later, when I get on him.

Walk to Ride

Riding should be simple and fun. Sometimes I think we try to make it too complicated. When it's too hard to do, it's even harder to enjoy, and that's true of any sport.

To me, riding is like walking. It's that simple. I relate the two by thinking of good riding posture as being much like my walking posture. We've all walked since we were about 2 years old or younger, so we already have great walking muscle memory built into our bodies. We don't consciously have to think about controlling our arms and legs when we walk; we do those things automatically. We can make good use of that same subconscious muscle memory when we ride. We might as well — it's there for the taking.

Many times, it seems, novice riders try so hard to follow the instructions they're given, that they don't use their bodies and muscle memory to advantage. They must make a really conscious effort to ride, which shouldn't be the case. There's an easier way.

When I let my riding happen in the same way my walking happens, the riding becomes so much easier. As I walk faster, my energy level elevates and my weight shifts forward. If I increase my energy and shift my weight forward when I ride a horse, he walks faster, trots or lopes, depending on how much I change my body. That muscle-memory process works the same on the horse as it does when I'm afoot.

Plus, it's so easy for me to become consistent with my body movements when I ride because I've used many of the same moves consistently for years while walking. That consistency's important to good horsemanship. The more consistently I handle my body when I'm horseback, the more quickly and better my horse learns to follow what he feels, distinguishing one of my actions from another. A horse can eventually learn to pick up on my subtle body changes, which makes riding him much simpler.

So I make it easy on myself. When I ride, I use my body just as I do when I walk. That helps me better position and balance myself in the saddle to more clearly and easily communicate what I want of my horse.

Of course, few people want to spend all their riding time fine-tuning their horsemanship. But if a rider spends only half his riding time consciously thinking and riding his horse, as opposed to just being a passenger in the saddle, he can make his horse a real pleasure to ride. Perhaps everyone should work on

his horsemanship for a little while, each time he rides, and then have some fun on his horse. He can always consciously work on his horsemanship again later.

When a rider takes that approach and works on his horsemanship a little each day, before long it doesn't take such a conscious effort to improve his horsemanship. Then he learns to ride well in a natural way by also having fun with his horse. Even though the rider at first must think harder about everything he does, pretty quickly all his riding moves seem easy and second-nature.

Getting the Movement

To make nice transitions from one gait to another, or within a gait, I first must get my horse moving. The second thing I do is control his spine's straightness so I can go where I want. However, sometimes when I get a horse's spine positioned so he can go straight to a tree or gate, I might lose his movement. Then I must work to get my horse moving again.

If I can't get the forward movement I want from my horse, I usually use my mecate, or McCarty, to get him going, rather than kicking him with my legs. Typically I ride with

I exaggerate my arm movement, when I must drive my horse forward with the McCarty lead, giving him every opportunity to move out...

.... before I spank down his hind leg with the McCarty lead.

As with the McCarty lead on the left, the tail of my rope can be used on the right side of the horse to encourage forward motion.

When my horse knows I mean it the first time, I don't have to nag him with the tail of my rope to maintain his forward motion.

my McCarty on one side of my saddle and have my rope with the tail hanging down on the other side. That way I can use either one to encourage my horse to move forward.

When a horse won't step forward and I must make him move, I usually grab my night latch and use the McCarty or the tail of my rope to spank hard down one of his hind legs. I don't want to do that again — I want that swat to mean something to him the first time. If it does, the next time I liven up my body and ask my horse to move, he probably will.

Occasionally, instead of using the McCarty or rope, I might pop my horse's elbows with the sides of my feet. My legs are long enough to do that, but not everybody's are. That pop usually gets a horse moving, too. Again, I usually take a good hold on my night latch before I pop a horse — he might buck, but he goes forward. I wouldn't try that, though, unless I felt secure enough in the saddle to handle whatever might happen.

When I use my legs to just kick my horse, as most people do, I kick like I mean it, too. Again, I want my leg cues to mean something the first time so I don't have to use a correction again.

DO IT YOURSELF

When I have a slow-moving horse who really doesn't understand how to go forward, I sometimes turn my colts or other horses into the arena and track them with the slow horse. As I follow the colts around the pen, the slow horse wants to keep up with them, so he has a reason to go forward. Don't do this unless you're reasonably confident that you can control the situation and safely work the other horses from the back of your mount, just like you work afoot with a horse in the round pen.

DO IT YOURSELF

If your horse doesn't want to go when you leave your barn, get somebody with a more willing horse to ride with you a few times. When the other horse leaves the barn, that gives your horse a reason to go forward — but you also must actively ride him forward. Don't just sit there like some people do, getting mad at the horse because he won't go. When the other horse drafts or draws your horse forward a little, really ride with a lot of life in your body and use that life to push your horse ahead. Put the same effort into it that you expect from your horse. Whatever you do transfers to your horse and shows in his response.

Whatever the method, I won't overuse it to the point that I abuse my horse. But I do let him know that I mean for him to move out when I ask him. He must get moving before I can direct his motion to take us wherever we need to be.

Using My Legs

When a rider doesn't properly set up his horse to make the transition to a trot or lope, he usually kicks with his legs to get his horse to make that upward transition.

But where does the horse's mind go? Right back to the rider's legs — not toward the place he's headed.

In a way, the rider almost contradicts his cue as far as the horse is concerned. On one hand, the rider wants to move more quickly across the pasture toward a gate or a cow, so he wants to keep his horse's mind on where he's going. On the other hand, the rider using his legs often distracts the horse's mind from his destination.

Using the legs probably aggravates the horse, too, simply because kicking tells him to do something that he hasn't really decided to do yet, probably doesn't want to do, or has decided to do so quickly that he's not comfortable with the idea. In any of those situations, a horse often pins his ears or wrings his tail.

I'm not saying I never use my legs to signal a horse, but I try not to overuse them. I keep my legs soft around my horse's sides, but not squeezing him. When I use my legs to encourage a horse to move, I usually bump with one leg at the time on alternating sides because

Using one leg at the time to encourage forward motion keeps the horse's mind on his destination, and not my legs.

using both at the same time distracts a horse's mind from what I want him to do.

That subtle horsemanship approach also applies whenever I use my legs on a horse. Again, it's all about doing less, rather than more, to get my horse to work for me. Instead of moving my entire leg, I want to be able to wiggle my toe and have my horse understand what I want. If, over time, I need to do more with my legs to get results, I'm probably doing the wrong thing with my legs and need to rethink my approach and become quieter and softer with my legs. Ultimately, when nobody can really see what I do to get results, that's what horsemanship is supposed to be.

To Spur or Not

It's fine with me if somebody uses spurs when he rides, but I don't think most people have the discipline to use them properly. Not everyone is aware of where his feet are all the time, so a horse frequently gets spurred when the rider doesn't even know he's done it. So often a horse just becomes dull and takes it, and some develop bad habits, such as pinning their ears, because many people misuse spurs.

Nowadays, spurs have become fashion statements more than anything. Everybody who has a horse has a pair of spurs, and straps them on because he thinks spurs are such a part of the cowboy deal. And they are, but most cowboys really understand how to use them. If someone doesn't, he ought to hang his spurs on the wall as a decoration, instead of wearing them.

The problem: For many people, their spurs are the first things that touch the horse. A rider should use his thigh, calf and ankle to signal his horse first, before using his spur. That way, he gives his horse all the chances in the world to do right before he uses the spur, which should be the last thing to make contact.

Many people don't pay attention when they ride and spur a horse almost every step of the ride, which eventually just makes

him mad. If he can feel a fly land on his side, spurring him all day is an injustice to the horse. That's why only an advanced rider should strap on a pair of spurs; he already knows how to concentrate on his foot position at all times.

When I spur my horse, I use little short, sharp jabs until he responds. That gives him

"By the time most people become good enough horsemen to use spurs, they probably won't need them."

time to think about what I want. However, the next time I spur him, I again start by using only a light touch of the spur. If that doesn't result in the response I want, I do it again with the quick, light jabs. Soon enough a horse learns to pay attention to that lighter touch. But, if I turned out my toe and punched a horse really hard with my spur, he'd probably just have a knee-jerk reaction. When he does, whatever training I do then seldom sticks in the horse's mind anyway.

I rarely ride with spurs because my legs are so long that it's really hard for me to get my spurs to a horse. But when I do use spurs, I use a short-shanked, dull-roweled pair. Used properly, spurs are wonderful tools, and I'll spur a horse's sides if he's really sour about something I ask him to do. But the minute he changes his attitude — his ears come forward or his tail stops switching — my spurs come off the horse's sides. He gets that release only when his attitude's good.

Unfortunately, most people spur and release when the horse's ears are still pinned and his tail's still wringing. As far as that horse is concerned, he thinks he just ran off the spur, the same as he would a fly, so the spur is only a minor aggravation to him.

By the time most people become good enough horsemen to use spurs, they probably won't need them. That's because they've become such good hands. Good hands usually understand more subtle ways to get horses to do what they want, so they seldom feel a need for spurs anyway.

Rating a horse's speed in the lope goes back to the foundation laid at the walk and trot.

UPWARD AND DOWNWARD TRANSITIONS

9

Cowboys use transitions between gaits and to rate the speed of each gait. They ride enough to understand, for example, changing a horse's gait from a slow walk to a fast walk is easier than getting him to go from a walk to the lope. They try to keep their horses' responses balanced, and usually work to keep upward and downward transitions equally smooth.

Any rider should be able to get his horse to travel steadily at whatever speed he wants and in any gait. When a person does those things well, he truly rides in balance with his horse, but it takes saddle time to get to that point.

Using the reins or leg cues to rate a horse's speed shouldn't involve a bunch of wacky stuff that everybody notices. When a top hand gets his horse to do what he wants, generally nobody can tell what he does — except for him and his horse. A good horseman makes things look easy because his cues are subtle, and that's a good goal for anyone to work toward with his horse.

A horse can learn to look for and feel the slightest cues, however subtle; when he does, everything the two of us do looks so easy — and it usually is. The really great thing about a horse learning to respond to my body motion by matching the feel of it with his own is that doing so becomes his idea, as far as he's concerned. In that case, my horse is mentally and physically ready for any change I want to make, so he usually goes where I want him to go in the

way that's best for him. The easier I can make it for a horse to understand what's happening, by letting him decide to make that change in direction or speed, the better. Then my horse is comfortable doing what I want and doesn't become cranky about it.

Of course, that's hard to do in the show arena, where an immediate response is necessary, no matter if the horse is ready to make a change or not. Anyone who wants to work toward that degree of finesse on his horse can. Usually, however, that much finesse isn't quite as important to the recreational rider or the working ranch cowboy.

The Walk

The walk is a four-beat gait. When the horse's left hind foot moves, it's followed by the movement of his left front, then his right hind and right foreleg.

When I want my horse to step out and walk, I act as if I'm getting up and out of a chair. That tells my horse to prepare to move. When I want him to take a step, it's almost as if I walk away from the chair. I take a breath, lift my upper body and tighten my stomach as I ask my horse to move, just as I would if I took a big step. My horse soon learns to follow that feel; when I increase my energy to move, he does, too.

I then act as if I'm walking at whatever pace I want my horse to go. When I want a slow walk, I act as if I'm walking around sightseeing. If I want my horse to have a medium walk, I act like I'm headed to the bank to make a deposit. When I want a fast walk, it's like I'm starving and headed to the table. I use different postures for each speed, and my horse learns to feel those differences.

Because I teach my horse to make transitions and rate his speed by the way that I ride, it's important that I stay balanced and don't bounce around in the saddle. When I'm balanced, my horse can more easily understand that there's a purpose to

"But I never develop that subtle response if I always poke, kick and prod a horse with my legs."

any subtle move I make; it means something specific that he needs to know.

When I start riding a colt, I work hard to get what eventually becomes a subtle directive across to the horse. I let the air out of my body slowly — whoooossshhhh — and the colt slows down. When I elevate my body energy, my colt learns to pick up his speed, sometimes right into a trot, just because the air and energy come back into my body so quickly.

But I never develop that subtle response if I always poke, kick and prod a horse with my legs. He can't think about the subtle, little things and respond to them because his mind always will be on the big, huge things — the kicking and prodding — and how to dodge or survive them.

When I walk a horse away from the barn, I don't smooch, kiss or kick him. Kicking is my last resort, and when I do that, I really use my feet with authority, as stated in the previous chapter. But before I kick, I first lift my chest and body and, as I do, look ahead and watch my horse's ears. When they go forward and he looks where we're going, that usually tells me he's made the decision to move forward.

Rating the Walk

When I rate my horse at a walk, he should willingly hold the walk at three speeds — a slow walk, his normal medium walk and a fast, ground-covering walk.

Ideally, my horse can walk slowly in the arena or on the trail. Then I know later, if I head home and he gets excited and wants to jig, that he can, in fact, relate to what I'm asking him to do. I know positively that he understands that he's supposed to walk slowly.

To get my horse to walk faster, I use my body just as when I walk faster; I'm a more active and my energy level is higher. That encourages most horses to step out faster. However, some horses simply walk slower than others. When asking one like that to walk faster, it's almost as if I take each step for him. Instead of kicking with my legs, I consciously think about picking up my feet and almost physically lift my legs to help the horse move forward faster. Sometimes I must really emphasize that at first to get the speed increase I want. That emphasis might not necessarily be obvious enough for anybody to see, but it's strong enough that the horse can feel it.

As soon as my horse walks faster, I leave him alone. At first he might slow down, and then I have to ask him to walk faster again. But the minute he does, I quit asking. That's his reward for doing what I want.

To get a slower walk, I let the energy in my body drop, sink back into my saddle and exhale slowly. If necessary, at first, I might even wiggle my fingertips on the reins just enough to rate the horse back to the slower speed. Again, the minute he responds, I leave him alone.

Obviously, teaching a horse to rate his walk isn't always a quick deal. Just as some people are more sensitive than others, some horses are more naturally sensitive to the changes in my body than others. But if I continue to rate my horse's speed by raising and lowering my energy level, in time my horse learns to respond more quickly to those changes.

The Trot

When I want my horse to trot, no matter if he's standing still or walking, I liven up my energy, as if I more quickly rise from my chair. I also realize that when I ride him faster than he's traveling, I become out of balance with him. Either he must speed up his body to catch up and stay in rhythm with me, or I must slow down to match his pace.

If using my body to tell my horse what speed I want doesn't work, I might then use a little leg to get more speed from him, or check him a bit with my reins if he takes off too quickly.

When I want a horse to jog, I simply walk him really, really fast. A horse is smart and wants to conserve his energy, so he soon decides to hit a trot on his own. Because he makes that decision, his attitude is always better and less cranky. His mind's already thinking about trotting somewhere; it's not on me kicking and prodding him to go faster.

The trot is a two-beat gait created by the horse's right foreleg and left hind leg, and vice versa, moving together on the diagonal, almost in a side-to-side motion. Many people try to sit absolutely straight and still when trotting, which usually makes them really bounce in the saddle. A horse is a dynamic, moving animal, and his rider also must be dynamic to stay in balance with him.

Some people always post the trot. They rise and fall in the saddle in the rhythm of the trot, because they want to keep from bouncing around on the horse's back. Obviously, when a rider bounces that much, he isn't in balance with his horse in the first place.

Another rider might post because his horse seems a little out of balance and has a rougher trot. That's why posting has become so popular — a lot of horses are out of balance.

However, from the horsemanship standpoint, I don't recommend posting the trot all the time. I'm not at all against posting —

Even the two-beat trot is easy to ride when a horse's body is well-balanced.

just not all of the time. Posting is a wonderful tool that came from military riders and cowboys who traveled long distances horseback. If they didn't post, friction in the saddle made their backsides hot, especially troopers trotting 7 or 8 miles in a straight line without doing other maneuvers to break the routine.

Instead of sitting absolutely still or always posting, I position myself well in my saddle and then pivot at my waist to let my hips alternately move up and down in motion with the horse's gait. Even though my upper body remains quiet, I must move my hips to maintain my balance atop my horse. When trotting, I think of myself as a slalom skier, who's learned to let my legs and hips take the shock from the bumps and turns, so the rest of my body can remain quiet and controlled.

As I easily ride the trot, pivoting my hips up and down, my body becomes more balanced with my horse's action, which, in turn, makes performing easier for him. When the trot's easy and comfortable for him, his spine softens and his gait becomes smoother. That's when a horse best develops an easy-to-ride trot.

Some transitions from the trot seem easier to make than others. The transition from a walk to a trot, or vice versa, probably is one of the easier transitions to make. My horse and I are moving slowly enough that we can think about making either the upward or downward transition smoothly and calmly.

But making a smooth change from a stop to the jog is a more difficult upward transition that requires practice and finesse to do well. It's really more a show-ring maneuver that judges use to help make their decisions.

Perhaps speed, or the lack of it, makes a downward transition from lope to trot seem so easy. When changing from a faster gait to a slower one, it always seems as though I have plenty of time to think and make a change.

But I think about transitions like many ranch cowboys do: If I need my horse to go from here to there in 15 seconds or less, so I can turn a cow, I don't care how my horse goes there — just as long as we get there to turn the cow. To cowboys, sometimes getting there in time is the big deal, not how smooth the transitions are.

Rating the Trot

My horse can move in a really slow, show-ring jog, which I don't use very much, trot at a more natural, medium speed or in a ground-covering long-trot. Teaching him to rate his speed at the trot is much like teaching him to

Obviously this horse has become braced and stiff, so I elevate my hands and use the reins to soften his jaw.

DO IT YOURSELF

To improve your upper-body control at the trot, make a transition from a fast walk to the trot, but stay in the trot for only a stride or two. Come back down to the walk before you get too far out of position at the trot. Regain your balance at the walk, and think about that correct, basic position you should use while riding.

Then swing back up into the trot for two or three strides more before coming back down to the walk again. Do this repeatedly, as if you're a pendulum, swinging back and forth between the faster and slower gaits. Each time stay in the faster gait a little longer. Before long, you learn to balance yourself well in the saddle at a trot.

rate his walk. Fast or slow, the first thing I do is find and stay in a balanced position so my horse can keep his balance.

When I want my horse to trot faster, I liven up my body to speed up his. Increasing my energy by riding faster encourages my horse to extend his trot.

When I want my horse to trot more slowly, I think about slowing down his front feet,

DO IT YOURSELF

To improve your upper-body control, stand up in your saddle and, as you do, let your weight sink slightly into your heels. Then you can easily move your feet in and out slightly to help maintain your balance and good riding position. At first really think about letting your weight sink to your heels, and hold onto your saddle horn as you stand and find your balance, so you feel safe and secure.

If you push down too much with your toes, your heels come up; you lose good position in your saddle and have an even harder time keeping your balance. Stand up in your saddle a few times while your horse is still, and then as he walks, before you try standing at the trot. When you can comfortably ride the trot while standing in your saddle, try doing it without holding your horn until you can maintain a well-balanced position on your horse. I trotted miles like that as a kid just because that's what my grandpa did, and it really helped me find my balance.

and I elevate his head by bringing up my hands just slightly. If necessary, I wiggle my fingers slightly, too, just to be sure the horse is soft and responsive in his jaw and not resisting my signals.

I don't lift my hands really high or bring them back to my waist. I might raise them only an inch or so, but even that slight change helps set the horse back just enough to bring his hindquarters underneath him. Then his spine becomes rounded and soft, and he can slow smoothly and easily.

Typically, when someone has trouble rating the trot, he can't rate his horse's walk either. I don't understand why people are surprised to learn that.

To better rate a horse's trot, I first work on rating his walk well, long before I ever concentrate on his trot. When he rates the walk well, he understands what I want.

Later, when I use the same cues in the trot, my horse isn't confused about what I want. It's much simpler then to teach him to rate his trot. Likewise, when my horse rates both walk and trot well, it's far easier to rate the canter, too.

Another reason people often have trouble rating a horse's trot, or any gait: The rider can't control his upper body. Without that control, his upper body pitches forward, and he's out of good position. That also weights the horse's front end, leaving him unsure of what he's expected to do.

A horse just wants to get comfortable, so his speed goes back and forth from fast to slow as the rider's upper body moves forward and back. The problem usually compounds, too, as the rider pitches forward because the horse often goes faster and this, in turn, only causes the rider to bounce forward even more with the next stride. That's a bad cycle that needs breaking.

The Lope

The lope is a three-beat gait, and a horse can take a right or left lead at the lope. In other words, when he travels to the right, his right foreleg and hind leg seem to be leading his left legs, and vice versa when he travels to the left. When traveling to the right, the horse's left rear strikes the ground in the first beat, followed by his right hind and left foreleg striking the ground in unison to create the second beat. The third beat occurs as the right foreleg strikes the ground and, again, vice versa when the horse travels left.

Many people have heard about loping a horse on the correct lead. However, for anyone to truly learn about leads, he first must be able to lope his horse consistently and be well-balanced in the saddle, without bouncing all over his horse's back.

When I ask my horse to speed up from trot to lope, I don't make him lope — I always try to let him decide to lope. That's an important point. When the transition happens that way, a horse is always happier about making it. I'm not headed to the show arena, where an instant response is a big deal, so I don't get in a hurry to make my horse lope. Instead, I let him learn what I want at his own pace, and in time his response becomes quicker and sharper.

I always pay attention to my horse's ears as I make upward and downward transitions. When my horse seems really good at making a change, it usually happens when his ears are forward, and his ears tell me he thinks that change is his idea. So I always watch and try to ask for a transition when his ears are focused ahead.

I don't think so much about making my horse lope as I do about elevating my energy so that I ride faster. I continue to think and ride "faster" until my horse breaks into a lope, no matter how far he trots. Then he thinks loping is his idea, and doesn't become cranky, pinning his ears or switching his tail. Striking a lope becomes easier each time I ask, and, in time, my horse breaks into a lope immediately, even from a walk or stop.

When I first lope a colt, I use a pendulum routine to help him become comfortable packing my body weight. I let him lope forward a few strides, bring him down to a trot, and then open the door for him to lope forward again, instead of trying to make him hold the gait for an extended period. That way, I also can be sure the colt responds well to the same amount of effort in his downward transitions that it takes for his upward ones. That's a safety factor that helps ensure my control should the colt become bothered and try to flee a potentially scary situation.

To slow my colt's speed after a few loping strides, I let my energy drop, gather my horse and check him back to a trot with my reins, if necessary, for several strides. When the colt feels balanced and secure at the trot, I ride faster until he lopes a few strides more, before I again bring him down to the trot. By swinging up and down between the gaits, my colt doesn't become scared and uncomfortable, and neither do I. Instead, I build balance and control a few strides at a time, and my horse can become comfortable learning that way, too.

The pendulum approach also helps a seasoned rider get in rhythm with a new mount, but it's an important technique for a novice rider because neither he nor his horse

DO IT YOURSELF

When you use the pendulum routine to swing up from one gait into another and then back down again, you and your horse learn about downward transitions, too. And you learn to make those downward transitions before your horse travels so fast that you feel out of control. Using the pendulum allows you to feel safe and secure as you learn.

The pendulum routine works on all transitions between and within the gaits. So don't ever overload yourself or your horse and force the two of you into a situation you don't feel prepared to handle. Try the new speed or gait for only a few strides at first, then rate down again, and with each cycle let your pendulum swing a bit farther. This is such a confidence-builder because you and your horse stay comfortable together as you speed up — and slow down. Then you never feel out of control.

becomes scared and uncomfortable with the change of gait and speed. A novice should never force himself to continue riding in a lope until he feels out of balance or control. Instead, he can build balance and control a few strides at a time, and his horse can remain comfortable while he does.

At the lope many people get into trouble because they bounce, which puts them behind the horse's action. Typically, the person then pulls back on the reins, as he tries to catch up with his horse and regain his balance, but he usually kicks the horse with every bounce. That's the most valid reason for finding good balance first at the walk and trot, before trying to lope, and why the pendulum approach is a savvy way to build the foundation necessary to lope a horse safely.

A rider should be able to slow his horse from a lope to the trot at any time because knowing he can make that transition gives him the confidence to lope in the first place. That transition isn't just a safety consideration; it's also a confidence-builder.

As for the downward transition from a lope to a walk, I don't think that change is quite so important for a trail rider or cowboy to make with any great amount of finesse. But anyone who's headed to the show arena should master that transition.

Leads

Because a horse loping to the right appears to lead the action with his right foreleg and rear leg, he's said to be on the right lead, or vice versa when he heads to the left. Leads are important when competing in horse shows, as criteria for judging, and important for a ranch horse to use effectively when tracking a cow.

But, unless someone heads to a show next week, there's no real reason to hurry and learn about leads. Imposing a time-frame on that skill usually just leaves a horse and rider frustrated.

It's difficult to ride a horse in the wrong lead, but it's not the end of the world, and it's

Here, it's easy to compare a shot of a horse loping on the left lead (at left) with another shot of him loping on the right lead (at right).

not worth ruining a day's ride. Few recreational riders compete anyway, and nothing terrible will happen if someone fails to get his horse on the proper lead — even though he might get a little saddle sore from bouncing around on the wrong lead.

If a horse doesn't understand that there's a correct lead when I lope him, I let him figure that out. And he will because when he's on the incorrect lead, he's out of balance and uncomfortable. When he doesn't take a right lead, for example, I continue to lope him to the right although he's on his left lead. That soon gets old. If he breaks to a trot before he takes the correct lead, I let him.

He might make a flying lead change, without breaking to the trot, and that's okay, too. Usually I can feel when he tires of the wrong lead and is about to make a change, so just before he does, I ask him for the correct lead. Then the horse associates my body action with the response I want.

But I don't *make* the horse do anything — he decides to do things on his own and learns to find the open door. Then the change is his idea, and I don't have to thump with my legs or pull on his head, so there's usually no problem with crankiness.

Canter Departures

Ideally in a canter-departure, I prepare my horse to lope with my hands, elevating them slightly and checking to be sure he's soft through his jaw. Then he can make a smooth transition to lope in a straight line.

For a right lead, I balance the horse by rocking him back just a little bit, then open the fingers on my right hand and open my right leg, moving it slightly away from the horse's barrel. My left leg stays where it is. Then I simply ride faster. If I've taught my horse to pay attention and respond to my body, he should lope on the right lead.

If I drop my left leg back to touch my horse's side, cueing for a right lead as horsemen traditionally have been taught, the leg motion only brings my horse's mind around to the left. Then his mind looks left when I want a right lead. That's why I worry less

about closing the door to the left, and think it's more important to keep the door open to the right. Then it's more likely that my horse's mind and body work well together for a smoother transition into the correct lead.

When loping on a right lead, I open the right side with my hands and legs, but I keep my horse traveling straight. I don't bend and correct him with the reins, but let him lope straight several strides. Then I slightly elevate my hands and sit back to bring him smoothly to a walk. After he walks a few steps, I open the left door with my left leg and try to lope him straight through it, to take the left lead. The straighter my canter departure, the more smoothly my horse can take the correct lead.

Rate the Lope

Most ranch-cowboy work is done at the walk or trot, which probably contributes much to a ranch horse becoming solid and responsive at any speed. A ranch cowboy makes many upward and downward transitions with his horse every day, slowly and easily, which builds a foundation for controlling his horse when things get fast and furious. That's an approach anyone can take.

Rating a horse's speed in the lope, again, goes back to the foundation laid at the walk and trot. When the horse rates well in those gaits, it's much easier to rate his lope.

To rate a horse's speed back to a slow lope, I sit back into my saddle more and, just as I do when rating his trot, I elevate my hands a little. If my feet go slightly forward as I do, that's okay, but I don't brace them in the stirrups ahead of me. I don't pull on the reins either because that causes my horse to brace and stiffen; I just wiggle my fingers to keep my horse's jaw soft and responsive.

As I lift my hands, I rock back slightly in the saddle, exhale and *slooowww* myself down. I hold up my slightly lifted hands until my horse slows to the speed I want, then lower my hands and let my body rhythm get in sync with his. Again, I think of myself as running around afoot, then slowing to find a place to sit down. If I've done my homework

When a horse is responsive to subtle cues, the downward transition from the lope to the trot is smooth.

DO IT YOURSELF

If your horse lacks rate at the lope, direct him into a large circle and then spiral him down to a smaller circle, which forces him to slow his pace. First, make sure there's enough space where you ride to guide your horse into the large circle, then gradually make your circle smaller and smaller. Once you spiral your horse into the smaller, slower, more controlled circle, either stop right there or, if you're confident, open him out into a larger circle again, to see if you have the desired rate and can maintain control.

Use this technique only at the lope. At the walk, you should have enough control without spiraling your horse, and if you have control at the walk, you should be able to get it at the trot. But at the lope, it's always good to know that you have the option of spiraling your horse down into a smaller circle to regain control.

at the walk and trot, my horse should relate easily to my body's movement in the lope.

The Back-Up

Backing softly probably is the most important control issue anyone can have with a horse because it's the ultimate downward transition. Working on the back-up is the most important thing I can do to help any horse become good in any downward transition. That's because a horse does the same things physically and mentally when going from the stop to the back-up that he does when going from a lope to the trot or the trot to a walk.

I learned that from Jerry Olson, who had the buffalo act and appeared at rodeos. Some performances he loped his buffalo to the far end of the arena and backed only two steps before starting his routine; other nights he backed his buffalo the length of the arena. That made it hard for me as an announcer.

This Paint Horse is somewhat stiff and resistant in the stop, almost pushing against the bit in response to my hand pressure.

The best way to improve a horse's stop is to back him until he learns to be soft and responsive in that maneuver.

When I finally asked him about it, he said, "I tell you what, kid. If I don't get control of this buffalo by backing him, you won't have an act to announce. You'll be talking for 20 minutes to fill the time until they can get me out of the arena because that buffalo will have run off with me."

It hit me then: If backing could help him control a buffalo — and he wouldn't go on with his act until the buffalo responded really well — then backing could help me control my horse even better.

Plus, it's easy to improve a horse's back-up because I can focus on straightness and softness without dealing with any forward momentum. When a horse lopes, for example, it's more difficult to feel his head elevate or his jaw soften, to help him find his balance. But it's so easy to practice finding that feel by backing my horse.

If I pull a horse back, he usually drags back stiffly and slowly. Instead, I elevate my hands slightly, shift my weight back and work my fingers a little. When I feel the horse's jaw soften, I know his spine softens, too, which makes it easy for him to back in a balanced way. Because I let the horse find his balance before I ask for the movement, his response becomes so much better. And if I need him to back faster out of a tight spot, all I do is work my fingers faster on the reins.

When a horse resists backing, he's probably been forced into the movement, and has never found his balance. So, at first, he might struggle with the changed way I ask him to back, and even resist the maneuver. If he does, I always first make sure that he finds his balance by softening his jaw and spine before I ask him to move. I also might need to bring up my energy, to help him start thinking out of the box and about what I want instead of what he's used to doing.

The minute the horse responds, I quit asking and give him a release; then he's more willing to respond the next time I

After backing a horse, it's best to take time to let the horse stand, relax and mull over things.

balance and back him. In time he responds to lighter cues instead of my initial, stronger cues. And that's the goal in horsemanship — to accomplish more things with less effort.

Many people are taught to use their legs during the back-up to direct the horse in an arc or to straighten his path of travel. But that's all after he's moving backward.

I've learned that when I use my hands to keep my horse's spine perfectly aligned, he must back straight. I watch his ears, too, because when his spine is straight, his ears are level. Only when his spine is out of alignment are his ears uneven and only then does he back crooked.

Now I put my effort into keeping his spine straight and his ears level as he backs, instead of using my legs to straighten him after he's backed up. When I do that, he usually backs straight and easy.

No matter if I back my horse in a straight line or a circle, I always keep my horse's head elevated; that tips his pelvis under, which helps him back more easily. If I need to back my horse in a circle, his spine and body remain straight although he bends more at the jaw than anywhere, and that helps loosen his spine for easy movement. I tip his head left or right to direct him as he backs in either direction. How much I tip his head depends on how sharply I want him to turn, but I usually see only his eyelash and nostril as I direct him in a circle.

Backing is one of the best ways to learn about the horse's spine. Learning to recognize a straight spine in the back-up has increased my understanding of and feel for straightness in his spine when a horse moves forward. As my understanding improves, so does my horse's back-up.

Stop

Often a ranch cowboy focuses on getting his colt soft in the back-up and later, when he lopes and asks the horse to make a downward transition, the colt buries his rear end and stops. Sometimes all the cowboy really has going for him at the time is the back-up, because he hasn't really worked on the colt's stop at all.

"It should take no more physical effort for me to back my horse than it requires to step him forward."

I've had that happen, too, and like most ranch cowboys, I've sometimes fallen forward over the colt's neck; as a result, he might never stop that way again. But the bottom line is that the colt understands the response I want when I work him on the back-up, and at the lope he really tries to give that same, correct response.

The first thing I do to improve any horse's stop is get the horse really responsive in the back-up. The back-up work is slow, so the horse and I can more easily get together to build the same responses I need for a solid, smooth stop.

That balance in the round-pen work is just as important here. It should take no more physical effort for me to back my horse than it requires to step him forward. When I consistently balance my transition work, a horse learns to stop as easily as he goes.

When I first ask a horse to stop, I do it from the walk. But no matter the gait, I always wait to ask for the stop until I'm sure my horse is relaxed. I first wiggle my fingers on the reins to be sure he's soft through the jaw. If he is, he's probably soft throughout his body and can easily gather his hindquarters underneath him to stop. When that happens, I'm fairly certain that his stop will be soft and straight.

Because my horse's jaw is soft and hindquarters are engaged as he stops, he's also prepared to move in any direction after the stop, if necessary. Like most ranch cowboys, I want a horse to stop and be prepared to go again. He must stop in a balanced position so he can move quickly to turn a cow. In a ranch situation that balanced stop — not a long, sliding stop — is important. I never want a horse to prop-stop hard on his front end either, but I do want him to stop quickly and in balance.

I don't say "whoa" for a stop simply because, when I worked around ranch crews, saying something to my horse every time I stopped seemed to add to the confusion. Too, all I can do with that voice command is say "whoa" for a quick, hard stop or "whoooaaaaa," like reiners do for long, sliding stops. When working cattle, I need more variables than that. My horse might need to coast to a stop with one cow or stop hard to turn quickly with another cow taking off in the opposite direction. It's not only important that my horse stop in a balanced position, but also that he stop slowly or quickly in response to however much pressure I put on him as I work a cow. Most horses usually pick up on that pretty quickly and respond to whatever amount of pressure they feel, which might be a little or a lot, depending on the cow. Either way, a horse can stay in balance, stay with the cow and be ready if she makes a fast move. Balance is the key to the stop.

The typical stopping problem occurs when a horse "pushes through the bit." In other words, he doesn't respond, relax and soften his jaw when I wiggle my fingers on the reins. As a result, his spine isn't soft, so he can't prepare to stop. He braces and stiffens his body, which also affects his overall balance and comfort level.

The only way for a horse to understand how to do anything well is by slowing and breaking down maneuvers for him. I can break down a stop for him by working on his back-up. Backing to build the correct stopping response is far less bothersome to my horse than running and stopping him repeatedly. The back-up also allows me to evaluate my horse's response throughout the maneuver, which helps me find any problems. I also have time to let my horse figure out the correct response.

Although elevating my hands is the first step in the back-up or a stop, softening my horse's jaw is the next step in either maneuver. That's probably where a horse is most resistant, and he's probably that way because he's been jerked to an out-of-balance stop. It all comes back to allowing a horse to find his balance before I ask him to stop or back. It takes time for a horse that's never been allowed to find his balance to develop the confidence to stop in a comfortable, secure manner, so I must be patient.

Only when his jaw is soft can I be certain that his spine is soft, too. Then he's in a balanced state, which is what I want before he actually moves. And only when he backs well in balance, do I focus on a balanced stop.

I don't immediately lope my horse and ask for a smooth stop. First, I actively walk and stop him several times to build his confidence that he won't be asked to perform in an unbalanced way. If I feel any resistance when stopping in the walk, I work more on

DO IT YOURSELF

To really improve communication between you and your horse for better transitions and stops, set a goal each time you ride. Make upward and downward transitions between the gaits five times whenever you ride. Or work on the back-up until your horse responds well; then make 10 walk-to-stop transitions each time you ride until he responds equally well there, too. After that, make 10 walk-to-stop and also 10 trot-to-stop transitions each time you ride. When your horse stops smoothly and squarely, you're ready to stop from the lope because your horse has the foundation to progress to that level.

the back-up and occasionally test his stop at the walk.

When my horse stops smoothly and consistently at the walk, I progress to stopping from the trot. I start by checking his response from a slow jog before progressing to a medium or long, fast trot. I never ask him to stop from a faster pace until he consistently stops softly at the slower one. That way I build his confidence as I build his speed.

When he responds well enough to try stopping from a lope, again, I don't hammer down on him at a hand gallop at first. Instead, I lope him slowly and quietly ask him to stop. If that seems to bother him, I drop back to the trot and stop a few times at the more comfortable pace to rebuild his confidence before returning to the lope. Only when my horse stops comfortably from a slow lope, do I gradually pick up the pace, progressively asking him to stop at faster speeds.

Anytime my horse's response is less than it should be, I slow his pace, find his comfort level and work there before again going faster. I take that same pendulum approach by asking him to stop from a faster pace and then a slower one, then again from the faster one. Doing that's a good way to maintain my horse's soft, smooth stop and his confidence.

I often see riders let a horse dribble to a stop, almost stopping, then continuing to walk forward. There's nothing responsive in that. The horse might start the maneuver nicely, but usually fails to follow through because his rider fails to follow through and complete the stop. Usually that happens because the rider's attention drifts, and he doesn't consistently complete the maneuver. As a result, his horse has a bad habit of almost, but not quite, stopping completely.

When a horse has that problem, I consciously focus my attention on him until he reaches a complete stop, and I feel him rebalance his body. Following through on the stop is like cultivating any other horsemanship technique. I might have to consciously work to remember to do this at first but, before long, it becomes a habit.

113

As this horse moves his hindquarters to the right, his left front is the pivot foot, and his left hind steps forward and across the right hind. My legs and hands are in proper position to keep the horse balanced.

HINDQUARTER TRANSITIONS

10

In addition to making upward and downward transitions, I also should be able to maneuver my horse's hindquarters smoothly to the right and to the left. I work on the hindquarter transitions before I focus on the final two transitions, moving his forehand left and right. That's because the more easily I can move his hindquarters in a balanced way, the better I can prepare my horse to move his front end smoothly in either direction.

Many people don't consider moving the hindquarters an important maneuver, but hindquarter transitions are good tools for helping any horse become better balanced to perform many maneuvers. Remember: When a horse is comfortably balanced, he seldom becomes cranky about performing because he feels secure. When he's secure, he's physically capable of anything.

For a ranch horse, especially one used for roping, moving his back end is necessary to maintain his balance without falling down. When a cowboy ropes a 1,000-pound animal, he has to keep his horse's spine in line with the cow he ropes. If the cow gets perpendicular to his horse, the cowboy's saddle might roll, or the cow might pull the horse completely off his feet. Even when the horse's spine is lined up with the cow's, all the pull comes right down on the horn at the horse's withers, so it's hard for him to move his front end to reposition himself. But he can move his hindquarters easily because

there's much less weight on them. That's an important skill for any ranch cowboy to develop in a horse.

Sometimes a cutter cocks his horse's head as he goes across in front of the herd. The rider's really cocking his horse's hind foot, moving his hindquarters just a step to the right, for example, so that his left rear foot steps slightly in front of his right rear. When the cow makes a big move in the other direction, the horse can step out with his left rear, stay balanced, and has power to sweep around with the cow. When the left rear is positioned behind the right rear, the horse must scramble to turn around.

Ranch cowboys pay attention to such things. It's as important to them as it is to the professional cutter that a horse always be ready for the next maneuver. If he's not, the cowboy might lose the cow. Even when he's not cutting or sorting cattle, and holding cattle in an alleyway, a cowboy often needs to move his horse's hindquarters to block the alley.

A team roper can use hindquarter transitions to set his horse in the box, and a trail-rider might use the transitions to maneuver through timber. Moving the hindquarters is another piece of the puzzle for more advanced maneuvers — a lead change, for example — and practical maneuvers, such as working a gate. Hindquarter transitions are good tools for most any horseman to have available.

DO IT YOURSELF

Become more aware of your horse's weight as you shift it forward and back by lifting yourself forward to shift his weight. Be sure your chest is slightly in front of the saddle horn or withers, your horse's natural point of balance. As you rock back, shift your weight slightly behind that point to bring his weight behind it, too. Watch your saddle horn as you lift forward and rock back, and you can see it move slightly, although maybe only a half-inch or so. That's a subtle change. If you move too far forward or back, your horse must take a step because he's totally out of balance again.

The teeter-totter is a great tool for learning how a horse feels when he shifts his weight, which is on the hindquarters in the approach, to the forehand.

Once the horse is balanced on the teeter-totter, the rider can shift the horse's weight back to the hindquarters and lighten his forehand.

The rider can then shift her weight slightly to shift the horse's weight forward onto his forehand.

Even though the teeter-totter moves only a few inches from the ground, some horses might find that unsettling.

Shift His Weight

The first step in moving a horse's back end is to shift his weight to the forehand; then he can more easily move his hindquarters left or right. Again, I think about my horse being on a teeter-totter. When his weight shifts forward, the teeter-totter comes up behind because the load there has been lightened. To move my horse's hindquarters, being able to shift his weight is important because that's closest to what my horse normally does on his own to move his back end. The closer I come to asking my horse to do what he normally does, the less resistant he is when I ask him to perform.

To shift my horse's weight forward, I act as if I'm riding him on a teeter-totter. To weight his forehand, I increase my energy and lift myself forward, just like I'm getting out of a chair, and open my fingers slightly on the reins. That opens the door for my horse to shift forward and bring the teeter-totter down at the front.

I practice this first step with my horse to prepare him for moving his hindquarters. I see how subtly I can shift my weight and still get my horse to shift his weight.

Move His Hindquarters

Once I shift my horse's weight forward, I can ask him to move his back end in one direction or the other. My reins are short, and my hands are in front of the saddle horn.

To move my horse's hindquarters to the right, I close my left hand to relax his jaw and get him to look across to the left. I don't want him to turn his entire head to the left; I want to see only his left eyelash and nostril.

At the same time, my left leg moves toward the back cinch ever so slightly, just to let my horse know it's there. I don't kick or bump him with my foot, but that slight motion also draws him to look to the left. I even like to see a horse cock his left ear in that direction, just to acknowledge that change.

I use my outside, right rein, to keep my horse from overbending through his neck. When he overbends, he weights his outside, or right, shoulder, in this case, too much. That unbalances him, causing him to brace and step forward to maintain good balance. I use my outside rein to prevent him from bending so much that he must take that step.

DO IT YOURSELF

Build your own teeter-totter, but be sure it's sturdy enough to support your horse's weight. Use 2-by-6-inch or 2-by-12-inch lumber and reinforce the teeter-totter with cross-members underneath. I first nailed mine together and then used screws.

My teeter-totter is $1\frac{1}{2}$-feet wide and 11 feet long. However, 10 feet is sufficient length. I also have a narrower, foot-wide teeter-totter, but the $1\frac{1}{2}$-foot width is easier when first accustoming a horse to it.

Don't put a huge log under the center of the teeter-totter; that's not necessary. A fence post works fine because the teeter-totter needs to come off the ground only 3 or 4 inches to help you and your horse learn about the subtle shifting of weight.

This is a great tool for working with horses, and is good bridge-training, too. But you must use caution and judgment when introducing your horse to the teeter-totter. Some horses have a hard time at first, just putting a foot on it, and the sound sometimes bothers them, too.

First, let your horse become accustomed to putting only his front feet on the boards. Don't ask him to walk on them with all four feet until he's comfortable with only two there. When he walks across the boards, don't be too particular about how he does it at first. He's uneasy just being there, and your criticism about how he does things will only worry him more. You must allow your horse all the time he needs to decide he's okay there on the teeter-totter. Only then can he be still and calm for you to achieve any finesse in shifting his weight forward and back.

A horse doesn't have to bend his body significantly to successfully cross one hind foot over the other.

Watching my horse's ears is one way I can tell when he's about to take a misstep. When his ears are level, he's balanced as he moves his hindquarters, and his front pivot foot stays in place. When his outside ear drops, that means his weight has shifted improperly, and he's forced to take a step to maintain his balance. Again, this doesn't really have anything to do with the horse's ears, or even his shoulder, but his spine. I can't see his spine, but I can watch his ears.

After he's balanced with his head tipped slightly to the left, ideally, my horse shifts his weight forward to his left front foot. I have his left eyelash and nostril in sight by using my inside rein, and my outside rein maintains the balance, so he doesn't overbend his neck or step forward.

Then I elevate my horse's head just a bit, and that's when he moves his hindquarters on his own to the right. And I won't have to wait for him to move. Usually when I must wait on a horse to move, it's because he's still out of balance and trying to find a secure position. But when his balance is good and he's set up right for the maneuver, there's

DO IT YOURSELF

To better understand how your horse moves his feet when moving his hindquarters, you must know where his feet are at the walk. That way you know which foot lands last. For example, when you move your horse's hindquarters to the right, you want his left front foot to be the last foot to stop because it becomes his weight-bearing foot in the maneuver. Then you don't have to shift your horse around so much to help him find his balance. That's thinking ahead to prepare your horse for the maneuver and make it easy for him.

no delay unless he's a really dull horse. In that case I might lift my rein slightly more and wiggle my foot to bring up a dull horse's energy.

The best thing: A horse won't be fussy about moving his hindquarters because he's balanced for the move and makes it himself. I don't have to kick him to make him do it. I won't kick then anyway because I don't want to distract my horse's mind from what I'm asking him to do. If I start thumping on him, his brain goes down to my foot, and he won't learn to keep his balance.

At first, I move my horse's hindquarters in small increments, so that he learns to find the balance. I might move him one step, rebalance, move another step and then ride him forward. Then I stop, rebalance him and ask him to move his hindquarters again. The end goal is to move his hindquarters around 360 degrees however many times I want.

I don't try to do this fast because my horse must continually rebalance himself. If I push him too fast, he gets bothered and starts switching his tail, so I work slowly to build a willing response.

When my horse feels balanced and moves his hindquarters smoothly to the right, I reverse my hand and leg cues and ask him to move to the left.

DO IT YOURSELF

Although your horse probably won't dig a hole in the ground with his front pivot foot when first moving his hindquarters, he might eventually. To see how his pivot foot augers as he moves his hindquarters, do the maneuver in soft dirt. If you look down at the left front foot, for example, it can help you understand the maneuver. Look down, but don't bend over or lean way out because keeping your body in the right position is necessary to make that maneuver happen. Just elevate your back and shoulders, stretching your spine so that you can see your toes without bending or leaning from the waist.

Hindquarter Transition Problems

The most typical problem in moving a horse's hindquarters left or right occurs when the horse walks forward during the transition. He can do that because the rider forgets to use the outside rein to check the horse's forward motion. More often than not, the rider concentrates on bringing the horse's head too far around to his knee, which isn't desirable either. He should concentrate on preventing the horse from stepping forward.

When I move a horse's hindquarters and he tries to step forward, I simply use my hands and body to put my horse back into place. Mentally I put him on the teeter-totter again to best understand how I need to make the correction. Consciously, I close the fingers on my outside rein, but I don't pull with them. That'll cause my horse to brace. Instead, I use the outside rein softly to keep my horse's neck straight and his weight shifted back. And, if he walks off my mental teeter-totter again, I just set him up to move his hindquarters and try it again.

Some people have an unresponsive horse that's dull to the rider's legs. When that's the case, I use my legs in one of two ways — as subtly as I can or really aggressively. I usually first try cueing a horse lightly by wiggling my boot. If that doesn't get the response I want, I sometimes use either my McCarty or rope to smack him down a hind leg, but timing is critical when doing that.

Although I seldom wear spurs, if I had a pair on in this situation, I might use short, small jabs to get an unresponsive horse's attention. Then I'd become like the old mare in the pasture who kicked the young horse — the next time I signal my horse, he'd probably pay attention.

Again, my goal in making this correction is to progressively use less pressure in the correction, instead of more. If I move my horse's hindquarters for 3 days and must use more leg pressure on the third day, I need to reevaluate what I do. Perhaps my horse's balance isn't quite right before I ask him to

To evaluate how well a horse moves his hindquarters, I first position him perpendicular to a fencepost.

As his hindquarters step across to the right…

move, and I should slow down and work on that first.

Whenever I correct a horse, I understand that a horse lives very much in the present. He doesn't hold grudges or harbor ill-will. Once the correction is made, and he responds, everything's over with no hard feelings.

Some people might think a horse just doesn't like them from one day to the next, but horses don't think that way. All they think about is surviving to get back to the feed bucket.

I also hear people complain that a horse works better to one side than the other, usually because of the way he was carried in the mare's womb. There might be something to that because that entirely stretches one side of a horse's body. But once a horse hits

the ground, I don't pay any attention to that, and I don't expect him to be worse one way than the other. All that's necessary is for me to do things correctly and be sure my horse is balanced.

In making these transitions, we're often too quick to pull and prod our horses. But we do those things usually because we have no idea what a horse normally must do physically to maintain his balance. So we hammer and pound on a horse when we don't fully understand things. That's rude to the horse, but a common problem.

We also often try to go too fast when working a horse — just for our own enjoyment because it's fun to whirl him around. But our rush bothers the horse all the more.

...he ends up parallel to the fence with his left front leg in line with the post.

For good results simply ask the horse for one step at the time, stop, allow the horse to rebalance and then ask for another step. If we work slowly and with balance, a horse eventually performs any maneuver much faster.

What's the hurry anyway? If I'm not on a show schedule, I don't have to impress anybody with how fast I accomplish things. So why would I ever get angry or ruin a ride because my horse doesn't keep his foot in the ground where it ought to be? I'm like everyone else who rides — I just want to have a good time, and I should never lose sight of that.

If it takes me 2 weeks to get that pivot foot into the ground just right, that's no big deal. Moving a horse's hindquarters isn't difficult when I slow down and break down the maneuver into component parts.

DO IT YOURSELF

After your horse responds well when you ask him to move his hindquarters, here's a way to better evaluate your success and perform more precisely in the transitions. Ride directly to a fencepost and stop your horse perpendicular to the fence line with his head or tail at the post. Then move his hindquarters a quarter-turn to the right. You should end up perfectly parallel to the fence.

If your horse is ahead of the fencepost, he stepped forward as he moved his hindquarters, and you can correct him by backing him until his nose is lined up with the post. If his rear end is closer to the fence than his forehand, you overplayed your hand and pushed him over too far. If the opposite is true, you didn't move his hindquarters far enough. The fence and the post are your guidelines. They reveal exactly how precise you are when moving your horse's hindquarters in either direction.

The horse already has shifted his weight and moved his left hind foot slightly back, all in order to move his left front foot to the side so that he ultimately can cross over it with his right front.

FOREHAND TRANSITIONS

11

Working cattle is the main activity in which a ranch cowboy uses a forehand transition. He turns his horse on his back end to move the forehand right or left to sort cattle, or block them in an alleyway. But ranch cowboys seldom ask horses for 360-degree turnarounds. A complete turnaround expends a lot of the horse's energy and isn't that practical for ranch work.

However, when a ranch cowboy enters a ranch-horse competition, being able to perform a 360-degree turnaround works to his advantage. The more smoothly and fluidly his horse completes the maneuver, the higher he scores. As far as most cowboys are concerned, though, the complete 360 is for the show arena.

Shift His Weight

Just as it's the initial step in moving a horse's hindquarters, shifting a horse's weight is the first step in moving his forehand right or left.

I like to think about my horse on the teeter-totter again. When his weight is balanced, his withers are over the center of the teeter-totter. For a turn on the hindquarters, which allows his forehand to move in either direction, I must first shift his weight back, behind the point of balance at his withers. As his weight shifts back on the teeter-totter, it goes down, and his front end elevates because it bears less weight. Obviously, that's what I want and need to make a transition on the forehand —

less weight, so my horse can more easily move his front end.

To shift my horse's weight back, I close my fingers a little on the reins, let my energy drop and sink back as though I'm sitting down in a rocking chair. This is the opposite of what I do to shift my horse's weight forward — open my fingers, increase my energy and act as though I'm getting out of a chair. Closing my fingers, dropping my energy and rocking back closes the door to the horse's forward motion and leaves the door open for him to shift back.

Before asking any horse to move his forehand, I practice shifting my horse's weight back and forth to prepare him for the maneuver, just as I practice shifting it to prepare him for hindquarter transitions. Again, I want the weight-shift as subtle a move as possible.

DO IT YOURSELF

Review the do-it-yourself tips in the "Shift His Weight" section of the previous chapter, "Hindquarter Transitions." This time, however, pay more attention to your saddle horn as you shift your weight back on your horse, rather than forward.

If you built a teeter-totter and introduced your horse to it gradually, as recommended, you probably already have mastered shifting your horse's weight to his hindquarters. If you haven't worked your horse on a teeter-totter before, read the cautions in the previous chapter about gradually introducing your horse to the tool. The teeter-totter is just that — a tool that can help you improve your horsemanship. But you must use good judgment with it. Your safety depends on it.

Move the Forehand

Most people forget about the horse's hind feet when they think about moving his forehand. In a turn to the right, they think only of stepping the right front foot over, then getting the left front to cross over it before the right front sweeps over again.

But, to me, the first foot that really needs to move in a right turnaround is the horse's right hind foot. It first needs to step back slightly to give the right front foot somewhere to go. As the right hind moves, the left rear foot momentarily becomes the weight-bearing foot that's the balance point, and then the right front can sweep over to the side, followed by the left front crossing over the right front. Then the horse resets his right rear, moves his feet through the sequence again, his right front reaching out and the left front crossing over it to make a forehand transition.

My left hand keeps the horse from overbending his body, and my right hand and leg open a door for his forehand to move to the right while my left leg creates impulsion.

But the left rear is the critical foot that helps the horse find and maintain his balance. For my horse to move his forehand fluidly, I must be sure he's comfortably balanced before I ask him to move. I do that by shifting his weight back to his left hind foot, and use my left rein to keep his neck straight. My left hand comes more toward my saddle horn, not to pull my horse back, but simply to give him a sense of direction and keep his weight shifted back where it needs to be.

My right rein opens only a little, as my hand comes back more toward my horse's right hind foot. Then I massage the right rein with my fingers until I see my horse's right eye and nostril.

At the same time, my right leg moves slightly away from my horse's side to do the same thing I do with my right hand — open a door for my horse to move through.

As for my left leg, I don't bump or spur with it although I usually wiggle my toe forward of the cinch, maybe only a half-inch. My foot wiggles just enough to give my horse impulsion, however much it takes. As I've said before: When I use a leg forcefully, that only brings my horse's mind back to my leg. Then he can't keep his mind on the open door because he can think of only one thing at the time.

When asking a horse to move his forehand, I don't hold my hands out to the sides of his neck because that can throw him off balance, and it also makes it harder to move a young horse into a full bridle, which I plan to use with one hand on the reins. However, if I start these maneuvers by keeping my hands as close together as I can, it's much easier for a young horse to go to the bridle because he's always balanced.

That's why I ride using my hands close together, as if my horse is already in the bridle. When I set him up to move his forehand as described and keep my hands together, he learns how to stay between the reins. Doing that also allows him to keep his spine lined up for the turnaround, and lets him define his boundaries by finding his balance. If he backs too much into the turn, he loses his

The horse shifts his weight back and lightens his forehand.

Then he steps his left front across his right front.

balance, just as he does by stepping forward too much.

I don't turn a horse fast on his hindquarters. For one thing, I don't show reining horses, so that isn't necessary. But the main reason I don't turn my horse quickly is because I don't want him to lose that beautiful balance in his body. If I worry more about his balance than speed, when I work a cow, I have the balance I need, and the cow can create the speed. I've already done my homework so my horse knows where to be in balance, no matter how fast a cow dictates we go.

It seems to me that turning around fast a lot makes most horses cranky. Maybe they don't like doing that because they don't naturally have a real need to do 360s. The only time I might turn a horse around fast is when he's really excited. For example, if a herd of horses runs off and mine wants to go, too, I might spin him just to get him busy and thinking about me, not the horses. Most of the time I turn my horse calmly and slowly. His turn stays smooth because it's a balanced ride, which is no big deal to the horse, so he doesn't get fussy about the maneuver.

After he makes a long reach with his right front, the horse repeats the cycle and again will cross the left front over the right in the turn.

To me, there are two ways to move the horse's forehand. One is the forward, reining-horse-style turnaround, and the other is the backing turn cutting horses often use to work a cow.

In the forward turnaround, the horse pivots on his inside rear foot. He can turn fast, but the faster he goes, the harder it is for him to stay on his inside hind foot. When I watch reining videos, it almost seems as if some of the horses are swapping ends, although some people might disagree with me. Ultimately the forward turn is faster and flatter, but it's not as true if the speed is too great.

When a cow horse backs into a turn, he keeps his weight more on his outside hind foot, using that foot for balance and power. He can stay in balance there and also push away quickly to head a cow. When a horse uses the more forward turn, a cow might get by him, but with the backing turn, he can always give room to the cow if that's necessary to work her. A competitive cutting horse learns to do those things because he must hold the cow on that imaginary line in the arena, so the horse learns to adjust forward and back to maintain that line.

Forehand Transition Problems

The most common problem when moving the forehand is keeping the horse's weight shifted onto his hindquarters. Most people just try to take the front end across in one direction or the other without giving the horse's back end a thought. Then the horse often becomes cranky about moving his forehand, probably because he's not balanced well to perform the maneuver. In that case, the rider must remember to shift the horse's weight back, so that he can reset the one hind foot and give the corresponding foreleg room to move.

However, many people never even try to shift a horse's weight back before they turn his forehand. As a result, they allow the horse to simply walk a small circle, and he never gets his balance back far enough to truly

I stop my horse perpendicular to a fence-post to check his accuracy as he moves his front end to the left.

move his forehand around his hindquarters.

The best solution for these problems is to learn to teeter-totter and shift the horse's weight forward and backward. It's the same old story: Break the maneuver into its component parts and work on them in sequence until the problem spot becomes clear. In this case, shifting the horse's weight back is the first step to turning him on his hindquarters, so unless I first master that, I won't be able to improve his forehand movement.

Another problem I sometimes see in moving the forehand occurs when the person doesn't turn the horse slowly enough for him to maintain good balance. I see that more often when people work cattle. For some reason the rider thinks — just because the cow's out there — that the horse should be able to turn as fast as the cow can. But when the rider expects that, he really throws the horse off-balance. There's a simple solution to that problem — slow down.

I also see many people literally drag their horses through a turn when they work cattle. The important thing in work-

I keep the horse's weight rocked back on his hindquarters as he crosses his right front over his left.

The horse's hind legs should be aligned with the fencepost at the turn's completion.

DO IT YOURSELF

Just as you did when making hindquarter transitions, use a fencepost and your fence line to evaluate how precisely you and your horse make changes with the forehand. Again, ride across your pasture and stop perpendicular to a fencepost with your horse facing it. Step his forehand a quarter-turn to the left. You should be parallel with the fence, and your horse's hind feet should be even with the post. Then again face the fencepost and try turning your horse in a 180, to face away from the post. You should be able to look back over your horse's tail and be right in line with the post. Using the post and the fence, you can test how precisely you and your horse perform a quarter-pivot, a 180 or a full 360-degree turn-around. This is a great exercise that you also can do using a barrel or pole in the arena, a tree in your pasture, a panel post upright in your pen or a spot on your trailer to check your horse's alignment.

ing cattle well and easily is maintaining the horse's balance, no matter how fast the cow travels. I work to do that, even if I lose the cow. Or, instead of letting the cow go, I might let my horse turn as slowly as he must to keep his balance, and then really hustle him back to the cow as soon as his body straightens from the turn.

However, most people tend to either drag a horse through a turn, or yank him through it with the bit. Either way, it's a novice-looking turn.

DO IT YOURSELF

Take a different approach to riding your pasture fence. Most people ride right next to it. Instead, try maintaining a 15-foot distance from the fence as you ride. Imagine that you get shocked anytime your horse is closer than that. When you come to a corner, stop and move either your horse's hindquarters or forehand to realign yourself 15-feet away from the other fence line. You can also use an arena rail in the same way you use the fence as a training aid to develop more precision as you work your horse.

When first teaching a horse to side-pass, it might be necessary to move his front end over.

ADVANCED MANEUVERS

12

With an understanding of the six transitions and some saddle time, almost anyone can help his horse become more responsive and willing to speed up or slow down and move his forehand or hindquarters right and left. And with these six transitions a rider can do almost anything, including more advanced maneuvers, such as a rollback, side-pass or flying lead change.

That's because the six transitions are the component parts that make up advanced maneuvers. The six basics never change; however, the sequence in which they're combined varies from one advanced maneuver to the next. Performing an advanced maneuver well is simply a matter of breaking down the maneuver into its component parts and using them in the proper order.

People seem to get tied up in knots about advanced maneuvers, such as lead changes. If someone's riding competitively, that type of maneuver is a different deal altogether, but the average recreational rider doesn't need to put so much pressure on himself and make such a big deal of them.

The Side-Pass

In side-passing a horse, for example, his forehand and his hindquarters move in the same direction at the same time. The side-pass is a handy maneuver to use in many situations — opening a gate or finding a trail through timber. When working cattle, it's often easy to side-pass a horse only a step or two and head a cow.

The side-pass is fairly easy to master for anyone who's learned the six transitions. The rider just fine-tunes the work he's already done while working on the transitions, and balances his horse's weight evenly before he side-steps him in one direction or the other.

When I side-pass a horse, again, I think about him on the teeter-totter. I want his weight equally balanced between his forehand and his hindquarters. That means the teeter-totter should be level, with my horse's strongest point of balance at the withers right over the teeter-totter's center.

....and then his back end across before combining the two into one maneuver.

DO IT YOURSELF

If your horse pins his ears or switches his tail as you work on any maneuver, back off. You're using too much pressure. When your horse gets that bothered in his work, just stop. Let him stand quietly for a few minutes because he needs to relax and become calm. When he is, he's ready to work again.

I prefer letting my horse stand quietly while he calms himself, to letting him walk away from his work. When working on a side-pass at a gate, for example, I don't want my horse ever to think he can escape his work by walking away. He might learn to do that every time he's a little tense.

After your horse stands still and calm for a few minutes, wiggle a rein to see if he braces against or resists you. The best way to determine that he's relaxed and at ease is to move him in any direction — forward and backward or his forehand or hindquarters to the right or left. If you can do that easily, your horse is relaxed mentally and balanced physically, and you can return to work on the maneuver.

To side-pass my horse, I simply stop any forward or backward movement and let his motion come out sideways. I open the door to one side, the right, for example, with my leg and let my horse look in that direction. If necessary, I use my right rein slightly to guide his head. I want to see only his right eye and right nostril; otherwise, his spine should be straight.

Before I ask my horse to move, I shift in the saddle, however much necessary, to balance my horse's weight evenly front to back. I continue using my right hand to keep his eye and nostril in sight, which means I lighten his right front leg and rear leg, shifting his weight onto both left legs. Then it's easy for his right legs to make that initial move to the right.

In this case, I use my left hand to prevent my horse from walking forward or bending his neck too much to the right, and my left leg hangs straight down. I open the door for my horse to move right by moving my right leg slightly away from his side. As I do, I wiggle

my left foot to get my horse moving. That should be all that's necessary to get some impulsion if my horse has learned to be responsive in the six transitions.

As soon as my horse starts to shift his weight to the right, I leave him alone to complete the step in that direction. Ideally, his forehand and hindquarters should come across to the right at the same time. When my horse steps right, his weight shifts right, and that lightens both left legs so they can easily follow. So instead of shifting his weight to move forward or backward, my horse simply moves sideways with his weight equally balanced on the forehand and hindquarters.

To side-pass to the left, I reverse my hand and leg cues. As with any other maneuver, I teach a horse to side-pass one step at a time and build on that foundation, and I always try to work him in each direction.

Side-Passing Problems

Sometimes people have trouble moving a horse's forehand and rear end together in the side-pass. Ideally, both should move at the same time. But absolute perfection isn't critical, especially at first, and there's no judge scoring the results.

When I have a problem like that, I take the best my horse has to offer at the time and work with him from there. I continue balancing him carefully and asking him to move his front and back ends together, and I do that as long as it takes for my horse to figure out what I want and how to do it. Eventually he will. The side-pass simply is a difficult maneuver for some horses to master.

Sometimes, in that situation, opening a gate is the best thing to improve a horse's performance. He learns to be more precise there, and I become more aware and can better evaluate how much pressure he can handle from me. When I use too much pressure, a horse usually jams my leg into the gate, or he won't stand still, and I must back off a little. Or I might need to use more pressure to help sharpen his response. Either way, the problems seems a little more obvious to me at the gate.

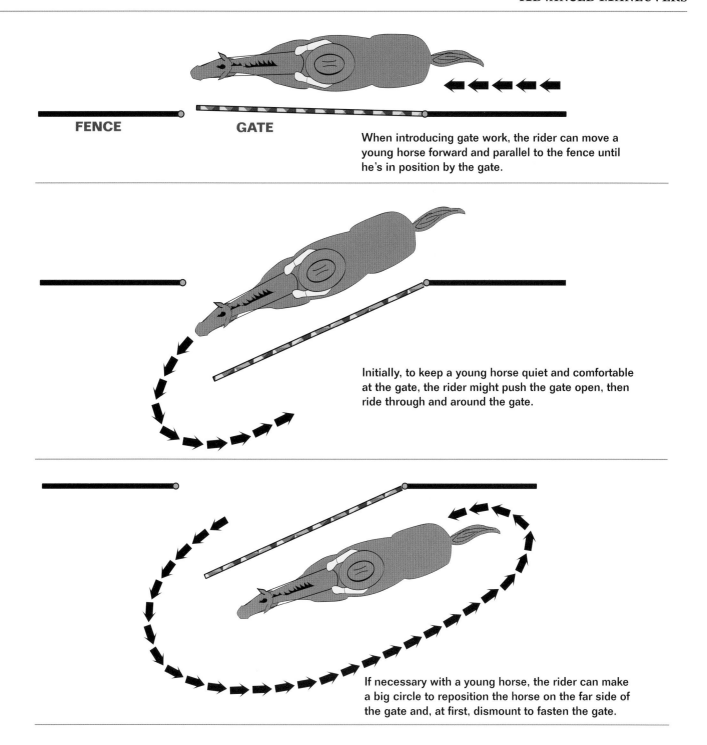

FENCE   GATE

When introducing gate work, the rider can move a young horse forward and parallel to the fence until he's in position by the gate.

Initially, to keep a young horse quiet and comfortable at the gate, the rider might push the gate open, then ride through and around the gate.

If necessary with a young horse, the rider can make a big circle to reposition the horse on the far side of the gate and, at first, dismount to fasten the gate.

I also can use the gate as a point of reference to help keep my horse's body straight. I can use a fence in the same way, too, but I prefer to use the gate, especially with a sluggish horse. Because many horses want to fade to or go through a gate, I might use that to advantage by letting the gate draft my horse into better position. When I work with only a fence, I make sure that my horse's nose isn't right against the fence because that can affect his good balance. Instead, I work him

about 5 feet from the fence.

Another side-pass problem: The rider often allows his horse to overbend through his neck and body. Then he's out of balance, and it's difficult for him to step across laterally.

When I ride a horse that overbends to the right, for example, I tighten my left rein to correct that. Again, I want to see only his right eye and nostril. If I see more than that, I must make a stronger correction with my

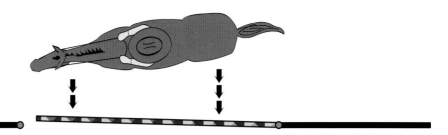

A green horse might be easily positioned alongside the gate but, perhaps, hasn't yet mastered the side-pass and must alternately move his forehand and hindquarters to move closer to the gate.

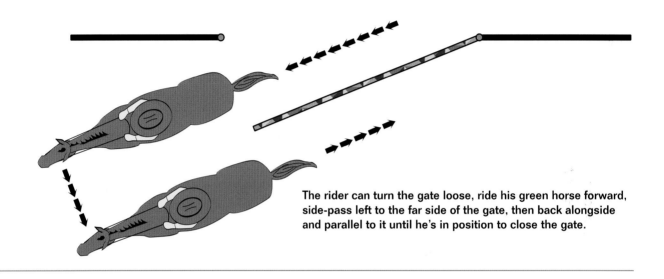

The rider can turn the gate loose, ride his green horse forward, side-pass left to the far side of the gate, then back alongside and parallel to it until he's in position to close the gate.

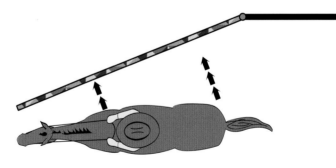

To close the gate from a green horse's back, it might again be necessary to first move the horse's forehand and then his hindquarters.

left hand, the same hand I use to keep him from stepping forward.

Whenever I work on the side-pass or side-passing problems, I pick the time and place to do my training. It's difficult to school my horse on the side-pass at a gate during a trail ride when other people ride off and leave me, even though that's not considered proper trail etiquette. When that happens, if I can get the gate shut horseback without a big struggle with my horse, I just do it. I don't worry about how sorry the job looks as long as I don't set back my horse's training.

Sometimes when the gate must be shut, the best thing to do is get off and work the gate afoot to avoid a real problem with my horse. If the other riders leave us, a battle with my horse at the gate can set me back in teaching him to side-pass. To me, a good horseman understands when it's better to work on something and when to avoid a fight.

Of course, a courteous horseman doesn't ride away and leave somebody at the gate, or the barn for that

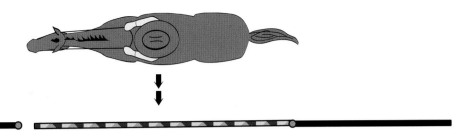

A finished horse can side-pass to the gate so closely that his rider can unlatch the gate from his mount's back.

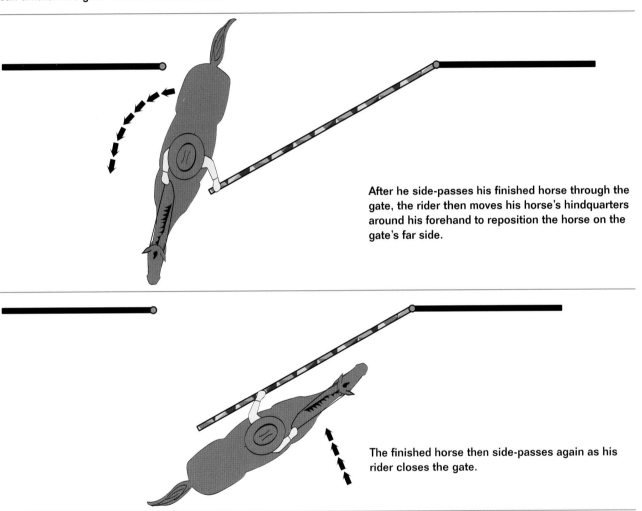

After he side-passes his finished horse through the gate, the rider then moves his horse's hindquarters around his forehand to reposition the horse on the gate's far side.

The finished horse then side-passes again as his rider closes the gate.

matter. That's a real part of ranch etiquette for working cowboys. They know how hard it is to work a gate or mount up when a horse is dancing and jigging because he naturally wants to follow the other horses. When somebody's delayed, for whatever reason, the other cowboys wait on him. It's the polite thing to do, and then nobody's horse becomes bothered.

Another thing ranch cowboys sometimes do, as a matter of courtesy, is try to help a cowboy riding a green colt through a gate. The cowboy on the more sea-soned horse usually rides through the gate, and then stops to provide a natural draw for the young horse. That gives the colt a reason to go through the gate — to get to his buddy on the other side.

The big problem for most people working a gate or teaching the side-pass is that they lose patience with their horses. Teaching a horse a new maneuver isn't a timed event, and the only way he figures out things is when the rider works one step at the time, one day at the time.

The horse is on the right lead...

Lead Change Considerations

Although leads and leads changes are big things in the show arena, they're important for ranch or pleasure horses, too, primarily for the horse's and rider's comfort. When a ranch horse changes leads each time the cow he's tracking changes direction, it's a smoother, more balanced trip for both horse and rider. That's equally true for the pleasure rider changing direction as he lopes across a meadow or down a winding trail. Otherwise, the horse feels out of balance as he goes, and neither horse nor rider feels comfortable and secure in his work.

Flying lead changes are such a big deal to so many people. They think that their timing must be perfect and that there are too many things to remember as they make the change. But flying lead changes are no problem if the rider's balanced in the saddle and stays out of his horse's way.

I know that from riding colts and I've learned it, too, from reading about military horsemanship. Some recruits weren't experienced enough horsemen to get leads or changes. However, they could do those things because they were taught to set up a horse for the maneuver, open the door and let the horse find his way through it. All the rider had to do was stay out of his horse's way, and because he did, the cavalry horse really learned to look for open doors.

A lot of ranch cowboys don't really know what a lead or lead change is, at least not as people studying horsemanship or showing horses do. But a ranch cowboy often understands leads and lead changes through practical application. He knows that a horse traveling to the right on a left lead is uncomfortable to ride and makes him feel out of balance. So he does something differently to find a better balance. He might steer the horse in one direction and then another to see if things improve, or he might slow to a trot and start loping all over again.

The cowboy and the cavalryman can get a horse to change leads because they open a door and let the horse decide when and how

...then makes the change...

...to the left lead.

to go through it. Neither rider forces the horse through the door or makes him go through it on the rider's terms, but instead lets the horse find his way.

Letting a horse find his way through any open door is a valuable tool in good horsemanship. When a horse finds his way, he's more naturally balanced because the rider doesn't "fix" him, but leaves him alone, so the horse learns to perform any maneuver well. Plus, he gets in time with his rider, rather than his rider having to get in time with him.

Something similar often happens when a ranch cowboy tracks a cow. He has one thing on his mind — the cow, so he's not trying to bend or fix his horse at the same time. As a result, his horse learns how to do his job in a way that's best for him, and the bottom line is that it's best for the cowboy, too.

It seems that many riders, who are taught to change a horse's lead in a schooling situation, must be excellent riders in the first place — they're expected to know which of the horse's feet strikes the ground with every beat. These riders also are expected to have excellent timing so they can cue their horses at the best, precise moment in his stride for the lead change.

It's no wonder that, for the average rider, a lead change hardly seems worth the effort. But the average rider usually can teach his horse to change leads as nicely as anyone, and sometimes better than most. That's because the recreational rider has no time frame within which he has to perform the maneuver. There's no pressure, so he and his horse learn to change leads at their own speed.

The Lead Change

Performing a flying lead change is like demonstrating that my horse works well in the bridle. No matter what anybody says, what somebody sees shows how well I've prepared my horse for the job. When my horse is prepared, things are easy to do. If there are holes in my preparation, my horse has trouble.

My approach to lead changes is a little different than most. It's a good one for the average rider or even a ranch cowboy. I really don't want to get in a struggle with my horse by putting a lot of pressure on him to perform the maneuver before he's balanced and ready to do it.

I don't need the lead change for the show arena, so it really doesn't matter if I do simple lead changes for 2 days or 2 months until my horse volunteers the change in the lope. He eventually can learn to make that change on his own, but only when he feels balanced to do it. So I wait for him to learn. Then, when he changes leads, he's seldom cranky.

For a lead change, the first thing I must do is get my horse moving. He should move forward freely and easily if I've done my homework on upward and downward transitions.

Straightness is the next element I need for a lead change. My horse must lope straight in his path of travel and with his body straight. Again, that shouldn't be a problem if he's responsive in the transitions. Other than setting up my horse for the change by making sure he has impulsion and straightness, I don't really work on lead changes per se. Instead, especially with a young horse, I lope him a short distance, for example, on the left lead, then bring him down to a trot straight and easy.

Then I use my hands and legs, just as I do in any transition, to open the door on the right side of his body. Next, I encourage him to trot faster until he decides to lope — on his own — in the right lead.

I continue doing simple lead changes like that for a long time, so my horse really understands that changing leads is no big deal. And he usually does, because I haven't put any pressure on him, and I've let him find his balance first — before he performs the maneuver.

Before long, when I track a cow or lope across a meadow, my horse changes leads on his own, just because he knows that it's a lot of work otherwise. All I do is keep him from dropping to a trot; then I have the change.

Practical Applications

One place a horse changes leads naturally is coming through a draw, so I might use that as a training tool. I lope my horse down a slight hill or slope, and as he comes up the other side, more often than not, he changes leads. That's because he gathers and elevates his forehand. A draw is a great place for us to figure out the perfect lead-change position.

Any natural obstacle, such as a small ditch or log in the trail, that my horse must jump, also offers a good opportunity for me to ask him to change leads. That's the ideal time for a change because, again, my horse naturally gathers and elevates as he prepares to jump the ditch or log.

That's collection, a big word that's become a big deal in the horse business, just like changing leads, but it doesn't have to be for the average rider.

To know how a collected horse feels, all I have to do is ride toward an irrigation ditch. That moment, right before my horse jumps it, he's collected. He elevates his head, which raises his withers, and his hindquarters drop. When they drop, his pelvis tips under, and his spine is soft. He's balanced. He becomes lighter on his front end and can spring forward because his legs are right underneath to give him thrust.

When a horse elevates his head, it actually lifts his withers, but doesn't necessarily hollow his back. That happens only when he pushes out his chin to brace against the rider's hands. The resistance puts the rider out of balance, and he and his horse struggle through the change. Eventually the horse becomes crabby and pins his ears.

When I watch a roper track a steer, his horse makes natural flying lead changes — and the roper's not even aware of it. He's too busy roping. But he and his horse are balanced, and the changes are smooth and easy. I could ask that same roper to change leads with his horse, and he'd probably start pulling on his horse's head, and his horse would brace in resistance and lose collection. The roper might've been trying to get in time with his horse to make the change, but nobody's that fast with his timing. That's why I think people can have better results when they let a change happen, rather than try to make it happen.

As for timing in the lead change, my horse and I can get in time with each other as long as I don't make the change happen, but let it happen. Timing my cues during my horse's stride is really difficult. Usually by the time I figure out where my horse is in his stride, it's past time to do the maneuver. If, instead, my horse and I just go with the flow, and I let my subconscious take over, rather than forcing my timing, we usually get in rhythm together anyway.

This seems such a simple explanation for such an advanced maneuver, but that's the way I work with a horse on lead changes. If I've allowed him to find his balance in the six transitions discussed previously, he already has the component skills necessary for the lead change. My horse usually learns to change leads so quickly because he knows how to find the balance he needs to feel comfortable and secure in the maneuver.

DO IT YOURSELF

Drag a log or telephone pole into your pasture to use when working on lead changes. Be sure there's enough room on either side for you to ride several strides straight to and from the log or pole.

Introduce your horse to the ground obstacle by letting him look it over first; then walk and trot him over it a few times. When he's prepared, point him straight at the center of the log or pole, and then lope him over the obstacle. He soon learns that he must gather himself slightly for his feet to clear it.

After your horse feels comfortable loping over the log or pole, ask him to change leads. When, for example, he lopes on the left lead, just as he gathers to go over the log, open your right hand and leg and close the door to the left with your left hand and leg. Your horse probably can change leads easily because his body is balanced and prepared.

PART 3
PRACTICAL APPLICATIONS

A solid understanding of the six transitions discussed in the previous section allows any rider and his horse to combine transitions in various ways to perform many precise maneuvers. Some maneuvers, such as multiple 360-degree turnarounds, are more for the show arena. Other maneuvers, such as the side-pass, are useful during competitive events and outside the arena. Cowboys, for example, side-pass their mounts when opening or closing gates, and kids often use a side-pass to retrieve mail from the box.

The next two chapters describe how to apply the six transitions in practical ways to maneuver a horse around common obstacles most any rider faces, sooner or later. Some of these everyday obstacles are natural, and others are manmade.

The following chapter discusses natural obstacles a rider might encounter as he trots through the woods, over a hill, across the pasture or down the trail. These include, for example, downed timber, poor footing, water-crossings, steep hills and even weather factors that sometimes become problems for horse-back riders.

Chapter 14 focuses on manmade obstacles, such as bridges, pavement, vehicular traffic and even the packs an outfitter uses atop what otherwise seems an ordinary mule. Hikers and bikers also contribute various manmade obstacles encountered on the trail.

The average person might have the perception that bold, tough cowboys will ride through anything like a fast-moving train. And cowboys, in fact, are bold and tough in many ways, but safety also is a big issue for them. Because they often work alone, and sometimes on relatively green horses, most cowboys try to anticipate problems before they become real issues for a horse.

Likewise, the recreational rider can plan ahead to deal with potential obstacles he might face on the trail. At home he can set up similar obstacles and prepare his horse for them in a safe, controlled situation, and without feeling pressured because he's delaying a group ride to work his horse through a trail hazard. Advance home preparation is easy to accomplish and requires only a few simple props and time. Best of all, this homework can be done at the rider's convenience and as often as it takes until he and his horse develop the necessary confidence to feel safe on the trail.

Stormy weather's a
natural obstacle that
few trail riders enjoy.

NATURAL OBSTACLES

13

Anything that causes a horse or rider to feel uneasy and insecure can become an obstacle. A natural obstacle might be a tree down across a trail, a boulder head-high to the horse or even a small creek or ditch in the horse pasture. Sometimes terrain that's never been ridden before, such as a mountain trail, might even be considered a roadblock to an enjoyable ride. Worse yet, any obstacle seems twice as large and hard to handle from the rider's perspective when a group of people wait for the rider to maneuver around, over or through the problem.

Instead of waiting to deal with obstacles in that stressful situation, it's far easier to prepare a horse for them at home. There, horse and rider can learn to deal with troublesome situations in a controlled manner and at their own pace. This relaxed setting allows trust and confidence to grow between the pair, which serves them well when they later encounter the unexpected on the trail.

Obviously, such preparation also increases the safety factor for a recreational rider, just as appropriate round-pen work reduces the risk when a cowboy rides a colt outside for the first time. Even though a problem might arise in either situation, odds are that horse and rider better weather the storm because of their solid advance preparation.

Granted, no rider can fully prepare his horse for every obstacle. But a rider can use every obstacle as an opportunity to build trust and confidence between him and his horse. That's what a ranch cowboy tries to do during his day's work. He can't spend a half-day, of course, until his horse becomes

extremely good at creek-crossings or working through downfall. So he just tries to work past any obstacle in such a way that his horse will be a little better about it the next time. That small improvement from time to time is what makes a well-seasoned, solid horse over the long haul.

A recreational rider can take the same approach at home. If he routinely sets up unfamiliar situations at home and successfully guides his horse through them, the horse soon comes to trust his rider to help deal with the unknown, wherever the pair might be riding. Likewise, the rider becomes confident and comes to rely on his mount to carry him safely past any potential hazard.

Understanding Trouble

A loose horse can walk by a big rock in his pasture every day without a problem. But put a rider on his back and the horse spooks at the rock every trip. In either case, the horse probably thinks something behind the rock can jump out and get him. His natural reaction is to fight or to flee, and the typical horse's response is flight.

The difference: The apparently unconcerned loose horse knows he can leave in a hurry, should he feel the need; no bridle reins or halter rope confine him. But the horse with the rider might not feel so free to leave if his flight instinct takes over; he knows the rider can use the reins to keep him there. So the horse then becomes twice as frightened — the first time by what he fears might lurk behind the rock and the second time by what he fears the rider might do to keep him from getting away from the rock, or fleeing to safety.

A human, on the other hand, responds differently to the unfamiliar; he tends to slow or stop when uneasy or frightened. A horse can sense that discomfort. When he does, and the rider then routinely stops, the horse soon associates those two things. The lesson he learns: When he's still, he should be troubled because his rider is.

When confronting an obstacle, a rider usually slows or stops because he fails to focus his attention beyond the obstacle, where he wants to be, and targets, in this case, only on the rock. He worries that his horse won't go past it and becomes tense and scared, which only further convinces the horse that the rock is a bad thing. Since a horse thinks of only one thing at a time, in this situation, he focuses on his rider's fear.

"A good rider... must create just enough pressure with his feet and legs to outweigh an obstacle's pressure on his horse... ."

Instead of worrying about the rock, the rider should concentrate on the open trail beyond it, and the good ride he's sure to enjoy. His horse might well follow his focus and travel right past the rock.

When that happens, it's okay if the horse travels a little fast the first time or two he passes the rock. At this point, he hasn't refused his rider outright, and the rider probably can soon bring that slightly hurried pace under control as he approaches, passes and leaves the rock.

However, the horse shouldn't run past the rock. If he does, that only means that the rock continues to put more pressure on the horse than his rider does. When that's the case, a horse often becomes worse about an obstacle instead of better.

On the other hand, if the rider has spurred hard to drive his horse beyond the rock, his horse might run in an effort to escape the spur pressure. Obviously, a hard-spurring approach, where the rider applies too much pressure, won't help a horse become better about an obstacle any more than the previous approach, when the rider applies too little pressure.

A good rider is always involved in a balancing act. He must create just enough pressure with his feet and legs to outweigh an obstacle's pressure on his horse and get the desired response, without creating too much pressure on his horse. The only way to find that just-right balance of pressure at the rock or any obstacle is to keep riding past the rock over a period of time and analyzing what happens there.

Another cause for potential trouble: Some horses are more reasonable about approaching scary things than they are about leaving them. A savvy rider realizes that's a possibility and plans ahead to deal with it.

Too often when a rider forces his horse past a frightening obstacle, the minute the pair are beyond it, the person feels so relieved that he quits actively riding his horse, who's still trying to flee the rock now behind him. So the horse's pace isn't controlled, and he breaks into a lope. This, in effect, teaches him to escape an obstacle by running away from it. That satisfies the horse's need to flee, but can compromise the rider's safety.

Instead, the rider must think not only about his approach to an obstacle, but also about what can happen once he's ridden beyond it. When he doesn't think ahead about how he can handle that situation, his horse might take off, overpower the rider and learn that he's the stronger of the two.

Although a rider's natural instinct in a troublesome situation is opposite his horse's, it's the rider's responsibility, as the thinking partner, to approach the unfamiliar in a way his horse can understand. Then horse and rider can both feel secure.

Understanding the horse's need to flee — in other words, move his feet — is key to helping him deal with obstacles. Although the horse shouldn't run away, if he's really bothered by an obstacle, it's okay to allow his feet to move in a controlled manner, if necessary, to satisfy his flight instinct. Doing so also gives the

DO IT YOURSELF

The biggest stumbling block for many riders troubled by obstacles is the inability to focus beyond an obstacle to the trail ahead. Even though you might never compete in a speed event, barrels and poles are good tools to help you learn to focus ahead on where you want to go and better maintain your horse's forward motion. Using the barrels and poles also helps gradually accustom your horse to going through narrow spaces at home, so you can confidently ride through tight spots on the trail.

Set two poles about 12 feet apart at first. Circle your horse first at a walk around one and then the other until he's relaxed. Then, without making a big deal of it, ride your horse straight between the poles. Look directly between the poles and focus beyond them on something across your pasture. You should still see the poles in your peripheral vision.

Notice that any time you lose your distant focus and look directly at the poles, your horse slows and loses his forward momentum. When that happens, don't look down at your horse or stop — look ahead, refocus and keep moving, using your legs to drive your horse forward.

When you've ridden between the poles several times and maintained your focus and your horse's steady pace, move the poles closer together and ride between them again. Over time, gradually move the poles until there's just enough clearance between them for your horse. Eventually, stop and let him stand quietly between the poles.

At the same time you learn to focus beyond an obstacle, you also prepare your horse to ride through closely spaced timber and other tight places on the trail. That's important because horses can be very claustrophobic.

Don't worry if you hit a pole as you pass between them, even though your horse might become startled the first time it happens. Just reset the pole and ride between them again. If the falling pole spooks your horse so much that he's hesitant to go between them again, temporarily move the poles a little farther apart and continue riding between them until your horse again relaxes. Then move the poles closer together and, again, follow the same routine.

You don't have to accomplish all this in one ride, one day or even a week. You might work with the poles at 12

feet the first day until your horse is comfortable, then enjoy a ride across the pasture. The next day, make a few passes at the 12-foot distance, then close the gap to 10 feet and work there until your horse handles it well. The third day start at the 10-foot distance, then narrow the gap even more. Your goal is to gradually increase your and your horse's confidence, and that's a solid foundation for trust.

Another way to build your horse's confidence is to do the same exercise using two 55-gallon barrels. Gradually move the barrels together, eventually so close that your legs brush the barrels as you ride between them.

Your leg brushing a barrel is like knocking over a pole — just another unfamiliar situation for you and your horse to experience at home, so it's no big deal. Soon you can stop him right between the barrels. Your horse learns he can get through a tight spot without rushing, which means he has no instinctive need to fear the situation — because he trusts you to guide him through it.

A horse should be allowed to look at the poles before being ridden between them.

Only when a horse is comfortable around the poles should he be asked to travel directly between them. Both horse and rider look ahead and demonstrate good focus here.

horse time to think his way through the unfamiliar situation and develop greater confidence in his rider.

The point where a horse wants to leave an obstacle becomes his flight zone. It might be 10, 20 or 30 feet from the obstacle, but it's the point when the horse becomes motivated by fear. At that point, it's best not to try to stop him altogether because a frightened horse often braces all the harder against the rider and sometimes tries to get away even more quickly.

Instead of dealing with the additional resistance a complete stop might bring, the rider should lift — not pull — on the reins to elevate his horse's head, similar to the emergency stop described in Chapter 4. That slight elevation increases control of the horse's spine and body, so the rider can slow the horse's feet enough for him to face and handle his fear.

Working through the fear often means riding the horse out of his flight zone until he calms, then matter-of-factly guiding him back toward the obstacle and, again, helping him as he approaches the flight zone. It might be necessary to go through that process several times before a horse accepts an obstacle reasonably well. As that happens, his flight zone decreases as the rider builds the horse's confidence to handle a scary hazard a little at the time.

Up- and Downhill

When working a horse on any obstacle, including a mountainside, it's important to go slowly. Slow is safe, and the best approach to mountain riding is to first become comfortable riding up and down smaller hills. Any rider with a balance problem in the hills isn't ready to ride in the mountains. They're not fun for someone uncomfortable with the terrain.

A horse raised and kept outside generally knows where to place his feet to best take care of himself and his rider — if the rider is confident to trust the horse. A trusting rider should simply guide his horse, stay balanced in the saddle and let the horse keep him safe.

A horse raised and kept in a stall or a young horse is an altogether different matter. In

A rider should maintain his balance over the horse's center of gravity to make it easy on the horse as he climbs uphill.

either case, it's best to use caution in the hills because the horse doesn't know physically how to balance himself, let alone his rider. Pushed too hard, before he learns how to effectively use his body to travel in such terrain, a horse can hurt himself or might even quit trying altogether.

A horse should never be put in a situation where it's so steep he might fall or fail to make the climb, especially a young horse. Sometimes a cowboy must ride where he really shouldn't because that's where a cow is, but the recreational rider has no cowboss back at the pen waiting for him. Ego and simply thinking that he has to go up or down a mountain because it's there are the only things that prevent most people from safely riding out of the mountains.

Anyone riding in steep country should pay attention to his gear. A breast collar's necessary when going uphill on a horse with poor withers. Using a breast collar beats tightly cinching a horse, which makes it even harder for him to catch his breath as he climbs.

As the saddle slides back, it's especially important to notice how far back the rear cinch moves. During a steep climb the saddle often slides so far back that the rear cinch flanks the horse just as he tops out of the climb, which makes a lot of horses buck then.

For a mutton-withered horse, going downhill is even worse than going uphill because

When going downhill, a rider keeps his balance by simply letting his body slide forward while maintaining his balanced position in the saddle.

the saddle can work up his neck. A crupper that attaches to the rear of the saddle and around the base of the horse's tail helps, or the rider can simply lead his horse downhill.

Riding up- and downhill without getting into trouble is a matter of using good judgment more than anything. Loose horses in the mountains don't go straight uphill or down because that's physically difficult. Instead, they usually "side-hill," or travel at an angle, and make frequent switchbacks in the trail, which helps save their energy. A game trail usually offers a good switchback route for horses in hilly country.

And as hikers do when climbing mountains, horses need to take breaks, too. Just because a rider's lungs aren't burning doesn't mean his horse's aren't. Regular rest stops are great places to enjoy the scenery while a horse airs up. It's frustrating when a horse is exhausted, sore or unfit for his work, and an unfit horse probably is the pleasure rider's biggest problem in the mountains, so knowing when to stop is critical. It's not rocket science either: When a rider must use progressively more effort just to keep his horse moving, it's time to stop.

Stopping at a somewhat flat spot makes it easy for a horse to rest, relax and blow, and it's safer, too. If possible, a horse should have all four feet on relatively flat ground, so he can relax without slipping or staying tense to maintain a safe balance. A horse tells his rider when the stopping spot's comfortable; otherwise, he won't stand there and squirms around. When it's time to move again, it's also best to let him take a few steps and limber his muscles, if possible, before again starting to climb up or drop down a mountainside.

A good trail horse climbs at a steady walk although he might have to lunge uphill at times. However, some horses are simply chargey climbers and want to get to the top too quickly. That's good in one respect: The horse's mind goes where the rider wants him to go, so it's easy to maintain forward motion. But it's still up to the rider to control the charginess.

Probably at some point in the past, the chargey horse became excited climbing uphill and was allowed to go faster and faster until he now anticipates the climb like a barrel horse does his pattern. Instead, if the terrain allows, before starting uphill it's best to try to change a chargey horse's attitude by riding in small circles until he relaxes.

Sometimes a horse that travels uphill quickly doesn't charge so much as try to catch up with the other horses. That's especially true of young horses and can work to the rider's advantage because the lead horses often give the young horse added incentive to climb the hill.

The rider's balance is important when riding in the hills. The rider should stay plumb, sit as straight as he can in the saddle and set his feet wide as a base for good balance. Uphill or down, a well-centered rider allows his horse to make the best use of his hind legs when getting across the terrain.

Going uphill, a rider should be slightly ahead of the motion, which means his feet might fall just a tiny bit behind his body. His position is like that of someone walking uphill; the steeper the hill, the more forward the upper body.

Using the horn when riding uphill is okay. But holding the horn with the knuckles up stiffens the arm. If the horse lunges, he can pop a stiff-armed rider right out of the saddle. Instead, it's better to use a night latch (see Chapter 6) and curl into the saddle.

A common problem for a novice mountain rider is that he sometimes tackles too steep a hill, and his horse tries to lunge and jump up it. The novice then typically gets thrown or falls behind his horse's action. And when a behind-the-action rider pulls on his horse's head, he runs the risk of pulling his horse over backward — again, because they aren't in balance. It's smart to pick a less severe trail.

If a horse traveling uphill loses his balance, it's best to turn him to face downhill instead of traveling sideways around the hill while he scrambles for his footing. Facing downhill, should the horse slide, he does so with his butt underneath him and can better regain control.

When traveling downhill, a rider shouldn't lean back in the saddle so much as he should slide into the front of it and let the swells hold him. Again, he can spread his feet wide, away from his horse's sides, for better balance, but pushing his feet forward hard against the stirrups braces his body too far back in the saddle. When a horse takes a misstep, it's harder for him to rebalance with a braced rider than with one who's relaxed.

DO IT YOURSELF

If your horse charges uphill when his buddies are at the top, deal with the problem at home on flat ground. The hillside probably isn't the only place you have that problem. A horse headed uphill to his buddies is no different from a herd-bound or barn-sour horse. But a steep hillside isn't the place to cure his problem; it's too dangerous.

Remember that everything about a controlled ride relates to maintaining a soft, responsive jaw as you ride through the six transitions. Before you head to the mountains, work your horse at home on level ground until he responds consistently and correctly when you ask for those transitions. Refer to Part Two as you fine-tune your horse's responses.

Understand that a more severe bit offers only a temporary fix. Solving any horsemanship problem always comes back to the basics — performing them correctly. You might be able to skip them if you ride only in a pen, but when riding cross-country, good control might mean the difference between life, death or injury.

If you don't master the basics and take time to resolve such problems at home, you'll probably continue to have trouble with your horse everywhere you go.

Some people don't think they need to zigzag as much when going downhill as they do when traveling up, but that also helps protect a horse from a fall. It might look western to slide a horse off the edge of a steep hillside, but that can be dangerous, just as side-hilling on too-steep terrain is.

No one should ever be afraid to dismount and lead his horse — before he starts rolling or sliding. It's also smart to lead him across rocky ground, especially if it's mostly shale, or a sometimes-icy northern slope. It's too easy to get hurt on poor footing; it's safest then to dismount and lead the horse.

A word of caution: It's also easy to get hurt while leading a horse up or sliding down a hill. A person directly in front of a horse lunging up or sliding down the hill can be run over. Instead, the handler should walk on the uphill side of his horse. That's another reason I like using a McCarty: The get-down-lead part of it is longer than a split rein, giving me plenty of room to stay out of my horse's way. Or, if necessary, when I'm afoot, I can send my horse by me in a bad spot, without letting go of the McCarty or jerking my horse's head.

Cowboy etiquette when traveling uphill and down is similar to gate etiquette: Riders at the top or bottom of the hill should wait in sight of, but out of the way of horses still traversing the hillside.

Going uphill, riders often crowd into a bunch, but a horse in the bunch has trouble maintaining his momentum. There's no room for him to keep moving forward, and he might have to veer off the trail into really tough terrain.

Instead, it's best to start uphill when there's plenty of room for a horse to travel at a swift walk and maintain his momentum, without being blocked by riders ahead. Once up the hill, a rider should move out of the way, but wait nearby for the others to top out.

Making a horse stand or stay put when other horses are leaving him usually causes a problem, but sometimes it's not as severe if the horse can see other horses ahead. However, holding back a horse can mean that the rider pulls a lot on the reins, which changes the horse's balance, and he might fall over backward. The horse at the bottom might even stand quietly for a few moments, but when he moves, it can be scary and fast. Rather than stop a horse completely at the foot of a climb, sometimes it's best, if the terrain allows, to handle him like a chargey horse and put him to work trotting circles.

The bottom line on mountain riding: It's some of the best riding ever, but only when good judgment and common sense are used. That means a rider should take plenty of time, look at the terrain, pick a good trail, and never be afraid to dismount before there's a wreck.

Riding Through Timber

Transition work pays real dividends when riding in the woods. A smooth stop is a plus, especially when a rider's about to hit his head on a limb or catch his reins on a limb. Responsive lateral transitions make it easy to work a horse through the trees or to move his forehand or hindquarters to clear a downfall.

When a horse is about to bang his rider's knee into a tree, few people realize how easy it is to push a 1,000-pound horse off a tree trunk. The rider simply can push against the trunk with his hand, which pushes his horse off-balance. That takes his weight off the foot nearest the tree, and when that happens, the horse must move away from the tree to rebalance himself. Because this problem-solver is strictly a balance maneuver, the rider doesn't have to be big and stout to move his horse — even a kid can do this.

Ducking a limb usually isn't that big a deal either. But sometimes as a rider leans forward to duck, he accidentally spurs or kicks his horse, causing him to jump. As a result, the rider sometimes hits the limb harder than he would've anyway, or the horse might jump into a downfall and get into more trouble.

With a really spooky horse, bending over might be dangerous. A rider bending completely over in the saddle to dodge limbs in heavy timber or thick brush can bang his head into a tree or even be knocked off his horse. It's no disgrace to dismount and lead an unsettled horse when that's the case.

Mother Nature provides many obstacles for improving horsemanship, including bushes to circle.

A ground pole or cross-tie can be used to teach a horse to pick up his feet when stepping over obstacles.

When leading a horse through timber, however, the saddle horn still sticks up higher than the horse's back and can easily catch on a limb. As a limb draws back against the horn and then pops free, the horse might jump forward, right on top of his handler. The same thing might happen if brush or a limb gets stuck under the back cinch or through a stirrup.

If a horse blows up when something touches his side or underbelly, he's not yet

DO IT YOURSELF

Even if you have no brush or trees at home, here are several exercises to help prepare your horse for traveling through timber. None of these maneuvers requires elaborate equipment; just use whatever you have handy at home to prepare your horse for whatever you might encounter in timber. Otherwise, you're just taking chances.

If your horse has never been in the woods, a tree limb rubbing on your jacket or coat, especially if it's nylon, can scare him. Take time at home to rub vigorously on your coat, even scratch it with your fingernails, until your horse becomes accustomed to the sound.

Limbs make noise, too, rubbing against each other and slapping against your leggin's or coat as you ride through the woods. At home, put on your chaps, chinks or slicker, then ride and slap your leg from time to time until your horse is comfortable with the noise.

When riding through the woods, somebody's hat always gets knocked off. Prepare your horse for the experience at home. Flip off your hat and let your horse get used to it flying through the air and landing on the ground.

Ride near a fence- or corner-post, then push against it with your hand, just as you'd push against a tree trunk in the woods to protect your knees. Feel your horse's balance shift as you go through the motion.

You can also hang a tarp or piece of plastic from the post. The tarp makes noise and moves just as a tree trunk can when you push against it, and your horse can learn to handle both the noise and motion.

Be sure your horse can tolerate things touching his belly, which might be the case if a limb gets caught under the back cinch. If you touch his belly and he jumps at home, he's sure to jump when limbs or brush hit him out on the trail. Take time at home to desensitize him, but be cautious and use good judgment as you rub his belly, first with your hand and later with a saddle blanket, slicker or an actual limb.

At home make a "forest" of poles and barrels so your horse is less likely to become claustrophobic in the woods. Randomly maneuver your horse through the barrels and poles, and don't forget to practice backing between and around them.

The do-it-yourself ground-sack exercise described in the water-crossing section of this chapter is also good to prepare a horse for low brush. He can learn to step over the sacks with confidence and without feeling that he has to leap over them.

A series of ground poles can be used to accomplish the same thing, and you can slightly elevate them later to introduce your horse to jumping. Remember, though, that stepping over obstacles is a good skill to have because that's sometimes safer than jumping them. Walking over an obstacle isn't so critical at home because you probably set your ground poles in a relatively clear area, and it's more fun to encourage your horse to jump them. But when you're in timber and your horse knows only how to jump the downfall, it's not safe; he might well hurt himself, at least skin and scrap his legs, or hurt you. That's less likely to happen when he understands how to walk over the downfall because you've taught him the difference at home.

Even though you might never plan to enter a trail class, set up similar obstacles at home for your horse to work. Use hay bales to teach your horse to side-pass over deadfall with ease, or ground poles in an "L" formation to sharpen the back-up and lateral transitions you need in the woods.

If you don't have solid downward transitions at home, you won't have them when you need them in the woods, so fine-tune your horse's rate and his stop as described in Part Two.

Crossing a natural obstacle, such as a log, can help boost a rider's confidence.

fully prepared to ride through timber. An excellent horseman might be able to deal with that situation, but few novices could. Before riding in the woods, a rider at any level must be honest about his and his mount's abilities and limitations; their safety depends on it.

Additionally, if there's no real reason, such as a lost cow, for putting a horse through heavy downfall in really brushy country, why do it? That's tough on a horse, and the brush is hard on his eyes. A big downfall usually includes sharp-pointed sticks that a horse must work his feet and legs around, and he can get skinned and scraped badly. A rider working through downfall can dismount and break off larger limbs, so they don't poke his horse in the belly, catch his legs or take him by surprise if he jumps a log. Obviously, if a horse and rider aren't capable of jumping downed timber, it's best to lead the horse or find another route. It's one thing when traversing a downfall is necessary, but whenever possible, it's best to avoid the really tough spots and make things as easy as possible for the horse.

The most common problem in timber: Horses often try to hurry through the brush and trees, and a claustrophobic horse in a hurry seldom gives his rider time to duck. Instead, he often falls back in the saddle, pulling back on the reins, which can cause a horse to rear. It's best to stay forward in the saddle, rather than behind the horse's action.

An experienced cowboy always plans his route through the woods, just as he does in the mountains. He looks for that random bare spot with no timber and little brush, especially when riding a young horse. Then he knows a place where he can safely regain control and circle his horse, should the horse become troubled.

To ride successfully through timber, a rider should have consistent control of his horse's mind and body, then trust the horse to slowly work his way through it; this isn't the place to rush. If a horse just wants out of the timber,

DO IT YOURSELF

When you and your horse are comfortable with the previously described do-it-yourself experiences, ride your horse through timber. Don't go through the heaviest stand of trees you can find. Pick a less dense area at the edge of the woods, then work slowly to control the situation from the start.

Gradually and calmly work your way through the trees. First ride between a couple of trees, and then circle several of them. As your horse becomes comfortable in the new setting, ask more of him.

Don't rush through the trees or hurry while going under a limb; that only tells your horse that trees and limbs are causes for concern. Then he rushes because he's uneasy and needs to move his feet to feel safe.

Sometimes necessity enters into riding decisions, and a horse might be asked to do something for which he's ill-prepared. A ranch cowboy usually asks such an effort from his horse because it's necessary to complete the day's work; he does the job and later fixes his mistakes with the horse. However, when a pleasure rider intentionally asks his horse to do something that's unnecessary and for which he's not prepared, ego drives that decision.

tries to leave and the brush is poppin', the rider hasn't done his homework. His horse isn't prepared for the obstacle. A horse seldom puts himself in all the situations a human puts him into, so the horse shouldn't have to panic to get out of a bad situation.

Nobody's lack of experience, or his horse's, should prevent him from riding through timber. It's simple to prepare a horse at home for that, and easy to do when good judgment is used to go through the woods one tree at a time.

Water Crossings

Some horses seem so afraid of water, which might be due to their poor depth perception, so a water-crossing is a good gauge of a rider's home-obstacle preparation. The home experiences are important because they build trust between horse and rider, and the horse learns to perform a maneuver when asked and not refuse.

Crossing water is like riding by the rock in the "Understanding Trouble" section — use too much or too little pressure and the horse won't cross. He might wheel or back away and learn to escape the rider's pressure, something he might never have known had his rider not

When crossing a creek, the most confident horse and rider should cross first since the other horses probably will follow.

given him the opportunity to learn it, and that's true at any obstacle.

Anything alongside a horse, such as water in a creek, causes pressure, and to drive a horse forward and across it, the rider must apply more pressure than the creek. Eventually the horse understands that when he goes where his rider directs him, he gets relief from the creek's pressure on either side.

Any time a rider approaches a crossing, he must focus on the far side of the water, then act and ride as if he'll get there. He also must be sure his horse's mind is headed in that direction before applying pressure. Perhaps that's why people seem to dread water-crossings; they don't know how much pressure to use or how to apply it.

A rider might become aggressive at crossings and, for example, spur a horse or spank down a hind leg with the bridle rein. When the horse is pointed toward the creek and he's looking at it, he'll probably cross. But when he's looking in a totally different direction, and gets swatted or spurred, he goes where he's looking — not across the water. The rider, in effect, drives his horse away from the creek.

That's why a savvy rider quits talking with his buddies 40 or 50 feet from the creek bank, and starts thinking and riding. Otherwise, his horse slows before he reaches the water, which adds even more resistance to overcome. Many people don't realize that happens until a horse spins around to leave. But by concentrating on his horse beforehand, a rider can more easily drive his horse through that slow-down before the problem escalates at the creek bank.

Although a recreational rider must consider the people on any group ride, his best option with a reluctant horse is to decide that the creek crossing is a wonderful place to spend the day. Then he has time to work with his horse without excess pressure. He can take an advance-and-retreat approach, if he wants, until his horse becomes totally comfortable with crossing.

But no matter the approach at a water-crossing or any obstacle, a rider should never be afraid to tell his horse, "Let's go." That might be necessary, and when it is and the rider reinforces his request, the problem's never again as serious an issue. Getting after a horse one time is much less cruel than picking at him at water-crossings, or any obstacle, for the rest of his life.

And that's real, just like the cowboy who spends all day gathering cattle and must cross a creek to keep from losing his herd. He puts his horse across the creek — even though it might take a firm hand and might not be a pretty maneuver. But he can smooth out the maneuver later, which probably will be easy because the horse wasn't allowed to escape or refuse the obstacle the first time. The great thing about a horse is that he forgives, and when a cowboy directs him across the creek the first time, a horse doesn't forget it. Riding a horse isn't always loving and petting him. Everyone would like it to be; then they'd never have to correct a horse. But if dealing with an obstacle means life, death or losing cattle, a top hand's going to do whatever it takes to get his horse across a creek.

That's an important mind-set for the recreational rider to understand and use anytime a horse challenges him. When a training job's done right the first time, it's always easier to accomplish the next time. When a person realizes that about horses, it's so much easier to make up his mind to get the job done. That's great, as long as he can be safe and not be too hard on his horse.

Sometimes having another horse across the creek can help draft a reluctant horse and motivate him to cross. Or a rider might join a group of seasoned horses comfortable with water-crossings, and then give his horse the chance to follow their willing lead. With a large group, a couple of riders on either side of the reluctant horse might herd him across, making it easy for him to go with the other horses' flow.

So often when other horses are drinking from the creek and a rider offers a reluctant horse a drink, as the other horses continue across the creek, the reluctant horse soon decides to cross without a big fuss. Sometimes he needs only those few minutes while he drinks to decide everything's okay about the crossing. Because the rider doesn't force him and because a horse naturally wants to go forward anyway, he just decides to cross on his own. But that happens only when a rider reads his horse well and doesn't push him too hard too fast.

Another option is to have another rider lead a reluctant horse across the creek. That's also better than having a big fuss with him, especially if other people are waiting, but sound judgment must be used in selecting the person to lead the horse.

Once across a creek, the typical rider often wants to ride through the water again, and that's when he can get hurt; he pushes the horse too much. The rider wants to do that again for his own ego, but it's best for the horse to keep riding and let the experience soak into his mind for a while.

Whether a horse jumps or wades through a creek sometimes depends on the bank or the type of crossing. Most horses understand boggy creek banks and want to jump across, but it's better to slow down and wade through a rocky crossing. A rider must be able to feel when his horse gathers to jump, so he can stop the horse, if necessary, by checking his forward motion. That shouldn't be a problem for anyone who's mastered downward transitions with his horse.

Although each rider must use his own judgment, it's often best to approach a steep or slick bank head-on. If a horse gets sideways to the bank, his feet might slip out from under him, but when his spine's straight with the downward slope's main flow, the horse might slip, but can slide straight down and remain balanced until he reaches the bottom.

The same holds true when trying to climb a slick bank. It's best to ride straight toward the top and not dillydally or stop the horse. He needs his momentum to get up the bank. All the rider must do is stay forward in the saddle and not pull on the reins, which could cause the horse to flip over backward, should he slip.

Any rider should be aware that horses often paw in water with a forefoot — right before lying down in the water. Not every horse paws, but most do; a savvy rider soon

DO IT YOURSELF

Use feed sacks at home to prepare your horse for creek crossings and other ground obstacles, such as low brush. Teach him to step between and over the sacks, so he understands how to handle pressure when you later ask him to cross a creek. Then at home he develops the habit of going forward through things, rather than stopping or running away from them.

Collect 10 feed sacks minimum. I prefer paper feed sacks because noise eventually becomes a factor as my horse walks across the sacks or throws dirt atop them, which also prepares him for splashing water and dirt flying up from the trail.

Begin with two piles of sacks about 12 feet apart. Place a few rocks on top of the bags, if necessary, to keep them from blowing away. First circle one pile and then the other, and ride your horse between the piles, just as you do with the poles and barrels in the previous exercises. Don't try to stop your horse on the sacks at first, just continue to ride until he's comfortable.

When he is, spread out the sack pile, allowing only about 10 feet between piles, and accustom your horse to that change. Then close the gap even more, eventually creating only a small trail between the sacks and, ultimately, closing the trail to ride across the sacks.

At first, your horse might spook or pick up speed between sacks as the distance narrows. That's because he hasn't yet learned to think his way through the obstacle or to let you help him. I prefer to walk through the sacks, but if your horse needs to trot at first to feel secure, that's okay as long as he moves forward without a refusal.

As your horse progresses, try stopping him between sacks. If he seems afraid, let him walk through the sacks to find his relief, which always is on the other side. But don't force your horse because that only creates more fear. Give him all the time he needs at home to learn that across the way — forward and through the sacks — is a good place to be.

Work effectively. Don't spend all your riding time at the sacks; spend some time trail or pasture riding,

Initially, the sacks are placed far enough apart that the horse doesn't refuse to walk through them, and the rider should focus beyond the sacks, as this rider does.

too, and have fun with your horse. Before long, dealing with the sacks is part of everyday life, and your horse is confident that you'll help him take care of himself. He learns how to trust you and not to panic.

On the trail, when you get to that first creek crossing, approach it just as you do your sacks at home. It's no big deal. Your horse can handle the sacks, so you should feel confident that he can handle similar obstacles on the trail, too.

As the sacks are moved closer together a horse often becomes more concerned about walking between them.

A little coaching never hurts when introducing a horse to something new.

A good kid's horse shouldn't be concerned about walking over sacks.

learns that, unless he wants another bath that day, he should drive his horse forward and clear of the water.

Poor Footing

Slick footing is why long ropes (50 to 75 feet) have become so popular with cowboys in my home state of Montana. They can stay out of a cow's flight zone, throw a long loop and not make so many quick moves on poor footing.

On any kind of poor footing a rider should stay balanced, calm and relaxed, so his horse doesn't panic or scurry to get away from the problem. When a horse scurries on good footing, he can leave, but when he scurries on bad footing, it only worsens the situation. His feet go faster, but he doesn't get anywhere, and soon loses his balance.

By staying calm, the rider helps keep the horse relaxed, too. That's so important, no matter if he's on pavement, muddy ground or ice. If necessary, the rider might "milk" his reins slightly to get the horse to relax his jaw and start thinking instead of panicking. When a rider's done his homework, his horse should look to him for help, rather than panic.

A rider's responsible for helping his horse as much as possible on poor footing, primarily because the horse probably would've avoided that bad footing anyway had the rider not put him there in the first place. So it's up to the rider to help his horse get out of that bad spot.

Horses that have run outside usually know, for example, about boggy creek bottoms. Sometimes the bogs are deceptive and appear to be firm ground, but they're not. Seeing a horse bogged down is terrible. If a rider isn't familiar with the area he's traveling, he should follow someone who is. A ranch cowboy often follows a cow through a creek because, wherever a cow can cross, a horse should be able to cross, too.

If a bog is unavoidable, a rider should give his horse his head, sit forward and hang on. The rider could dismount and let the horse find his way out, but that's a touchy call and a good way to get into trouble. It's dangerous because the horse starts lunging and might panic. Then he can hurt himself or get on top of the rider. Sometimes a bogged-down horse literally climbs over his rider to get out — he tries to leave that hard. It's the worst situation.

On a group ride, the first riders down to the pond or creek bank generally avoid the mire that can develop as a group of horses waters or crosses. Even then a rider should use his horse's best judgment. If a horse doesn't want to cross in a particular spot, there's probably a good reason, especially if he's crossed there before and is generally good about water crossings. Something's wrong. The rider can work up and down the bank to find firmer ground, and the horse can drink cleaner water upstream or down anyway because the group hasn't yet mucked it up.

Recreational riders also must consider the damage 30 or 40 horses can do to a stream bank; nowadays if trail riders don't, they'll ultimately have trouble ensuring their right to ride in many areas. Riders can spread out and cause less impact, or they can water a few head at the time to prevent stream-bank damage.

As for rocky areas, a horse usually can pick his way through them, but a rider should never ask him to hurry, especially if the horse isn't familiar with the country. Instead, the rider should slow down and rely on his horse to deal with the poor footing, then relax and stay balanced in the saddle so he doesn't affect his horse's balance.

In some parts of the country, even grass can be dangerously slick when it's wet with dew. In other, more arid regions, grass can be dangerously slick because it's so dry. In either case, the amount of traction a horse has depends somewhat on the type of shoes he wears. But it's always best — on wet or dry grass —to slow down before turning a horse. Otherwise he can lose his balance and footing and fall.

The same holds true when riding across feeding or bedding grounds slick with hay or straw. They should be handled as any slick footing would be — stop straight, turn, then go forward again.

If a horse has ever been on ice, and must cross it again, he knows how to be light on his feet and put them down slowly and easily. The

A group ride isn't a problem when horses have been prepared at home.

With any questionable footing, it's safer to ride as straight a path as possible, especially when moving at a faster pace. If a turn's necessary, a rider should rate his horse's speed slowly and carefully, and then make the turn. Turning on slick ground is dangerous, and a horse's feet can easily fly out from underneath him. In that case, when the horse falls, it's difficult for the rider to free his leg underneath the horse.

If a horse starts to go down, the worst thing a rider can do is pull the horse even more off-balance by pulling on the reins. The horse needs his head free to balance himself; if the rider lets him have his head, a horse might work his way back upright. That's another reason I'm not crazy about tie-downs. They interfere with a horse's natural balance in a bad situation like that.

When a rider feels his horse's front end going down, he should balance back in the saddle so the horse can bring up his front end. By pushing back and staying out of the horse's way, the rider also has a better chance of getting off cleanly should the horse go completely down. When that happens, the momentum sends the rider out past the horse, just as if his saddle's an ejection seat. But if an off-balance rider pushes to one side or the other, he can pull down his horse. The best advice for slick footing is to go slowly and stay balanced with the horse.

Snow also causes footing problems because it tends to ball up in the bottoms of a horse's feet. People have tried all kinds of things to keep the snow from balling up — everything from axle grease to cooking spray — but those remedies work well for only about 5 minutes. The best thing developed so far is a shoeing pad that pops with every step, like the safety lids on food jars at the grocery, but it's easiest to just stop and clean a horse's feet when they need it.

The worrisome thing about snow is that a rider can't see what's underneath; he could hit a patch of ice or ride into a big drift. If that's the case, the horse lunges; to stay aboard, a rider must balance just a bit ahead of his horse and go with the flow. It's almost like riding a bucking horse, and if a rider gets behind

rider, too, should be as light in the saddle as possible, and never afraid to dismount and lead his horse across ice.

When a ranch cowboy in the northern states or mountains has to work on ice, he usually has the proper footwear for his horse. Most cowboys weld borium on their horseshoes for better grip. "Sharp-shoeing" is the old-time term for that, and nowadays a cowboy can buy shoes that already have little grips on them. The main thing: Ranch cowboys ride in icy weather only when they must. Working like that's a necessity on some ranches, but there's no real reason for a recreational rider to be out when the ground's icy and conditions are dangerous.

Cowboying in springtime in colder country always is hard on riders. The ground might be thawed for the most part, but still have frozen spots in shady areas. A cowboy often trots along on good footing, then hits a slick spot, and he and his horse go down. That's why so many cowboys in the north have broken legs in the springtime.

his horse's center of gravity, he usually goes right over the front of his horse. That's very dangerous because the horse could lunge right on top of his rider.

The bottom line on riding across poor footing is simple: Slower is safer. If a rider doesn't think he can handle it, he should dismount.

Weather Concerns

Weather conditions are natural obstacles of sorts. At any time heat, cold, lightening, wind or humidity can be big concerns to a horseman.

The important thing when riding during cold weather is not to work a horse so hard that he sweats heavily and breathes hard. When his hair coat's wet, the horse loses his insulation, and hard breathing might cause respiratory problems in extreme cold. Sometimes a ranch cowboy must ride, even when it's below zero. It's so difficult to doctor cattle then because his fingers don't work so well, and he sure doesn't want or need to deal with an overheated, hard-breathing horse as well.

Horses also seem more prone to injury when working hard in the cold, for whatever reason, and getting a horse to drink enough water during extreme cold is sometimes difficult. That's why heated tanks and buckets have become so popular. Even a pasture horse drinks more if he can get to a spring, where the water's warmer.

On the other hand, heat and humidity can be just as hard on a horse as the cold. A rider must take care not to overheat his horse to the point he can't cool down in a reasonable time. A fit horse that's had heavy exercise should be back to a normal pulse, temperature and respiration rate within about 5 or 10 minutes following the work. If not, he should be cooled out slowly, and a bit more caution should be used when he's exercised.

It's also miserable to be horseback in severe rain or hail, when it's best to dismount and find shelter. If that's not possible, the horse should at least be able to turn his hindquarters to the wind, and then all horse and rider can do is tough out the weather. Hailstorms are as bad, if not worse than rain, and sometimes cause wrecks because some horses just can't handle the hail hitting them. They just want to leave — and in a hurry.

Although nobody likes to ride in the rain or hail, the real danger is from lightning. Experts tell people not to get under trees during storms, but when riding in the high country above tree line, where horse and rider are totally exposed to the elements, moving back down into the trees is preferable. Once below tree line, a rider should find a low spot, because he sure doesn't want to be a target out in the open above tree line.

There's an old saying about not training horses on windy days. A horse is a prey animal, extremely uneasy and on alert on windy days. A savvy rider is aware of that. Many horsemen try not to ride young horses in strong wind at all, but sometimes they can't avoid it. Wind 35 or 45 miles an hour is tough unless there's a place behind a ridge line, for example, to ride. Even then, it's usually miserable riding, and a long coat or slicker can spook a horse when the wind pops it or blows a horse's tail between his legs.

But no matter the weather, the do-it-yourself exercises in this chapter should help prepare a horse for whatever the average rider might experience. It always helps in any potentially hazardous situation when a rider feels like he can relax and trust his horse to follow his lead.

Kids never allow natural or rough terrain to get in the way of having fun.

Rather than dismounting to open a gate, a rider can use this manmade obstacle to improve his horsemanship.

MANMADE OBSTACLES 14

Obviously, riding horses on pavement or near automobile traffic is dangerous; a horse could slip and fall, be hit by a car or even run into a parked vehicle. In an ideal world such things wouldn't be problems, but few people live in ideal riding situations. Most riders eventually face such manmade obstacles if not in their neighborhoods, then during local fairs, playdays or parades.

Riders also encounter manmade obstacles on the trail, such as the bulky packs an outfitter uses on his mule string. Unpacked mules might seem quite ordinary, but mules wearing packsaddles and panniers appear altogether different, which can frighten a horse. In a similar way, a hiker on multiuse trail, carrying a backpack with bedroll on top, seems totally strange when compared to the humans a horse routinely sees at home. Unlike a motorcycle, a bicycle creates little noise to forewarn a horse and rider of its approach, which only adds to the startle factor when a cyclist suddenly rounds a bend in the trail. Even a stall gate at home can become an obstacle if horse and handler have a problem going through it safely.

As with natural obstacles, it's possible to home-school a horse to face many manmade hazards he might encounter away from home. As stated in the previous chapter, home preparation allows a horse and rider to learn to cope with potential obstacles in safe, relaxed ways and, in the process, develop greater confidence in each other.

Pavement and Traffic

Pavement is so dangerous because it gives a horse a false sense of security. It looks like good footing to him, but it's not. Riding on pavement is similar to riding on ice; the faster a horse travels and the more he turns, the more apt he is to fall. One slip or spook, and he's down. When on pavement, a rider should slow down and keep his horse on as straight a path as possible. It's also critical for a rider to maintain good balance so he doesn't interfere with his horse's balance.

Ranch cowboys run into similar problems on concrete alleyways and in feedlots, which also are often slick with cow manure. Because the cattle are confined in a smaller area, they tend to run a little harder or be a little more ready to challenge a cowboy horseback. If his horse is the least bit cowy, he's attuned to the cow and not thinking about poor footing, so the cowboy must. Worse yet, when his horse starts slipping, he has little maneuvering room as he tries to regain his balance, which can also be the case when riding in traffic.

If it's necessary to ride on pavement or near traffic, it's better to ride on the left and into oncoming traffic, rather than in the same direction as the traffic flow. When riding with the flow, even though a horse initially might see a car or truck behind him at a distance, once it moves closer, then into and out of his blind spot, it still can startle him, and he might jump into the road.

Roadside riding isn't that much fun anyway because, in addition to traffic, a rider must watch continually for glass, wire or

Even a four-wheeler approaching in a pasture can scare a horse.

anything that can hurt or frighten his horse. That includes people in vehicles, too, who often shout or honk as they pass, which also can frighten a horse.

It's surprising there aren't more accidents on pavement at fairgrounds or during parades. All too often people take chances on pavement, while riding horses that aren't prepared for that situation. Often, when a horse at the fairgrounds or show gives somebody trouble, the person slaps the scared, spooked animal on the neck and says, "Stop that!" But that's the worst thing to do. That only tells the horse that there's something to worry about when he's most like a scared child who needs reassurance.

Instead, the rider can rub the horse, lift a bridle rein to encourage him to relax his jaw or do anything that he's accustomed to and understands. And, if possible, it's always a good idea to put more distance between the horse and whatever frightens him, even if it's for only a few minutes until the rider can regain control of the situation.

However, when a horse in a parade gets scared, there's really no place for him to go — cars, floats and bands are in front of and behind him, and a crowd lines both sides of the street. Only a very broke, gentle horse can accept that much pressure.

But so many people think they can get the job done horseback on parade day — even when they can't relax or control their horses at home. That's not facing reality. Should a horse prove unmanageable on the parade route, at best, the rider's embarrassed; at the worst, the horse, rider or spectators can be injured. Either way, the horse probably becomes worse to handle at such events, rather than better.

Again, working with a horse at home is the best way to ensure safety, as much as

DO IT YOURSELF

Before riding alongside a road or in a parade or horse exposition, ask yourself these tough questions and answer them honestly.

1. Do I have a good reason to be riding on pavement in a congested area?

2. Am I putting myself and my horse in danger?

3. Am I putting other people in danger?

4. How badly will I embarrass myself should I lose control of my horse? (Although most people think this the most important question, safety should, in fact, come before any other consideration.)

DO IT YOURSELF

At home realistically evaluate your horse's suitability for any event, such as a parade. He'll tell you if he's ready for it. You might already know he isn't, but just hope that maybe he'll change before the big event. Don't take that risk. Instead, keep your riding program on track and you and your horse safe.

Use common sense. If you aren't sure how prepared your horse is for a parade or public event, ask friends who are good horsemen to help you set up a similar situation at home. Be sure to use good judgment in choosing your helpers and to use caution throughout the entire experience.

Park vehicles in close formation, then ride your horse between them to see how well he responds. Is he quiet, or does he rush to go between them? If

he rushes at home, he'll probably panic even more in the confusion of an event away from home.

Have someone ride a bicycle around your horse, but be sure the person first approaches from a distance and has been cautioned about riding the bicycle into your horse's blind spot.

Perhaps someone can shoot a cap gun, starting some distance away, then gradually moving closer until your horse becomes accustomed to the noise. Loud noises are common during parades and grand entries.

If a grand entry or show requires riding inside a coliseum, haul your horse to a covered arena or indoor pen beforehand, so you know what to expect.

Analyze and evaluate the way your horse responds to these unusual things. If your control remains good at home, and your horse continues to respond well there despite the strange, new circumstances, you might well attend a public event and come away from it without a major problem.

If your horse doesn't deliver the immediate, calm response you want, work on the six transitions to improve your control. When you have no control over your horse's transitions at home, and know that any horse — not just yours — can panic in an unfamiliar situation, there's no real reason to think you'll be safe riding him at a public event. It's not worth the risk.

possible, in a less-than-ideal situation because horse and rider can learn how to rely on each other — before they ever face anything scary. By setting up manmade obstacles at home, the rider helps his horse learn to cope with out-of-the-ordinary things, and can later use the same techniques to help his mount relax, for example, at the fairgrounds. At home the rider also can take a lot of time to slowly introduce new obstacles while offering his horse a reassuring cue. He might simply back his horse a step or two or slightly lift or "milk" the bridle reins, cueing his horse to relax his jaw and, as a result, his body. A rider might even use his fingers to slightly roll the skin on his horse's neck and regain his attention when he sees something spooky.

Because a horse can think of only one thing at the time, when he's in a tight spot, the rider should be able to use such cues to refocus the horse, bringing his mind back to his rider, rather than having it focused on traffic or midway rides. But only by practicing these cues at home can a horse and rider become confident in one another. When they are, and

travel away from home, the rider can then offer the reassurance his horse needs when he's upset, and his horse can accept that reassurance and respond to it.

The important thing: When the horse encounters something scary and looks to his rider for support, the rider can't quit his horse. He must do those little things that tell his horse everything will be okay.

Bridges

Bridges can be dangerous obstacles, especially if a horse spooks while crossing one. Although few horses fling themselves over the railing, bridge surfaces often have poor or slippery footing.

A big problem with bridge-crossings is that so many folks start the ride by thinking that they won't get their horses across the bridge. By the time the rider actually reaches the bridge, he's seldom mentally where he wants his horse to go — across to the other side. Instead, the rider already has hesitated so often in his mind that he barely keeps his horse moving.

DO IT YOURSELF

Build your horse's bridge-crossing confidence at home by using the teeter-totter described in the chapter on forehand transitions. It's great at-home bridge preparation because, as the horse's hoofs strike the teeter-totter, they create noise similar to that a horse experiences when crossing a bridge.

Another way to better prepare your horse for a bridge crossing is to lay a sheet of heavy-duty plywood on the ground. It appears similar in sight and sound to a bridge, as far as most horses are concerned.

As always, take your time and work at the bridge obstacles a few minutes each day, then enjoy a relaxing ride on your horse.

It's okay at first if your horse puts only his front feet on the teeter-totter or plywood. If he responds well to the previous transition work, you have the tools you need to position him on the obstacles. If your horse doesn't respond well as you direct him onto the wooden objects, return to the transition work until he responds more consistently. Then go back and try the bridge work.

Gradually work with your horse until he's comfortable with all four feet on the plywood or teeter-totter. Your ultimate goal is to matter-of-factly walk your horse across the plywood or teeter-totter without him trying to evade the obstacle. Take time to ensure that your horse's bridge preparation is solid.

To increase the degree of your homework difficulty, make a bridge of heavy-duty lumber and fasten it on a base of, for example, landscape timbers. This slightly elevates the obstacle and creates an even more realistic, hollow sound as your horse walks across it. Be sure that the lumber and the base can adequately support your horse's weight.

When approaching a bridge or any obstacle, a rider must think ahead and ride more actively forward, as if there's no doubt his horse will cross. The rider also must focus on the road or trail beyond the bridge, where he wants to go next; otherwise, he'll never get his horse there. Crossing a bridge is similar to crossing a creek in many respects, and many of the tips in the previous chapter also are appropriate to prepare for bridge-crossings.

As with a creek-crossing, there's nothing wrong with dismounting and leading a horse across a bridge, or asking other riders to allow a reluctant horse to draft off theirs. Sometimes an inexperienced horse follows other horses right across the bridge. As ranch cowboys know from working horses and cattle, movement creates more movement, and a savvy rider uses that to advantage, letting the power of the other horses' movement sweep his horse forward.

Anyone who plans to spend an hour or more to successfully teach his horse about bridge-crossings should first find a bridge with little traffic, for safety's sake and for an effective training session without interrup-
tions. Trails, rather than highways, sometimes offer the best, least-traveled bridges for such training.

Then the rider simply takes whatever time's necessary to successfully cross the bridge, no matter what method, such as approach-and-retreat, he uses to help his horse become comfortable at and on the bridge.

Here, again, as with any obstacle, a rider using poor horsemanship as he approaches a bridge teaches his horse how to wheel and evade the bridge. And once a horse has committed to crossing the bridge, a poor horseman also can teach the horse to flee the bridge by allowing him to hurry across and away from it.

Successful bridge crossing begins with the basics — how responsive the horse is in the six transitions and to the application of pressure. A rider must have solid transitions to position his horse well as he approaches and crosses the bridge and to maintain control should his horse try to flee the scary obstacle. When the rider applies pressure to drive his horse forward and across, he must be sure his horse is looking toward the bridge before he applies the pressure. If he is, he should go right where the rider wants him — across the bridge — in response to the pressure.

Pressure plays the same role in this that it plays in crossing a creek. The rider must always apply slightly more pressure to the reluctant horse than the bridge exerts against the animal. No one knows exactly the correct amount of pressure to apply to a given horse at a bridge or any obstacle. That's determined strictly by trial and error.

A bridge is just one of many obstacles that ultimately might require a rider to cowboy up and insist that his horse move forward. That's sometimes tough, but in the long run insisting on a good response pays off. For one thing, a horse becomes more pleasant to ride on a daily basis, and for another, his quick response might one day be critical for safety in a dangerous situation. Whenever a rider experiences success at any obstacle, he paves the way for future success at other obstacles. Each obstacle experience helps build his horse's trust and confidence. The horse realizes that the rider can help him in any unfamiliar situation.

Packers, Hikers and Bicyclists

More and more horsemen, packers, hikers and bicyclists share multiuse trails. Backpacks, packsaddles, panniers, llamas, goats and the like appear alien and strange, creating spooks for horses on the trail.

The more aware a rider is of his surroundings, the sooner he sees a pack string ahead, and the more time he has to prepare and help support a horse that's bothered by it. The easiest thing to do, if possible, is to ride off the trail a distance, where the horse can still see the pack string, yet not so close that the horse is frightened by it. It's even better during a pack-string encounter if the horse is allowed to keep moving, either along the trail or in a small circle, if possible. That controlled movement often satisfies the horse's need for flight yet keeps horse and rider safely in control. With time and exposure, many horses

DO IT YOURSELF

Seek out unusual animals in your neighborhood, such as sheep, llama, buffalo or emus, and introduce your horse to the strange creatures gradually. It's safer to prepare for such encounters at home, rather than on a steep, narrow trail.

Be aware, before you approach strange animals, that they look, smell and sound different than more familiar dogs, cats and ponies. Your horse probably is afraid and wants only to turn and run from the strange creatures.

Plan in advance how to handle that situation. Are your downward transitions and your horse's confidence in you so solid that you can stop him and he'll stay right there even when he's scared? Maybe all you need is space to circle your horse a few moments to maintain control. With a plan, you're never caught by surprise. You know what you'll do, and because of that your horse probably stays calmer than he would otherwise.

Try to keep your horse facing up to whatever scares him until he finally comes to feel brave about the situation. If necessary, you might zigzag, like a cowboy holding the herd, while your horse checks out the strange creature. That satisfies his flight instinct, but not in an out-of-control way.

When he relaxes and accepts the situation, don't force him to do it all day. Ride somewhere else. You can take him by the llama pasture for a little while the following day and the next.

The best way for the horse to gain confidence around a four-wheeler, bicycle or hiker is to allow him to drive the "spook" away.

DO IT YOURSELF

Make arrangements with a neighbor to familiarize your horse with bicycles. First, pick a safe place to work on a quiet trail or in the pasture. Be sure the neighbor understands that a safe distance between him and your horse is just beyond his flight zone and that the neighbor's aware of the blind spots directly behind and in front of a horse.

Start by letting your horse track the bicycle from behind and at a comfortable distance for him. Don't force him closer to the bike; simply allow him to advance nearer as he becomes more at ease. Once he appears comfortable following the bicycle, your neighbor might then ride off to one side at a distance and back toward your horse, then turn and ride away until your horse realizes there's nothing to fear. Ultimately your neighbor can approach your horse from behind — always at a safe distance — then pull out to pass your horse just as a cyclist on the trail might.

become accustomed to pack strings and other unfamiliar things. Again, whenever a horse can move his feet, he thinks he's getting away from whatever scares him, and it's easier to maintain control. The difficult part is for an uneasy rider to fight his urge to stop dead still at the same time his horse needs to move.

In some places trailing behind a pack string is the only option available to a horseback rider. However, doing so allows a horse a good, long look at the string. More often than not, a horse's curiosity surfaces, and he often steps forward, closer to the string. If that's the case, he should be allowed to work his way closer, but not forced into it. Even if the rider's patient with his horse, he might take a few steps toward a llama, for example, and then retreat quickly to escape. A savvy horseman often allows his mount to repeat the cycle until approaching the llama is no big deal.

That same tactic often works to accustom a horse to a bicycle on the trail. When a horse comes upon a bike from behind, he might even think he's chasing the bike away and become really brave about it. It's a similar process to "hooking" a horse onto a cow and soon it's the horse's idea to go to the cow or the bike.

Although some might think dismounting is

the good option when meeting a pack string, that can be dangerous because a frightened horse might run over his handler. An experienced rider thinks ahead to find a safe place, and goes there as soon as possible. He also knows that, mounted or not, a frightened horse might well run under a tree limb while trying to escape the spooky string, and always looks for a small area where he can circle his horse if necessary.

No matter the options when meeting a pack outfit on the trail, a savvy rider tries to keep the experience as low-key as possible for safety's sake. He maintains his composure, so that his horse becomes better about such things with each encounter, instead of worse, and does whatever he must to maintain control. With that control, he can later go back to an obstacle and do the approach-and-retreat thing, for instance, if he wants. But he should go back only on his own terms and after he's safe. Safety is the No. 1 priority.

Ranch horses usually become accustomed to these trail spooks wherever they're encountered during the course of the day's work. But a pleasure rider can introduce these things at home, where he has far more control over the situation and his horse.

DO IT YOURSELF

To your unseasoned horse, a tent set up alongside the trail, a haystack with a loosely attached tarp or a horse-trailer awning appears to be a horse-eating monster. You know these things are harmless, but your horse doesn't. Teach him that at home to increase the odds that you'll have a safer, more pleasant experience away from home.

Hang a tarp or old slicker on the fence and let your horse become accustomed to it blowing in the breeze. Let him advance and retreat in and out of the flight zone at his pace. Eventually you should be able to ride right by the tarp without it spooking your horse. It doesn't matter how long it takes for him to get used to it; the main thing is that he does. Then there aren't any spooks in the tents your horse sees and hears flapping in the wind alongside the trail.

When one rider dismounts to open the gate for others…

… cowboy etiquette requires that the others wait for him to remount before riding away.

Working a Gate Horseback

Opening or closing a gate doesn't seem such a big deal; after all, everyone leads horses through gates at home almost daily. But not everyone takes the time to work the gate horseback, and that's one of the best training opportunities available to any rider. In fact, that's probably why so many feedlot horses are so maneuverable — cowboys open and close gates on those horses all the time.

A gate is a great place to work on forehand and hindquarters transitions, and an ideal place for a horse and rider to learn patience with each another. Even though few riders associate working a gate with riding a horse through the woods, the maneuvers used at both obstacles are much the same. Another plus: A rider working a gate uses only one hand on the reins, and that's good for any rider to master, especially if accustomed to riding with two hands and a snaffle. The gate also is a wonderful testing ground for horse and rider to develop more precision in their work while relating to a real job. Effective gate work also adds to the safety factor. Anytime

the rider needs his horse to move precisely to be safe, the horse knows how to respond. Obviously, anyone who accepts the challenge of working a gate horseback is on his way to developing a more responsive and safer horse.

When introducing gate work, a horse needs the best chance possible to succeed at the maneuver and to have a safe and pleasant new experience. That's why the type of gate used for such training is an important consideration.

Too often people try to ride a horse through a gate that doesn't allow enough clearance for a horse and rider. If a gate's not wide enough to allow a horse to pass comfortably, the rider's sure to bang his knees as he rides through the narrow opening.

Another risky approach is to ride against the flow of a narrow gate. The rear cinch can catch on the gate or latch and ultimately result in a horse becoming hip-locked between the gate and gateposts. That's a bad deal because that destroys the confidence between horse and rider. It's always best to ride with the gate's flow, rather than against it.

A walk-through portable-panel gate design doesn't provide enough overhead clearance for a rider, who risks hitting his head should the

DO IT YOURSELF

When you ride and come to an open gate, ranch etiquette dictates that you leave it open; if the gate's closed, leave it closed. Cowboys always leave a gate the way they find it unless instructed to do otherwise. That's the No. 1 rule on ranches anywhere.

Should you close it, always make sure that the gate's secure. Nothing's worse than losing a bunch of cattle because somebody didn't close the gate well. If the gate's in bad repair, try to fix it, or at least tell somebody that it needs repairs.

Another important part of ranch etiquette: When somebody dismounts to handle a gate, especially someone riding a young horse, wait for him to remount before you take off. That's just common courtesy.

It isn't considered polite cowboying to have somebody else hold your horse. In ranching circles, it's good manners to hold your own horse. He should be broke enough that you can hold him and open or close the gate. Somebody might offer to hold a horse, but a cowboy never assumes they will.

horse give him trouble. However, most panel manufacturers also offer ride-through gates, which have adequate clearance and easy-to-open latches. But if a latch is a little sticky or difficult to operate, that's not necessarily a bad thing; it simply means that the horse and rider spend more time working at the gate, which is a good thing in the long run.

Although it's sometimes tempting to try to open a wire gap or gate from horseback, rather than dismounting, that's never a good idea. It takes such a high level of skill to handle wire gates horseback that it's far too easy to get into a wreck and for a horse to step into the wire. It's best to dismount, open the gap and lead or send a horse through it, all the while remaining aware of the wire, especially in high grass.

If a gate doesn't swing well on the hinges, it might not be ideal for working horseback. When a rider has to lean over and pull hard to move the gate, or if it drags on the ground, he often accidentally kicks his horse in the side. When he does, it affects the horse's balance — he often loses it. Then he's not balanced before he makes his next move, which is just opposite of what should happen — balance first and then movement.

To first prepare a horse for gate work, it's a good idea to ride alongside a fence, then stop, reach out and touch it. If a horse won't stand quietly at a fence that doesn't move, he's not ready to stand quietly at a gate that will. It's smart to spend a few minutes standing at the fence and prepare him for the gate.

When parked parallel to a gate, the first thing to do is allow the horse to relax and stand quietly. When the rider reaches for the latch, should the horse move, he simply stops, allows the horse time to relax and starts over again.

The main thing about working any gate horseback is to keep the horse quiet and relaxed. The slower and steadier the rider at a gate, the less risk he takes and the better his horse becomes about working a gate.

If a horse becomes nervous or fretful at a gate, the rider should slow down and help him become mentally quiet before continuing. A horse usually becomes excited at the gate because he's had too much pressure put on him there before, or the gate has been allowed to hit his legs. Either way, as he moves closer to the gate, he begins to anticipate how he'll escape the mental or physical pressure he knows is coming. Sometimes, especially when a young horse can't yet handle much pressure, it's better to dismount, open the gate, send the horse through it, close the gate, remount and then try again to open the gate from his back. After all, a quiet response is the goal.

Sometimes a horse tries to lean on the gate, which also usually means he wants to hurry through it. Then it's time to stop and stand him up squarely on four legs so he's not leaning on the gate and out of balance to take the next step.

The same correction works when a horse tries to leave the gate area altogether. If the rider's paying attention, he notices when his horse drops an ear or shifts his weight; both signal that the horse is ready to leave, just as both do when a person saddles an untied horse as described in Chapter 2. When working a gate, it's critical that the horse stands balanced evenly on all four feet. Then he and the rider are never out of position to handle the gate no matter which direction they must move.

A rider succeeds in building quiet responsiveness at the gate when his movements are precise and when he gives his horse an opportunity to respond to each cue. Granted, at first a rider might have to compromise a bit on the quality of his horse's response, but a good horseman always works toward that precise, perfect response. As he does, his horse becomes a little better each time they open or close a gate.

It's hard to be precise and achieve the correct response if a horse isn't good at the six transitions mentioned in Part Two, "Cowboy Horsemanship." Too often people rush to work a gate horseback before they've done their homework, especially for forehand and hindquarter transitions.

When a rider fails to prepare his horse and hurries through gate work, a horse often becomes confused and excited. Then the rider usually becomes frustrated and even pushy with his horse; he'd be better off to push less and take more time right there and then. The gate isn't a place to hurry a horse.

Likewise, a rider shouldn't rush away from the gate the moment he's opened or closed it. Instead, his horse should stand there quietly for a few moments. If he becomes fidgety or, for example, tries to rear, it's safer to move away from the gate, regain control and then return to the gate. However, there should be few problems when a horse has been prepared for the job.

Having a game plan before riding to and opening a gate is smart. A good horseman seldom uses the same pattern or approach each time he works a gate. If he does, the pattern becomes a habit to the horse, and then the rider isn't truly in control.

A top hand might bring the gate toward his horse, to encourage him to side-pass away from it, until the gate is open several feet. Or, instead of riding around the end of the gate, he might ride forward, back his horse down the other side of the gate, and then side-pass him to close the gate. Rather than move the horse's front and rear ends at the same time in a finished side-pass at the gate, the rider

DO IT YOURSELF

When a ranch crew works a large pasture, but the cowboys can't see each other all the time, each cowboy signals that he's in the pasture by leaving a rock on a post by the gate. He then removes the rock from the pile when he comes out of the pasture. Or he might do the opposite and leave a rock on a post as he leaves the pasture. Either way, the ranch cowboys know how many people are still out horseback.

That's a good signal for trail riders to use as well. Always plan a place to meet — at a gate or trailhead, for example, and then decide in advance what a rock by the gate means. This is an important safety consideration, too. It's a terrible thing to see a horse coming back without anybody on him.

might first move his horse's forehand and then the hindquarters, just to keep from developing a pattern.

If a horse responds slowly, the rider can use his leg, hanging straight down, in an almost rhythmic, tapping motion to encourage the horse to move his forehand, hindquarters or both. As with any other cue, the moment the horse responds, the rider should stop and relax before taking another step.

Opening and closing gates well really comes right back to the six basic transitions, just as almost any maneuver does. The better a horse and rider become at those six transitions, the better they automatically become at many things, including gate work.

Anything, in this case a rolled-up irrigation dam, offers an opportunity to help a horse become more comfortable with obstacles.

PART 4

ROPE- AND CATTLE-HANDLING BASICS

Sooner or later, almost everyone who rides horses wants to play cowboy and sees himself gathering and roping cattle. For many, the cowboy life is still the stuff dreams are made of because, unfortunately, not everyone has the opportunity to live that lifestyle. However, many recreational riders get a taste of it when they attend a local team-penning practice, help a neighbor gather cattle or take up team roping. This section is for those people, including the ones who aren't there yet, but would like to be.

For many pleasure riders, the chance to ride horseback around cattle seems the ultimate experience. But when the opportunity arises, they don't take advantage of it, primarily because they don't want to appear silly or foolish and embarrass themselves. There's not a ranch cowboy, roper or team penner who hasn't felt the same way at some point. When a newcomer to a roping or penning practice or gather is honest about his ability,

few hold a lack of knowledge or experience against him, and most, in fact, find a way to make him feel welcome.

Part of being comfortable in any situation where cattle are involved is having a rope-broke horse because someone at the event or activity is sure to be swinging a loop. However, it's not necessary to rope cattle to rope-break a horse, and it's an excellent way to add to a horse's seasoning so that he becomes a solid and dependable ride. Chapter 15 describes how to combine basic rope-handling and horsemanship skills to create a more broke horse.

Although a book can't replace actual cattle-working experience, where horse, rider and cow are on the same wavelength, Chapter 16 describes how most anyone can relate standard horse-handling skills to working cattle. Plus, this chapter also describes typical ranch work and includes a bit of cowboy etiquette so no one's caught off-guard during the first ranch visit.

No matter where horse and rider
are positioned when roping the
dummy, the roper should follow
through after he delivers his loop.

ROPE-HANDLING 101

15

Although ropes and how they're used vary from one region to the next, rope-handling skills are essential tools of the cowboy trade. A Great Basin buckaroo, for example, might use a 60-foot or longer rope and dally it around a slick horn without rubber wrapping. Other cowboys might dally a 35-foot rope around a rubber-wrapped horn for a better grip. Yet a cowhand in Texas might not dally at all, but tie his lariat hard and fast to the saddle horn.

I learned to handle a rope as a kid in Montana and worked on ranches around home before and after I married. My wife and I have always kept a few cattle, and use our roping skills to work them or help friends and family work their cattle. Our children also are developing good roping skills.

That's all well and good, but the average recreational rider can learn to use a rope — and never build a loop — to help his horse become more broke. By swinging only the tail end of a rope, if that's as far as somebody chooses to go in developing his rope-handling skills, a recreational rider can make a better-seasoned horse, which is why this introduction to rope-handling skills has been included.

Although I discuss building a loop and dallying on the saddle horn, how to do these things is included to help the recreational rider become comfortable with a rope in his hand, not necessarily because he wants to become a ranching professional or competition roper. For that he needs to continue his education by reading the *Western Horseman* booklet *Ranch Roping with Buck Brannaman* or the *Western Horseman* book, *Team Roping with Jake and Clay* by the professional rodeo cowboys, watching videos or participating in a roping clinic.

Why Rope-Breaking?

Rope-breaking presents another opportunity for horse and rider to develop confidence and trust in one another. Even though a weekend pleasure rider might never become a roper, he doesn't want or need a horse that's scared of a rope; he and his horse could encounter someone swinging a loop almost anywhere they go. On a trail ride, somebody packs a rope to drag wood to the campfire or entertains himself roping a hay bale, just as competitive ropers practice swinging their loops at the local arena. By developing minimal rope-handling skills, a recreational rider and his horse can learn to feel safe and comfortable around ropes, first at home and later anywhere they go. Then there's no cause for alarm when a cowboy trots by swinging a rope — they take it in stride.

Starting Out

Anyone who picks up a rope for any reason must understand that it can be dangerous when mishandled. If a horse gets a foot hung in the coils, he might panic and take off through a fence, or the rider can catch his hand in a dally. Any number of things can go wrong unless a rope is given proper respect by the handler.

169

I always recommend attending a clinic to learn how to handle a rope correctly from the start. A clinic provides hands-on instruction and the immediate feedback necessary to correct mistakes quickly before they grow into bad or potentially dangerous rope-handling habits that'll have to be changed. It's usually easier for people to learn with that type of hands-on help.

Anyone who wants to rope-break his horse must learn how to coil a rope and

"A rope is a good tool to get a horse broke when working him afoot and from the saddle."

how to get free of it without becoming tangled in it; otherwise he and his horse aren't safe. Even the rider who never plans to throw a loop at a cow must learn at least to swing the tail without hitting himself or his horse in the head.

A kid's rope works well for most beginners because it's short, easy to handle and soft in hand, but an old extension cord works just as well, and might even be safer because there's no loop to worry about. A novice can coil the cord, swing it overhead and even throw the tail of it because the plug's weight helps carry the cord toward a target. Also, using an extension cord is a great way to learn how hand action affects a rope and to develop precise rope-handling skills.

Sacking Out a Horse

A rope is a good tool to get a horse broke when working him afoot and from the saddle. I prefer using a rope to using a sack or flag at the end of a pole to work a horse in the round pen. With a rope I can keep pressure on a horse until he mentally overcomes a problem, whatever it might be. Then he learns to think his way through a problem, rather than panic and run from it. But the minute a horse overcomes his problem or fear, I always release my rope.

A horse can run away from a flag or sack, which sometimes seems only to make him more afraid and reinforces his idea that being handled is a bad thing. But with a long lariat, I can put on or take off as much pressure as I want, even release the pressure completely, and do it whenever I want. Rope pressure is much easier to regulate than that from a sack or flag. The horse can learn to work through the bother of the rope, but he can't totally escape it as he might the pressure from another tool.

Although I use a rope to sack out a horse, some cowboys use a saddle blanket or a feed sack, which is where the term originated. Sacking out's an old-time practice that nowadays means allowing a horse to become accustomed to something potentially frightening, but in a controlled way so he learns to rely on his handler's direction. A century ago a horse's acceptance might've been more forced than anything, but that's not the case among good horsemen now. Instead, the horse learns at his own pace that a rope won't hurt him, and simply gets used to and accepts the feel and sight of it.

It's important to know there's a blind spot right around a horse's withers, just as there's one directly behind him. When something's in a blind spot, a horse strongly feels the need to get away, to escape. Although he can see things to the sides and farther to the rear or ahead of his shoulder, the blind spot at the withers causes many horses to fear a rope or even the saddle.

That's why I start there when sacking out a horse. Because it's the first place he learns to accept the rope, it becomes the most comfortable place for the rope to be. Later, as I do different things with my rope around a horse, that area at the withers becomes neutral, or the place I take the rope back to anytime a horse seems bothered by it.

When sacking out a horse afoot, I have a halter on the horse and the halter rope in one hand. Starting at his withers, I first put my free hand on the horse, then act as if the rope I hold is simply an extension of my hand. If necessary at first, I might actually put the rope on top of my hand, rather than hold it, so the horse is reassured by my hand being between him and the rope. Then when the coiled lariat actually touches the horse, I support him, again, by touching and rubbing him with my hand.

I then take away the rope and bring it back to touch the horse in the same area again, so that the rope moves in and out of his blind spot. Coming directly at a horse with a rope and forcing him to deal with it is hard for the horse to handle. Touching him with the rope and backing off slightly is far more tolerable. Even though the horse knows the rope is there, he can't quite see it all the time, so I continue touching him with my hand to reassure him.

Although I might have to back off a bit if the rope coils scare the horse, I back off only to the point he's no longer afraid of the rope. Then I immediately touch him with the rope again. This isn't exactly an advance-and-retreat deal as most people know the term because my rope is always touching or close to the horse. Otherwise, it's too easy for him to think he can escape it.

However, that's what often happens when people take away the rope altogether — the horse escapes, so the person quits, and the horse learns how to escape. Rather than being removed completely, the rope should be moved away only far enough that the horse is no longer afraid.

There's only one time to take away the rope completely — when a horse realizes there's nothing to fear. Then, because that's the response I want, I remove the rope and release the pressure, which the horse already understands from his previous training.

When a horse accepts the rope at his withers on one side, I move to the other and do the same things until he accepts the rope there, too. Next, I rub the horse on both sides with the rope, swapping from one side to the other. I also rub the rope up toward his shoulders and back over his rump.

I also lead a horse around as I rub him, too, occasionally draping the tail across his back or around his rump. I do everything slowly and advance only when the horse is no longer afraid. Anytime he seems bothered by a change in what I do with my rope, I take the rope back to his withers to reassure him and also touch him with my hand.

Sacking out a horse with a lariat is fine, but the halter rope works well at first for that, too, as long as there isn't a snap on the end to bang into the horse's sides or legs. After a horse is comfortable being rubbed with the halter rope, I can then advance to the lariat rope and work with it as described above. But anytime the horse becomes afraid, no matter what type rope's being used, I take it back to his withers, which by now has become the most comfortable, familiar place for the rope to be. Moving the rope back there tells the horse that everything's okay.

Rope-Breaking the Horse's Feet

When a horse is comfortable with a rope touching his body, I move to his feet with the halter rope or lariat. This helps prepare him for hobble-breaking, helps him learn not to panic should his legs become tangled in something and also makes cleaning his feet and shoeing him easier.

Although most people don't mind picking up and cleaning a horse's front feet, many are leery of handling the hind feet. Rather than immediately trying to do that, it's better to first spend a couple of days picking up a horse's feet with a lariat rope. Doing so simply creates an additional safety factor that anyone can build into his horse program. If a problem develops when handling the horse's feet with a lariat, the rope can be turned loose to keep both horse and handler safe. Once a horse is accustomed to having his feet picked up, cleaning his hoofs becomes an easy chore.

The horse is haltered when I first put a rope on a front foot, but I don't put a tight loop around his pastern right then. I sometimes start by doubling a lead rope around one of his front feet, and holding both ends in my hands. If there's a problem, I'm not hung up and neither is my horse.

Rope-breaking a horse's feet prepares the horse for the hobbles and teaches him not to panic if he gets tangled in wire.

Rope-breaking the feet also prepares a horse for easier shoeing.

DO IT YOURSELF

When you have only 15 or 20 minutes to spend with your horse, don't think you must rush through a quick ride to accomplish something good with your horse. Instead, spend that time handling his legs with a rope. Pick up each of his feet with a halter or lariat rope, or try to lead him forward with a rope around a front foot. You can even teach a horse to lead with a rope around a hind foot if you like.

This helps reinforce the good things rope-breaking teaches your horse. It keeps his rope-training fresh by reminding him not to panic, but to think through problems.

Come back to such lessons from time to time to keep your horse good about everything he's already learned, and he'll be even more responsive for longer periods of time.

With a halter rope or lariat around my horse's front foot, I apply just a bit of pressure to see if I can get the horse to shift his weight and think his way through the situation just enough to take one step forward. I don't want to make the horse leap forward quickly or take several steps; I just quietly ask him to lead forward by a rope on his front foot. I also can use the halter and lead on the horse's head to help the horse figure out what I want him to do.

Eventually, I put the rope around each leg individually and pick up each leg. In the process I learn a lot about the horse, and he learns a lot about a rope. I learn if he'll panic, strike or kick with a rope around his leg, and how well he thinks his way through things. Primarily, I learn how that horse responds when a rope goes on his leg; that's his "getaway," what he uses for the flight response. The goal is to teach the horse to think his way through the problem of having something around his leg, and not panic. Later, if he gets tangled in a wire fence or caught in a cattle guard when I'm riding him, that might save his life, or mine.

Hobbling

Done properly, hobbling is simply an extension of rope-breaking a horse's feet. Most ranch cowboys carry a pair of hobbles on their saddles and can hobble their horses anywhere because they can't always find a place to tie a horse. Hobbling also is a good skill for the pleasure rider to teach his horse because tying to trees is prohibited in many recreational riding areas. By learning to stand hobbled, a horse learns how to stand quietly without pawing a hole in the ground.

The first part of the hobbling process is using a rope to pick up each of the horse's feet and leading the horse by a front foot, as previously described in "Rope-Breaking the Horse's Feet." With a helper standing at the horse's head and holding the lead rope, I can freely move around the horse and use a lariat to pick up each front foot, just as I would when cleaning them. Then I step forward,

bringing the foot to the front, just as it would be if placed on a shoeing stand. If the horse bends his knee and tries to lie down, I simply hold his foot.

The important thing is that the horse learns not to push forward against the rope, but to yield his foot to the rope's pressure. When he can do that, he knows how to yield to the hobbles, wire or anything else he might get around his legs.

I even pick up my horse's back feet and do these same things, moving his hind leg forward and back. That's a good idea, especially if I want to hobble and sideline a horse, too, or hobble one by the hind legs, as the old-timers did.

Before using a three-way hobble, or sidelining a horse in addition to hobbling his front legs, it's important to put the rope on each foot and bring it forward and back until the horse no longer resists the pressure. If the horse won't yield to the rope, he's not ready to hobble yet. I prepare a horse for hobbling by rope-breaking his feet before he's hobbled — not after a wreck.

When the horse readily yields to a rope around his feet, it's time to hobble him, preferably in a soft, sandy area. Things go smoothly if a helper stands at the horse's head until the hobbles are fastened. The helper holding the halter rope should stand on the same side of the horse as the person doing the hobbling. Should something go wrong and a handler overreact when he's standing opposite the other person, it could send the horse right on top of the person doing the work, whether it's hobbling, shoeing or veterinary work — and that's usually the person with something in his hands who could be hurt. If both people stand on the same side of the horse, he has somewhere to go should his flight instinct kick in.

Before putting hobbles on a horse, I always tie my stirrups up on my saddle. If the horse goes down when he's being taught to hobble, that can be uncomfortable to him — and it could break the stirrup. But with the stirrups tied, neither of those things can happen.

I prefer a double-ring leather hobble for the front feet.

The third hobble on the left hind foot has a ring to use for attaching the rope to the front hobbles.

This shows the complete three-way hobble.

As shown in the hobbling photographs, I first use an ordinary set of two-ring hobbles and add a third hobble to the horse's rear foot to sideline him. The third hobble strap is thick, wide and well-padded. It buckles always snugly, not tightly, around the horse's hind foot, and has a D-ring and rope attached. After fastening the front hobbles and the third hobble strap on a hind foot, I bring the rope from the rear hobble forward and over the hobble strap between his front legs, then back to the rear-hobble D-ring, and tie the rope with a half-hitch or clove-hitch. Some people use a snap there, but that could break.

After the horse is hobbled, I drape the halter rope over the saddle horn, where I can easily reach it should I need to. Then I step a short distance away from the horse. If he tries to move too much in resistance, I can step in and stop him if necessary, and follow with more rope-breaking foot work before hobbling him again. Otherwise, I let the horse test the hobbles. If I've done my homework correctly, rope-breaking his feet thoroughly, the horse usually tests the hobbles and then yields to them and stands quietly, just as he did with the lariat rope.

From there, it's an easy progression for the horse to become gradually accustomed to spending more time wearing hobbles. However, it's never a good idea to leave a hobbled horse unattended for long periods of time, especially one relatively green to the experience.

DO IT YOURSELF

Here's a simple way to tie up your stirrups that works when you hobble a horse, load a saddled horse into a trailer or lead one through a tight gate. Simply flip the near side stirrup over the saddle. Then bring the off-side stirrup up and over to rest on top of the near-side stirrup. I use a rear saddle string, because it's handy and always on my saddle, to tie down the top stirrup, which holds the other stirrup in place. A piece of hay twine works just as well to tie the stirrups.

A horse in a three-way hobble could fall down, so I prefer to tie up my stirrups and keep a watchful eye on the horse until he's accustomed to being hobbled.

Rope-Breaking from the Saddle

I don't swing a rope around a horse much when I'm afoot; I'd rather he get used to a rope when I swing it from his back, but immediately swinging a rope overhead scares most horses. Because a horse can really become bothered by that rope right overhead, where he can't see it, I first coil my rope, mount a horse in the round pen and sack him out with the rope from the saddle, just as I did earlier from the ground.

I first rub the horse all over with my coiled rope. Taking my time, I also rub the rope on either side, over and down his back end, then back up to his withers and beyond, all the way up his neck to and over his bridle path. However, I usually don't rub a horse's ears with the rope right away, but gradually work up to that area.

Because I do these things in the round pen, I don't have to control the horse's direction; he's confined anyway, so I can really focus on what I'm doing with my rope. If the horse becomes bothered by anything I do with the rope, and needs to move his feet a little to feel comfortable, he can. The goal is to work with him until he can tolerate being rubbed with the rope, no matter if he's still or moving.

I'm never too quick to shake out a loop or swing my rope because at this stage that might make a horse even more afraid of a rope. Then he'd just be worse about the rope the next time I tried these things. Only when a horse is totally comfortable with being sacked out from the saddle do I swing a rope from his back.

When I do, I don't immediately swing a rope overhead. I first drop my arm down to the side and build a loop in my rope. Anyone who's uncomfortable with the idea of using a loop can simply use the tail of his rope for the experience, and eventually swing it overhead just as I do a loop.

With the loop down by the horse's side, I swing the loop back and forth, letting it move up toward his head and back to his tail. I'm careful not to hit him in the head with it. I stop anytime the horse seems bothered by the loop, and then resume swinging it back and forth again, however many times it takes, until the horse is comfortable with the loop swinging at his side.

A horse should be sacked out with a rope from the saddle, as well as from the ground.

A good hand rope-breaks the horse's feet from the saddle, too.

Next, I throw my rope on the ground to the front, almost under my horse's nose. I'm careful not to hit him with the rope, but I do want him to become accustomed to the rope touching him across his shoulder as I recoil the rope. When I first start to recoil, I pay attention because a horse sometimes can be frightened by the rope on the ground moving toward him. If that's a problem, I keep throwing my rope out on the ground and gradually pulling it to me until my horse is comfortable with that. Only then do I progress to other rope work.

Once I recoil the rope and rebuild a loop, I again hold it to the side of my horse, first taking a half-swing or two with it as before, and then finally swinging it all the way around, but still in a side-arm swing. I make one revolution and stop. I don't swing it overhead because the horse isn't yet ready for that. A horse can see the rope all the time with a side-arm swing, but can lose sight of the rope in an overhead swing. Then, as the rope comes back into his field of vision, the horse can become startled unless he's fully prepared for the overhead swing.

When a horse is totally relaxed with the side-arm swing, I gradually start to bring my loop from the side to a more overhead position, as I continue to swing the rope. If the horse seems troubled by the loop's changing position, I return to the side-arm swing, which at this point is neutral position, the one I return to whenever the horse becomes uneasy and the one I work from as I gradually bring the rope overhead again.

I do all these things with the horse standing still, and progress to do them while he walks or trots. Before long, a rope swinging overhead means nothing to him; the horse totally accepts that and is comfortable with it.

The main thing: A horse should never be scared by the rope. However, if he truly becomes scared, I won't totally take it away from the horse because ultimately he must learn to accept a rope, not escape it. That's why it's important to establish a neutral position — his withers when I'm working afoot and the sidearm swing when

Before making a complete swing with the loop overhead, it's best to use a sidearm swing to introduce a horse to the rope.

After the horse is accustomed to the rope swinging, the rider can start to gradually bring his loop more overhead, where he can learn to flatten his loop.

I'm in the saddle. That's the safe, comfortable place I always return to whenever a horse becomes bothered. Although he can't totally escape the rope, he feels less pressure with the rope there than at the newer overhead-swing position, for example.

Logging

Once a horse is comfortable with a rope touching him, logging is a great way to keep him fit and provides another opportunity for him to work through a potentially troublesome situation in his mind. When logging a horse, a rider drags something behind on a rope and usually dallies his rope around the saddle horn, although not always. In addition to a log, a rider could drag a small piece of firewood, 5-gallon plastic pail or a fencepost.

No matter what's used, the object is for the horse to become comfortable with a rope dragging behind him. It's not safe to try to log a horse until he's prepared for the experience. First, he must be rope-broke as described above and then introduced to a rope dragging behind him.

When a horse is rope-broke, I mount and simply hold one end of a rope, dragging it around the pen. Even though nothing's attached to the rope, I work in a safe place with good footing, and that's the smart thing to do when logging a horse anywhere. This is another situation where working in a pen allows me to concentrate on the rope to minimize and control the pressure on my horse until he learns to cope with it.

It's easiest to ride forward in a circle with the rope dragging at an angle to the inside, where the horse can see it. I also can start dragging the rope with it in hand, high over the horse's hip, and then gradually drop my hand to let the rope work down

Gradually feeding the rope out behind a horse allows him to get used to it dragging behind him.

Rope-breaking a horse for logging also gives a rider ample opportunity to practice coiling his rope.

For safety reasons, it's best to first let a horse face a drag, back up and pull it while he can see it.

After a horse is comfortable facing the drag, it's time to work him in a circle and let the drag fall behind while being careful not to scare the horse.

toward the horse's hock. That approach seems less frightening to most horses.

Should the rope bother the horse, I must be able to stop him, move his hindquarters away from the rope and then back him a step or two, or turn his front end to face the drag if he gets scared. Obviously the horse must be good at hindquarter or forehand transitions. I also must stay focused on what my horse does and where the rope is in relation to the horse, and that's another good reason for working in a pen; a rider can't learn to do those things at first when he's busy trying to dodge trees and rocks outside.

I can rope both left- and right-handed, so dragging a rope or logging a horse in either direction is easy for me. A right-handed person usually starts by dragging a rope in a circle to the right, with the rope in his right hand, and vice versa for a left-handed person. Either way the horse can see the rope on the ground and get used to it being there. Ideally, it's best to drag the rope to both the right and left so the horse is comfortable with the rope on either side.

As a horse becomes accustomed to the dragging rope, I gradually straighten his path of travel, which allows the rope touch him on his thigh and hock, and then I take it away, by moving back onto the circle. I do this a number of times to be sure my horse is okay with the rope touching his hips and legs. Again, if I've done a good job in introducing the rope from the ground and the saddle, the rope touching him probably won't be a problem. At this point, it's so easy to move the rope in any direction because there's no weight attached yet.

When a horse gets good about dragging the rope to one side, I use my hand to really flip the rope to the other side so he experiences the same things in another direction. When he's good about traveling in both directions with the rope behind him, it's time to attach a light drag.

I first drag a piece of firewood or something that weighs only 5 or 10 pounds, and isn't so heavy that it'll sore the horse to pull it. A 3- or 4-foot 2-by-4 works well. No matter what's used, it must be light

A counterclockwise dally should always be made with the thumb up.

enough that I can hold the rope in my hand and easily pull the drag. By using my hand at first, I can better control the drag, pulling it nearer to the horse or letting it fall back farther away from him. The closer I bring the drag to the horse, the more pressure he feels. So I gradually bring the drag closer, but when the horse becomes bothered by it, I let the rope slide through my hand so the drag drops back away from him. Then I again bring the drag closer and let it fall back several times to ensure the horse is comfortable with it trailing him.

DO IT YOURSELF

Here's a controlled, safe way to learn to dally a rope around your horn.

Hang a tire from your highline or in the barn doorway about 4 feet from the ground. When you want to practice dallying, attach a rope to the tire, then get horseback. Have someone hand you the rope after you mount your horse, or hold the rope in one hand as you mount, but be careful that you and your horse don't get into a wreck.

Then, holding the rope in one hand, pull the tire toward you and your horse. Then, as you let the tire swing away from you, take one counterclockwise wrap around your horn with your thumb up for safety. The tire provides just enough weight on the end of your rope to make the experience seem real.

As I log my horse in a circle to one side and the other, I adjust the inside rein just a little shorter than the outside rein. Then, if my horse spooks, I can always turn him to the inside, and his legs won't get wrapped in the rope. The rope and log are to the inside, and if I turned the horse to the outside, it'd be far easier for him to get his hind legs tangled. Plus, dragging a lot to the outside of the circle brings the rope more directly across the rider's thigh and that can be uncomfortable.

I always want my horse's hindquarters to move away from the rope, to the outside of the circle. When circling to the right, for example, the horse's hindquarters should move left, away from the rope and not into it. That's another reason hindquarter transitions are important. When those transitions are solid, I can move my horse's hindquarters and get the response I want, no matter if there's a cow or a piece of firewood on the end of my rope.

It isn't necessary to log anything heavy to make a really broke horse although a rider working to improve his horse's fitness can gradually add slightly more weight over an extended period of time. Most people get into trouble with weight because they usually try to drag a too-large piece of firewood to a campfire, for example, or the saddle doesn't fit the horse well and is pulled out of position by the increased weight. It's so easy to sore a horse, and then he never wants to pull again.

A rider should never drag anything so heavy that his horse quits pulling; a too-heavy load only teaches him that he can't pull. That's why using a slick horn, without rubber wrapped around it, is a good idea. Should a horse be overloaded, his rider can let out more rope to slip around the horn. This takes some of the direct pull off the horse, giving the rider time to stop the horse before he quits. Then the horse doesn't know he's defeated and doesn't learn to quit pulling. Once a rider makes a mistake with a too-heavy load, he can't take it back. But if he can slip rope, he can get out of that bad situation and still leave his horse a winner. When that happens, the rider immediately should change his load.

A ranch cowboy can get in a similar situation when he ropes a balky 1,200-pound cow. So he slips her a little rope, quits trying to drag her and just holds the cow instead, and his horse still wins. Usually slipping the additional slack into the rope gives a slight release, which the cow feels, so she quits resisting as strongly, and that's easier on the horse. Ideally, a cowboy prefers to drive that cow, rather than pull her, so he keeps trying to do that. But when she resists, he can take advantage of his slick horn and slip rope to give his horse some relief.

I don't log anything heavy and probably never will, unless it's a cow that I must work for some reason. I usually drag something lightweight that I can pull with my hand if necessary. And I certainly don't pull anything heavy behind a young horse. The point of logging is to get a horse more broke; it's not a contest to see how much weight he can pull. When a young horse or any horse is overloaded, he usually quits pulling.

After using the 2-by-4, I sometimes drag an empty bucket simply because it makes more noise. Best of all, once a horse is accustomed to all this, I might use him to pull a sled for my kids in the winter. That's great fun, but I'm always sure the horse is prepared to do that; otherwise the sled can scare the horse and my kids could be hurt.

It's best to learn to dally a rope around the horn before trying to dally a rope with something on the end of it. The dally, or wrap around the horn, is made counterclockwise, and the rider must always keep his thumb up — if he doesn't want to lose it when a dally pulls tight against the horn. Someone learning to dally should first get the feel of bringing the rope from right to left around the front of his horn — thumb-up — and later practice taking only one wrap. A second wrap usually isn't necessary when using a lightweight drag.

Only when a person's comfortable with taking a dally — and turning it loose — should he try to dally with a light drag at the end of his rope. Again, the drag shouldn't be heavy, maybe only a stick that the rider can easily control with his hand. Only when a rider knows how to make the appropriate moves with his rope so well that it's second-nature and only when his horse is totally comfortable with the entire process should anything heavier be used as a drag.

Someone dragging firewood through timber, for example, must be careful and stay aware of the many places his rope and the wood might get hung. That's why it's so important to dally — and not tie — a drag. Then, if the rope or drag gets caught anywhere, there's no reason for the horse or rider to be in a bind. It's so easy for the rider simply to release his rope, let the dally come off the horn, then pick up his rope from the ground and start all over again. And neither he nor his horse becomes frightened when the rope catches on something.

Logging a horse is a great way to develop a broke horse, but approached improperly, logging also can be dangerous. Too much weight and the horse gets sore; a thumb pointing down when taking a dally can result in no thumb at all. When logging a horse, it's

It's important to become adept at dallying correctly before roping live cattle to minimize the risk of losing a thumb.

always best to err on the side of caution, rather than risk injury to horse or rider.

Roping the Dummy

Even though a rider might never rope competitively, he also should learn to rope the dummy while horseback simply because that's another experience that contributes to making a well-seasoned horse.

Roping a dummy from a horse benefits the horse and rider in so many ways. And, again, a rider doesn't actually have to swing a loop and catch the dummy for his horse to benefit from the experience. Anyone who's

After making a small loop in my McCarty rein, which provides more immediate contact with my horse, I hold the small loop and rein in my left hand, along with the rope coils.

I release the honda and pull the rope toward me with my right hand to build a loop.

One-third of the finished loop makes up the spoke, which runs from the honda to my hand.

I start my swing with my palm up, so the honda's to the rear of the horse.

I roll my hand and the rope in a counterclockwise motion.

I continue the counterclockwise motion, rotating my wrist to bring my rope overhead.

I complete one rotation with my knuckles up and without hitting my horse with the rope.

The most common throw is an overhand delivery.

After roping the dummy, I begin to pull my slack by drawing the rope straight back, toward my horse's tail, with my right hand.

I push my left hand straight up the horse's neck to allow room to dally counterclockwise around the horn with my right hand, and try not to look down, but stay focused on the dummy and my horse.

DO IT YOURSELF

Sometimes a rope doesn't pop off a breakaway honda as easily as it should. To keep my kids safer when they were learning to rope and ensure that the rope pops free, I simply file the plastic honda slightly, making the gap in it just a bit wider. That way the rope pops right out of it.

The breakaway honda, made of plastic, pops off a rope when pressure is applied.

For added safety I file the opening in a breakaway honda slightly.

To reuse the honda, I simply snap it back on the rope.

not comfortable swinging a loop has an option. He can simply swing the tail of his rope and aim it at the dummy.

When I ride colts, dummy-roping's the last thing we do before going back to the barn. It provides a time for us to slow down and relax, which is good for me and the horse. Most people are in such a hurry when they get to the barn; they jerk off their saddles and turn out their horses. But taking a few minutes at the roping dummy is a great way to end a ride on a quiet, pleasant note, which helps ensure that the next ride starts well, too.

Roping a dummy also improves a person's ability to ride one-handed. He must learn to shorten his reins with one hand and keep his horse in position. So he learns to do those things, but it's no big deal at the time because his attention's focused on the dummy. He also learns to use both sides of his body at one time; one side handles the rope, and the other controls the horse.

Here's how I handle my rope and my rein. I can rope with either my left or right hand, which I'm using in the photographs. Someone who ropes left-handed can simply reverse left and right in these instructions.

I use a McCarty rein, so I make a small loop in the rein that I carry in my left hand with my rope coils. I want the coils to hang on the left side of my horse's neck.

The metal honda on my rope swivels, so I never have a problem with a kink in my loop. The honda is the small eye through which the tail of my rope passes to create the larger loop for roping, and a honda can be made of metal, synthetic materials or rope.

To build a loop, I hold the rope with my right hand directly behind the honda, and have my left hand just in front of the honda. I use my right hand to slide the honda back along the rope, release the honda and reach back to my left hand and again grasp the rope to pull it back toward me. I repeat the process until the loop is the size I want.

No matter the size of the loop, the tip of the loop hangs down at the bottom, toward the ground, and my right hand grasps the top of the loop and the tail

"Catching the dummy's not all that important — it's all about the horse and the horsemanship."

running back to my coils. The distance between the top of the loop and the honda is called the spoke, which should be about one-third of the overall loop size.

To start my swing correctly, the palm of my right hand is up and out to the side. I don't grip my rope tightly, but hold it loosely. With my palm up, I start my swing, rolling my hand forward until my knuckles are up. I continue to swing the rope around and back toward my body until I make one revolution, then stop the swing with my knuckles up and my loop down at my right side.

A novice with a rope should practice the hand motion one swing at the time until he builds correct muscle memory. That way he learns to set down his rope, or stop the swing, so he doesn't hit his horse. Once he's learned how to keep from hitting his horse in the head with a rope, he can progress to swinging the loop a couple of times before he stops.

After the swing is good, a novice can simply try to "lay" or throw his rope out on the ground in front of him, releasing the loop with right hand and feeding out or releasing his coils with the left. Then he gets more practice at recoiling his rope and riding with one hand. As when logging, when roping a dummy, the rider can shorten the inside rein just a bit so, if the horse becomes scared, the rider can turn the horse's hindquarters and have him face up to the rope without getting caught in it. A

novice roper should just ride for a while, throwing a loop out ahead, feeding out his coils, and recoiling while, at the same time, getting a feel for riding with one hand.

When he can operate both his rope and his reins easily and well, it's time for the rider to position his horse behind the dummy and try throwing a loop to catch the dummy. Most people who get this far with rope-breaking a horse probably are enthusiastic enough about roping that they've thrown a loop from the ground at the dummy anyway, and developed their aim. Again, it's so easy to learn to do those things — without developing bad habits — by attending a roping clinic, but not at all necessary for someone who only wants a more rope-broke horse to ride.

At first, a novice should stop his horse in one place and throw several loops at the dummy to get his bearings and develop his aim before he changes position. Then he should move around to rope the dummy from every direction — straight in front, straight behind or off to either side. He can ride in close or drop back farther away. It isn't necessary that the horse and rider are absolutely still while working at the dummy, and it's really better, as they become more accomplished, to walk around the dummy and change positions while practicing. That's a good opportunity for a rider to sharpen his one-handed riding skills, practice recoiling his rope and let his horse see the dummy from every direction.

The key to roping a dummy is to always make sure the horse is relaxed before throwing the rope; he shouldn't be stiff through his spine or neck, have his ears pinned or show any signs of tension when the loop is thrown. Then roping practice is always a pleasant experience. So not only does a rider learn to handle his horse more precisely at the dummy, he also learns to notice when his horse relaxes. That's a big part of having a broke, gentle horse. Catching the dummy's not all that important — it's all about the horse and the horsemanship.

The breakaway honda is a great invention

for novice ropers. It provides a safety factor for kids or anyone learning to rope, and allows repeated roping practice without requiring much help from other people with the cattle.

The breakaway honda is plastic, and is made so that, when the rope draws tight against it, (i.e., there's a calf on the end of the rope) the pressure from the taut rope breaks it completely loose from the honda. A novice roper can recoil his rope, pop it back on his honda, build a loop and start all over again. Although he later can add dallying to his roping program, using a breakaway honda gives the novice a good way to start roping live cattle and stay safe — out of his rope and with his fingers and thumbs intact. And the honda makes roping practice so easy.

From this stage a novice can advance his roping skills to whatever level he wants. The point: Slow, easy roping preparation is a great way to settle a horse and get him focused on a job, and the horse becomes well-broke and gentle in the process.

Roping Live Cattle

When a rider becomes really good at roping the dummy, and his horse remains calm and can be positioned anywhere, it's time to rope live cattle — if becoming a roper is part of the overall plan. If not, the recreational rider can stop at dummy roping and know that he has the tools to develop a well-broke and gentle horse.

Before a novice roper tries live cattle, he should be handy at dallying his rope. Attaching a rope to a tire, as described in the do-it-yourself section, is the best way to get a feel for that motion, build the muscle memory to make the correct moves and learn how to be safe before ever having a live animal on the end of the rope.

If a novice has never handled cattle before, he needs to read the next chapter, so he'll have some idea about how to get along with practice cattle and work as many cattle as he can. He also needs to watch practice ropings or pennings, partic-

When somebody's ready to rope live cattle, a slow, gentle steer like "Poncho" is best. I'm roping left-handed in this shot.

ipate in those activities or volunteer to help put them on to increase his cattle-handling savvy.

When a novice feels ready to rope live cattle, it's best to start with gentle cattle — old, worn-out steers that hardly move or slow Holsteins. The rider can put old, slow cattle in the round pen or a small arena, track them and try to throw his rope on them. The best and safest approach at this point is to find a knowledgeable roper who can provide hands-on guidance as the wanna-be roper and his horse progress.

Nothing's more fun than riding a horse that really works a cow.

CATTLE-WORKING 101

16

"Cattle-Working 101" is for the pleasure rider who might want to go to a local club team-penning practice and enjoy the experience without feeling foolish or appearing totally ignorant about cattle. This chapter's also for the rider who might be invited to a branding, yet doesn't feel he knows enough to help out — and maybe even less about how to stay out of the way of those who do understand the work.

In any case, the opening ranch etiquette section might help keep a person in good stead with area ranchers and from unknowingly stepping on a rancher's toes or those of the people who work for his outfit.

As for the actual cattle work, many riders might be surprised to learn that they already possess a few basic cattle-handling skills. They just don't yet understand that because they haven't applied what they know about horses to cattle.

This chapter also explores other cow-working basics, such as holding a herd or sorting cattle, for example, and takes a quick look at a few typical branding-pen jobs.

Ranch Etiquette

There are a few unwritten rules that most ranch cowboys follow — especially if they want to continue riding for the brand or be invited back to a neighboring ranch. People who've never had the opportunity to work on a ranch might be unaware these rules exist; after all, there's no etiquette book for ranch hands. But, just as in any workplace, ranch cowboys have their own code of professional conduct, and top hands play by the rules.

In most cases, ranch etiquette isn't so different from that practiced by most people in any work or social setting; it simply reflects common courtesy and consideration. However, ranch etiquette also has been adapted somewhat to consider the nature of the horses and cattle in the workplace.

Granted, nowadays not all ranches and their cowboys pay strict attention to range etiquette, as the old-timers did. But most cowboys continue to follow two main rules.

The first rule: A cowboy never rides off and leaves another cowboy afoot at the headquarters or at a gate. Nothing's worse than trying to mount a horse that jigs and dances because other horses are leaving him behind; he naturally wants to follow. To head off trouble instead of inviting it, at least one cowboy, if not the entire crew, waits for the last man afoot so that his horse stands quietly. Each cowboy, when it's his time to be afoot, knows the others will extend the same professional courtesy.

Another part of this rule is that it's not considered polite for the person afoot to ask someone else to hold his horse. A cowboy might offer, but not necessarily. It's best that a horse is broke enough his rider can hold him while opening or shutting a wire gap or gate. Any good cowboy prefers to hold his own horse anyway; he doesn't want to worry about somebody else not paying attention and letting his horse get hung in wire.

The second rule: It's considered impolite to ride in front of somebody and cut them off,

DO IT YOURSELF

Before you can play cowboy, you need to understand the lingo describing different classes or types of cattle. One ranch might be a cow-calf outfit, and another might background or prepare yearlings for the feedlots. Be sure you understand the differences between them.

A cow is a mature breeding animal, and a pair includes that cow and her calf, no matter if it's a heifer (female) calf or a bull (male) calf, which might be castrated to become a steer. Weaned calves are, of course, those no longer nursing, and they grow to become "short" yearlings and later "long" yearlings 7 or 8 more months down the road. Unlike the quieter, slower-moving mature cows, yearlings get "trotty," when they're gathered; they're more apt to spook and run longer distances faster than grown cows.

Bulls, obviously, are mature, breeding-stock males. A rancher might not castrate all of his bull calves, but allow a few better ones to mature into replacement bulls that'll later run with his herd. Replacement heifers are young females that are kept to maturity to replace older cows in the breeding herd. When replacement heifers are bred the first time, they're usually called first-calf heifers.

Once you understand the different classes of cattle, you might want to learn more about the various breeds. Some breeds might be favored in your region because of its particular climate or terrain, and any cattleman or ranch cowboy can tell you which breeds those are.

just as it's impolite to cut off somebody when driving on the highway. It's courteous to ride around behind another person instead of in front of him. That's as true for trail riders as it is for ranch cowboys.

It goes without saying that anybody joining a cattle gather should be on time and allow enough time to saddle his horse beforehand. Allowing a few extra minutes to have coffee with the crew is also a good thing to do because it might offer an opportunity to learn the lay of the land or get a better idea of how that outfit handles its cattle.

Other rules of ranch courtesy concern dogs, for example, and parking at the ranch headquarters. In either case, a lack of consideration can mean additional trouble and/or inconvenience for the rancher and his hands.

It's great when the invitation comes to join a neighbor's cattle gather. It's not so great around the cattle pens, however, when a guest parks his truck and trailer in front of a gate or loading chute or blocks the road with his rig. If a guest isn't sure that he's parked in an out-of-the-way place, he should ask someone the best place to leave his rig.

No one invited to a ranch gather should ever assume that his dog is welcome, too. If the rancher wants somebody's dogs on the work crew, he'll suggest that; otherwise, dogs should be left at home. Just as strangers don't always work well together, neither do cow dogs. A confused or unresponsive dog can wreck havoc in a herd of cattle, which wastes the ranch hands' time and effort and unnecessarily stresses the cattle, too.

Whenever a guest joins a ranch crew to gather cattle, he should hang back and wait for the cowboss to tell him how things will be handled. If everyone asks him individually, the man has to go over the same information 15 or 20 times before the gather even starts. A good cowboss is usually a good leader and tells everybody what's expected of them.

And just because a rancher handles his cattle one way in Montana doesn't mean that cattle are handled the same way in Idaho or Texas, or even 30 miles down the road. That's why it's best to saddle up and first see how the "Romans" handle the cattle on that ranch before bailing in there and doing things the way they're done at home.

Obviously anyone gathering cattle should be dressed for the weather and prepared for a long day. That might not be the case, but it could be a long time until supper, so it's a good idea to pack a water bottle or take a big drink before leaving the headquarters. And this goes without saying — no alcohol.

Anyone who joins a gather should be prepared for his horse to act differently around strange horses and happenings that he's not used to. The horse might be a little fresh or excited at first, but that'll probably disappear once he's jogged far enough across the pasture.

That jog is about as fast as things get during a good gather. Most people think that moving cattle is a fast and furious job, as shown on television. That just runs weight off the cattle. Good ranch hands barely get their horses and the cattle into a trot because it's so important to keep as much weight on the cattle as possible and keep them settled to work.

When the hands gathering cattle are assigned certain areas to ride, one hand usually doesn't ride into another hand's territory. Each just works his own turf, does his own job and lets the other cowboys take care of theirs.

It's best not to yell, scream or whistle at the cattle, or use a bullwhip when working another man's cattle. If things are moving along quietly, be quiet. It's that same old less-is-better approach.

Once the cattle are gathered and moving toward the pens or another pasture, one of the worst things people do — and I'm guilty of it, too — is take down their ropes and start roping calves at the back of the herd. That's fun, but the cowboys who do that better be skilled enough to keep one eye on the herd at all times and know what's happening with the herd.

Everyone wants to have fun at a cattle gather and enjoy the experience, but it isn't a game. It's the rancher's livelihood, and that makes it serious business. Out of respect for the livestock and the person who owns the cattle, everyone at a gather should take the job seriously and do the best he can. The people who try hardest to do a good job are the ones who'll be invited back. Those who cause wrecks or problems probably won't.

Round-Pen Parallels

The average rider who's never had the opportunity to gather cattle might say that he doesn't know how. But if he can successfully work afoot with a horse, he can work cattle. That's because the same principles that work on horses in the round pen work with cattle. If a person relates what he knows about one to the other, he probably won't embarrass himself too badly the first time he helps at a neighborhood gather.

The Breaking Point

To control a horse's movement in the round pen, a person must be aware of his horse's breaking point, which is around his shoulders or withers. A cow also has a breaking point somewhere behind the shoulder blade. When a person moves in front of that spot, the cow stops or turns back, just as a horse will. When a person moves behind that point, he, in effect, drives the cow or horse forward.

When a cowboy tallies cattle through a gate, he doesn't do it from behind. He slows down or speeds up the flow of cattle through the gate by stepping his horse forward or back slightly, which puts him ahead of or behind a cow's breaking point. That's the same approach a cowboy takes when bringing one cow out of the herd. The key is knowing where to be along the animal's side, where that horse's or cow's breaking point lies.

A Herd of One

It works well to think of the entire cow herd as one animal and relate to it the same way anybody relates to one horse in the round pen. The front 10 percent of the herd is the head, and the herd's back end is the hindquarters. The middle of the herd is the body, and a good hand finds the herd's breaking point there, just as he finds that point on one head or one horse.

To find the herd's breaking point, a cowboy must watch the entire herd without focusing on any one animal in it. A good hand always uses and works the whole herd. He first directs the front, and works back behind the breaking point to move the herd forward, or ahead of it to better direct the herd. He never stays in one spot as he works, but always tries to figure out where he needs to be next to keep the cattle moving. That way he doesn't react to a situation, but sets up the herd to have the right thing happen. It's penicillin-versus-vitamin-C-style-horsemanship applied to the cow herd.

Pressure Behind

No one can control cattle or horses by working directly behind them because then he's behind the breaking point. All he can do

Patience is required when driving through a bog.

from there is speed up the animal, and all the cow or horse thinks about is getting away from the person. A person should step or ride behind a cow's breaking point, toward her tail, only when he wants to move her forward.

However, he should be cautious about getting directly behind the cow in that classic blind spot. Then the cow must turn her head one way or the other to see the rider. When she does, she veers or hooks, as the cowboys describe it, in that direction. Just as a horse veers to the left when he sees a person behind him with his left eye, a cow hooks right if she sees a rider coming behind in her right eye.

When a lead cow in the herd knows a rider is behind her and hooks one direction or the other, she's going the wrong way. That's when a rider often runs up to straighten the lead cow, but going with her movement that way usually stops the movement. Then the rider must get the cow straight and start the movement all over again. The bottom line: That rider spends a lot of time fixing problems he

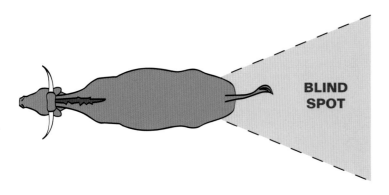
A cow has a blind spot directly behind, just as a horse does.

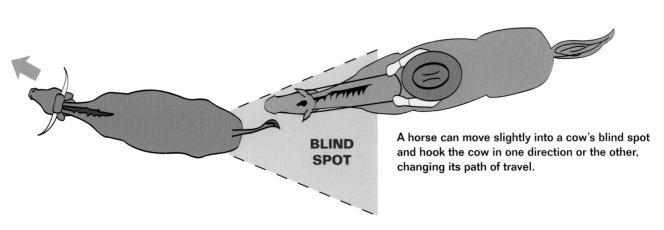
A horse can move slightly into a cow's blind spot and hook the cow in one direction or the other, changing its path of travel.

192

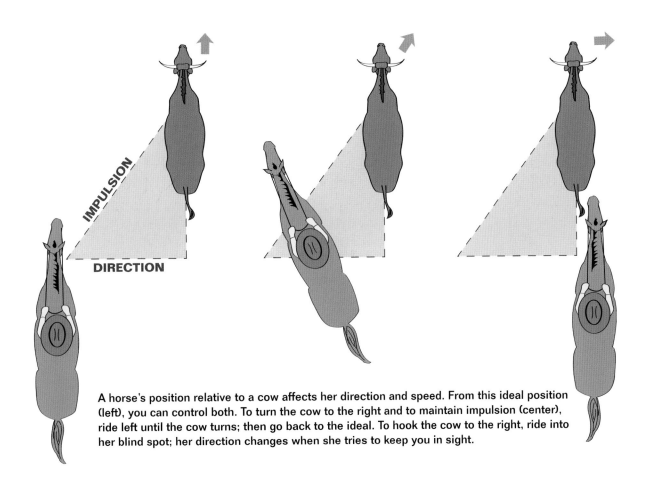

A horse's position relative to a cow affects her direction and speed. From this ideal position (left), you can control both. To turn the cow to the right and to maintain impulsion (center), ride left until the cow turns; then go back to the ideal. To hook the cow to the right, ride into her blind spot; her direction changes when she tries to keep you in sight.

caused simply by working too directly behind the cow in the first place.

Pressure in Front

When a person approaches a horse from behind, to catch him, the horse can walk off, but when a person approaches from the front, ahead of the horse's breaking point, the person can stop the horse's movement. Even though the horse can turn around, the person also can move around to stay in front of him.

A similar approach works with cattle to control their movement. A rider might start from the front of one cow or the entire herd, and then can move toward the side and the breaking point if he needs to. He can ride forward ahead of that point to slow a fast-moving cow or herd, but that doesn't mean he moves directly in front of the cattle. Instead, he should angle toward the herd.

The approach is important in relation to how fast the cattle move, just as it is when working a horse afoot in the pen. When somebody moves forward in an acute angle as though he's attacking, the horse or cattle probably move away quickly. But if the same horse or cattle are approached like a visiting neighbor, they won't leave quite as fast. A savvy cowhand drifts in toward the cattle at a less acute angle so they move quietly and calmly.

Smooth Transitions

By working alongside a horse, a cow or the herd, a person can change position as necessary to slow or speed up the animals, simply by moving in front of or behind the breaking point. The key to maintaining good-handling cattle is to make these transitions as smooth as possible, just as a good horseman achieves calm, quiet transitions when he changes gaits or direction.

A good cowhand can see it coming when a

cow's about to break into a trot, so he works to one side and in front of her breaking point. The cow feels less pressure with the rider there than behind her, so she slows. So the cowboy stops a stampede before it ever starts, instead of chasing a cow after she's already gone.

When a cow lags back, the cowboy drops behind the breaking point, moving toward the rear and the animal's blind spot, to put more pressure on her, and the cow speeds up in response. But the cowboy doesn't whoop and holler to get the job done. Instead he works to achieve another smooth transition, and his approach works just as well with the herd as it does with one cow.

The Flight Zone

Those smooth transitions ultimately result in cattle that are quiet and easy to handle. Ranch hands can achieve those nice changes because they understand the flight zone in cattle, no matter if they're dealing with trotty, flighty yearlings or mature, mamma cows.

Just as a good horseman understands his

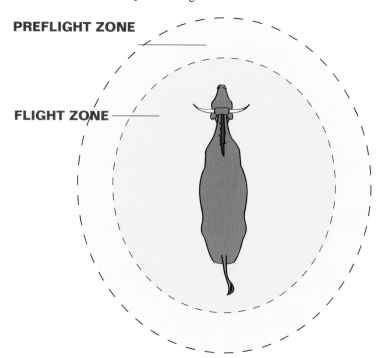

PREFLIGHT ZONE

FLIGHT ZONE

Understanding a cow's preflight zone allows a rider to better position himself to direct the cow and change its course smoothly. The zone's shape and size changes with the environment — for example, in a corral, against a fence or on a hillside.

mount must find relief or a release from pressure, a savvy cowhand knows that when he pressures a cow, he invades her flight zone, and that she must be allowed to move to get away from the rider's pressure.

However, if a rider doesn't wait for or allow a cow to move when he rides into her flight zone, or if the rider continually tries to stay in her flight zone, during the course of the day's drive she usually becomes immune to his pressure. The cow becomes dull, just like a horse that's been kicked all day becomes dull to his rider's leg cue. The cow might even turn around and fight when she's unable to find any relief from the rider's pressure.

The same thing holds true of cattle being pressured up the chute. If, even when they move, the pressure's never released, cattle become dull to the pressure or turn around and fight. In effect, they learn to fight, and people teach them that, instead of teaching them how to respond to the pressure and go up a chute or through a gate.

Few people really think of training their cattle in that respect. Driving cattle across the pasture is a great place for livestock to figure out that, if they move forward, the pressure releases. Just like a horse, a cow can learn to move away from pressure, and when she does, she becomes better to handle, instead of worse. But that holds true only when she gets some kind of release. If she doesn't, why should she do what the cowhands want the next time?

Having said all that, the crucial thing is learning where that flight zone is in order to know where the preflight zone, or area right before the flight zone, is. The reason: If a rider penetrates that flight zone too quickly, he makes the cow leave, but has no control over her direction. Finding the preflight zone allows a rider to position himself to get the cow to leave smoothly and to direct her where he wants her to go, just as he would do when making an upward transition on his horse. As with a horse, a cowboy has to get into the cow's mind first in order to move her feet. When a cowboy finds that preflight spot on a cow, he's ready for any move she might make, but he's not pressuring her to the point of leaving.

But when a rider penetrates the flight zone too quickly, the cow's already going where her mind is — away from his pressure and that bunch of cattle. And the cowboy's working too closely to her to stop her. Like a tennis player working too closely to the net, he has no room to maneuver. But if he rides too far back from the cow, she can build up a head of steam as she leaves, and he'll have a hard time heading her off.

That's why it's best to read a cow's flight zone and try to stay just beyond that point while working her. That might be 10 feet with some cattle, and a half-mile with others. In the corral a cow's flight zone might be a greater or lesser distance than it is in the pasture. Knowing the distance comes with experience and reading lots of cattle, and a cow will tell a cowboy where her flight zone is.

Making the most of a cow's preflight zone is also where good horsemanship enters the picture. The cowboy who can move his horse slowly and precisely can work just outside a cow's flight zone far more effectively than a rider with a less responsive horse. Not only does the hand riding the good horse have time to react to any move the cow makes, the cow also has time enough to react to him.

Cattle, like horses, always tell a cowboy when there's too much pressure on them or not enough. If the cows, for example, stop to graze frequently, there's probably not enough pressure being applied to keep the herd moving. On the other hand, if most of the cattle

DO IT YOURSELF

Here are a couple of ways to learn about cattle and how they handle pressure.

At your local cattle auction watch the sale-barn employees handle the cattle as they move through the alleyways and when they go through the ring. You soon see that some cattle have a greater tolerance of pressure than other cattle, and that some cattle have little tolerance at all. Those are the ones that run at the sale-barn employees instead of away from them. Of course, you can't learn everything about cattle by watching someone else work them, but the local auction barn is a great place to gain a better understanding.

Another way to better understand how cattle respond to pressure is to work a few head afoot. Cutting and team-penning professionals sometimes recommend that people do this to better learn to read cattle before they ever work a cow horseback. When a few head slip past somebody working afoot, and he has to walk to the far end of the pen to bring them back, the person usually begins to develop some cow savvy. He becomes more aware of the cattle earlier in the game, to save himself some steps — just as his newfound awareness can help save his horse steps.

No matter which method you try to better savvy cattle, the important thing is that you observe what the cattle do, then think about and analyze it. If you don't, you won't gain any expertise in handling cattle.

have their heads up, almost in an alarmed way, and seem trotty, there's too much pressure. They're about to scatter, so it's best for the cowboys to back off and let the herd slow, before the riders start losing cattle.

Handling trotty yearlings in the brush teaches kids to become better hands and more aware of the yearlings' flight zone.

A typical problem, when a cow does break from the herd, is that 10 people go after the one cow — and then the whole herd leaves because nobody's left to watch them. That's a common problem with people new to working cattle, but one that seasoned hands are aware of and try to prevent.

There are always stragglers when driving a herd of cattle. Some cows can walk only so fast, no matter how much pressure is put on them to keep moving. And some that are continually pushed eventually want to fight the horse and rider pushing them. If a cow can't keep up, the cowboys must be patient. Depending on the particular situation, a slow cow might be dropped back from the herd or she might be loaded into a trailer coming behind the herd.

The main point is not to push the cattle until they're on the prod and want to fight. That's a no-win situation that seldom works the way the hands want it to. Moving cattle isn't a high-speed activity. It's more like John Wayne described it in *The Cowboys*, when he said that about 10 miles a day was perfect for putting weight on cattle on the move. Most horses walk about 4 miles an hour, so that gives a good idea of how slowly cattle should be moved.

Gathering Pairs

Here's the thinking behind how cow-calf pairs, for example, often are gathered. A good hand knows that an animal can think of only one thing at the time. If the animal's a cow, for example, who doesn't know where her calf is, that's all she has on her mind, and every time she's pressured, she goes wherever she thinks her calf is. When she finds the calf, it usually just follows along.

That's why it's so important when gathering cows and calves to mother up the pairs before they're moved. That's also why

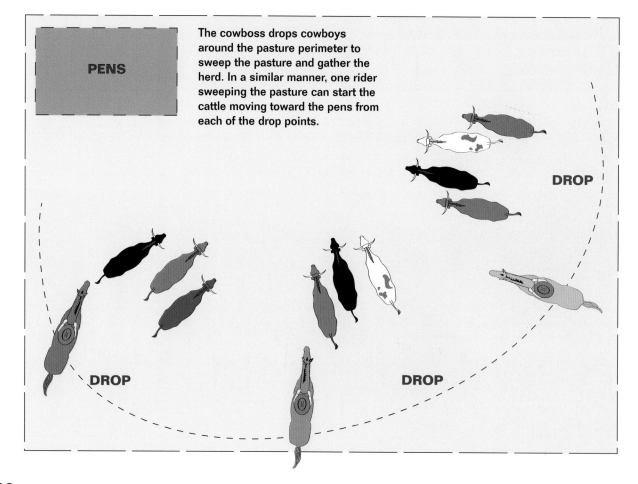

The cowboss drops cowboys around the pasture perimeter to sweep the pasture and gather the herd. In a similar manner, one rider sweeping the pasture can start the cattle moving toward the pens from each of the drop points.

PENS

DROP

DROP

DROP

The rider must decide the best place to be when penning a cow. He might ride around the cow to head it and drive it through the gate, but that could hook the cow to the right, drawing it away from the gate.

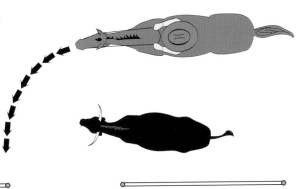

Or, the rider could follow closely behind the cow and slightly to the left and hook the cow to the left from its blind spot.

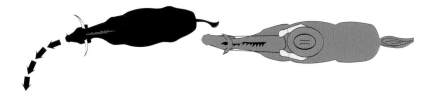

Changing pastures is a common occurrence on a ranch.

When the cattle are moving willingly, there's no need to crowd them.

the old-time cowboys started their gathers before daylight; the pairs usually stayed together because the calves hadn't yet sucked.

Later in the day, the calves have sucked and lay back down with full bellies while the cows wander off to graze. When the crew starts moving the herd, the cows don't have time to go back and find their calves. It's like a fire alarm at the mall; everybody's rushing, but nobody knows where the kids are, so all the mammas run back into the mall. It's the same with a cow. She keeps running back to find her calf, and the calf has panicked or runs back to the last place he saw his mamma. It's really difficult to pair cows and calves and keep them all moving ahead to another pasture or bedding ground.

When a crew gets to the cattle later in the day, and the cows already are grazing, it's best to slowly approach the herd. Most cows, when they see riders coming, will go back to their calves if allowed. Instead of riding directly to the cattle then, cowhands sometimes ride toward the herd at a flatter or longer angle. That gives the cows and calves time to mother up before the herd moves, which is so important for a smooth drive.

Holding the Herd

Cattle often are gathered, then held in a pen or pasture corner while they're sorted for whatever reason. Holding the herd while the cattle are sorted is an important job although

it can seem a little boring at times. When holding the herd, it's crucial to read what a cow's thinking about doing before she does it — and then stop her from doing it.

Herd-holding can be a hard job, too, because when one cow quits the bunch and a cowboy goes after her, he leaves a hole for the other cattle to escape. Then the cowboy's zinging around everywhere, but never catches up with all the cattle and has spilled his part of the herd.

But a savvy cowhand stays just far back enough that the cattle don't try to blow by him. Then he watches. When he sees a cow pick up her head and unweight one foot, he moves just enough to put her weight back down, like a horseman does when he's working on turnarounds, for example. All a good cowboy must do to stop a cow is stop her front feet.

A herd-holder also has another consideration as he does his job. He not only tries to hold his part of the herd, but also tries not to pressure the cattle so much that he runs them over the top of the cowboys on the other side of the herd.

Herd-holding can be such a dynamic deal. A rider might need to be in one cow's face to keep her in place, yet stay far away from another cow to keep from putting too much pressure on her. The herd-holder learns how to work just outside the edge of a cow's flight zone and just how much pressure to apply and when to release it to best keep his part of the herd in position.

The cowboss drops his hands to hold the herd.

The kids hold the rodear while pairs are sorted.

Sorting Cattle

The rider who'd like to be able to sort cattle at a local team-penning practice or help a neighbor gather his herd without looking silly probably can, if he follows a few guidelines when bringing a cow out of the herd. Sorting cattle is like a chess game. All the players must be set up right to win the game.

Some people are great at gathering cattle in the pasture, and use the best horsemanship to do it, but when they get to the pens, things seem to fall apart, and their horsemanship becomes poor. Maybe it's the pressure of feeling as though they and their horses should be at their best when doing corral work.

The first thing the rider must do is assess his skill level and that of his horse. If he has to think of every move for his horse to make, it's best to keep things really slow and not

break out of a walk. Otherwise, things move so quickly that he can't think and ride fast enough. Then his horsemanship suffers, too.

Slower sorting is better, especially when someone's learning about this job; he can learn much more, recall and retain it much better and doesn't need to jerk on his horse to do it. However, sorting isn't a job typically offered to a newcomer at a gather. The rancher and the cowboss usually know the best hands for getting the sorting done quickly and effectively.

It's best to build cow-sorting skills slowly and gradually. Then, when things speed up, no matter if prompted by the cattle or because a person's riding in competition, his sorting skills come to him so naturally. A rider might speed up things in a real competition, but probably not. Most top hands know that slower is almost always faster in the long run when livestock's involved.

When sorting cattle, a rider can scoop a cow off the edge of the herd or go deep into the herd in pursuit of one head.

The need for slow, quiet work means that it's important to have a horse that'll relax. The sorting pen isn't the place for one that jigs and dances; that'll only stir up the cattle. Cattle don't like to be in a really tight group, so a horse that operates quietly can ease through the herd, like a snake, and make a path to the cow his rider wants and bring her out with minimal fuss. The same principles about working the breaking point on a cow when moving the herd apply to sorting cattle, too. The better the rider's understanding of a breaking point and pressure on cattle, the more smoothly he's able to maneuver a cow clear of the bunch.

An important thing to remember: The first time the cow moves off, the rider should momentarily release the pressure on her before reapplying it. That way the cow learns how to be driven. Too, when the rider gets her free of the herd, if she doesn't understand how to be driven and that the rider can release the pressure on her, she doesn't yet know that the rider's in control. So he must apply enough pressure to drive her away from the herd, then momentarily release it before reapplying more pressure to keep her moving.

A savvy cowhand has from the time he sorts a cow to the edge of the herd to get her trained, but most cows that've been handled a lot already have that figured out. Too often, however, a cowboy just tries to force a cow from the herd without releasing the pressure. That works at the time, but the next time that particular cow's worked, she'll be harder, rather than easier, to handle. Anybody riding a horse at almost any skill level, even a green

Slow, quiet work keeps the cattle handling well.

It's easy to be in the right place at the right time and make a split to separate cattle when your horse handles well.

colt, can sort cattle if he approaches the job properly and moves slowly.

A cowboy can let a cow learn to work at the edge of the herd, but without getting into a cutting-horse-type situation. If he's done the job right, he's trained the cow to drive, and taught her what to do when any pressure's released, so a cutting horse shouldn't be necessary at this point. It's nice if one is available in case a mistake occurs, but that's having the best of both worlds.

The important thing to remember when sorting cattle is that the horse comes first. Maybe that's in the code of the West. That pen of yearlings will be gone in the fall, but the horse remains on the ranch. If he doesn't stay as good as he is, or become better than he is now, every pen of yearlings he works from this point on becomes harder to handle. It's so important to take care of a horse and help him become as good as he can be because that's the only way the cattle remain good to work.

Branding

The traditional style of branding cattle by roping them and dragging them out of the pen can be a most humane way to do things, if done properly, or it can be inhumane if not done well. That's why it's so important that people learn how to correctly work calves out of the corral, rope them and wrestle them. Then the job's so easy on horses, riders and cattle.

It works well to corral or at least corner up the cattle, then peel off the cows. That way, as soon as a calf is worked, he can immediately go to his mother and fill up his belly, and she can start soothing him. If the cow is left in the corral and the calf is taken out, worked and turned loose, it might be an hour or more before he and his mamma get back together, so it's best for him to be able to go right to his mamma after being stressed.

A bridle horse doing what he does best.

I'm taking a long shot to keep from startling the calf.

Roping

At a branding, people should be brutally honest about their roping abilities. So many people who can barely swing a rope go into the branding pen, and that's not good for the cattle. No one should go into the pen unless he's an expert roper, who can dally well and handle his horse while he handles his rope. He shouldn't stir up the herd, get in anybody's way or get twisted in a rope. Those things only slow down the day's work.

Expert ropers try to take sure shots because they know that every time they throw and hit a calf, but don't catch, the cattle get spookier. Then, late in the day, the final bunch of calves is really juiced up and flighty, and good ropers are a necessity.

Some of the best ropers always try to rope from the front of the herd. That way, they don't catch a calf clear at the back of the pen and have to drag him farther, which is only harder on the horse and stirs up the whole herd when he comes through it.

Ideally, the roper should have both of the calf's hind feet in a loop. Many cowboys don't even think a calf should be brought to the fire by one foot because that's harder on the calf. Then he tries to run around, and somebody gets into trouble.

Even a cowboy using a 60-foot rope can have his calf only 10 feet out on his rope, which is good. The more distance between the saddle horn and the calf, the greater the chance of having a wreck.

If an inexperienced roper feels confident enough to go into the pen, he might find an experienced roper willing to help him through the situation. So many times a novice doesn't really understand how much activity's going on and gets everybody in a wreck. He hasn't yet learned to see the big picture of what's happening elsewhere in the pen while he's so focused on what he's doing.

Wrestling and Doctoring Calves

Most novice or unskilled ropers end up wrestling calves at a branding. Done right, it's an easy job.

If, for example, a left-rib or left-side brand is used, the two guys wrestling the calf lay him down with that side up. The tailer gets on the right side of the calf and pulls to the side opposite the brand. The other ground person, who's on his feet, grabs the rope and pulls it the opposite way, in this case, to the left. When the two people wrestling calves get into the rhythm of doing that, it's effortless because they both use the momentum to advantage.

At some outfits the rope stays on the calf's hind feet, and the roper holds it. At other outfits, the ground man takes off the rope and holds the hind feet. One man on the ground works the calf's hind legs, and the other handles the front end. Certain techniques work better in each position, and a seasoned hand will show a novice how to handle the calf in a way that's not stressful and allows it to be doctored as quickly as possible.

The century-old tradition still works to doctor cattle today.

Branding work happens so fast that it sometimes seems chaotic, but usually isn't because everyone there knows his job and does it. The critical thing is for the ground crew to be sure that each calf has all his shots, his brand, ear tag, is dehorned or whatever. That's the ground crew's job.

A newcomer at a branding also might be asked to give shots or even hold a bucket of disinfectant. Whatever the job, he should do it because they're all important and need to be done. Nobody who attends a branding should be a spectator; he shouldn't be afraid to get his hands dirty.

Tie or Hobble?

When the actual branding and calf-doctoring begins, many people who'd been horseback earlier in the day find themselves working on a ground crew. Often there aren't really good places to tie horses around the pens, and when people do, their gear sometimes gets broken. A horse shouldn't be tied to the fence when loose cattle and horses are wandering nearby, and portable panels aren't always secure enough for tying. One good wreck and the panels might come apart or be dragged out of position. That's when having a hobble-broke horse works to advantage. He can be safely out of the way of the work yet still be close by when it's time to ride back to the ranch headquarters.

If there is a place to tie a horse, it's best to use a halter or a get-down rope; reins are expensive to replace. The big thing: Should a horse tied with the reins set back or be spooked, he can ruin his mouth. That's usually more important to a cowboy than the reins being broken because he has to live and work with that horse's ruined mouth every day.

I don't like to ground-tie in this situation or any other because it's too easy for a horse to run off. Doing that sometimes seems to work better when a horse and rider are by themselves and not in a crowd, but I'm not a big ground-tying fan.

DO IT YOURSELF

Many people would like to have a few head of cattle, just so they and their horses can learn about working cattle. That's a great idea, but it can be expensive entertainment. In addition to the initial cash outlay for the cattle, routine feed and health-care costs must be considered although having an inexpensive feed source in your area really helps minimize maintenance expense.

The problem with such sport cattle, as cattlemen sometimes call them: They become sour after they've been used a period of time. Then it's necessary to buy fresh cattle to keep you and your horse from developing bad habits in response to working soured cattle.

Although routine cattle expenses continue, and you're out the initial cost of your cattle, here's an idea that might be helpful in keeping fresh cattle to work. It's called buying and selling cattle on the same market.

For example, you buy five head of cattle at 75 cents a pound at the local cattle auction, just to learn how to head and drive cattle horseback. But after about 6 weeks, the cattle become sour and don't handle well anymore, so you decide to sell your five head and buy more fresh cattle on the same market. In other words, no matter what your original five head sell for, you spend the same money you receive that day when selling to replace your original cattle.

You might buy another five head at the same 75-cent-per-pound price. But the market might be down to 60 cents. So you sell your cattle for less than the purchase price, and spend only that same money to buy replacement cattle at 60 cents a pound — however many head that is. Or, if the price is up, you spend the same money and take home fewer instead of more cattle. Only when you sell your last set of cattle do you really make or lose money on your initial investment, the original purchase price.

Understand that your cattle also lose or gain weight, which affects the sales price, too. How much your cattle gain or lose depends on how hard you work them. Chase your cattle fast and furiously, and they won't eat as well and, obviously, won't gain weight. On the other hand, with slow, quiet work, the minute you're through playing cowboy, your cattle are ready and willing to eat.

Not everyone wants to spend the time or the money to maintain cattle just for his own entertainment. But, if you do, you might consider buying and selling on the same market to ensure that your cattle are fresh enough for you and your horse to benefit from working them.

PART 5

RANCH KIDS AND COMPETITIVE COWBOYS

This final section addresses a couple of things that usually become near and dear to any ranch cowboy's heart — kids and competitive entertainment. Horses play important roles in the ranch lifestyle, not only as a way to get the cow work done, but also as a means of entertainment for kids and adults alike.

At almost any cow outfit in the country, children are horseback much of the time. In part that's because ranch kids in more isolated areas are usually home-schooled; a horse often becomes a child's best buddy and his only means of transportation to the nearest fishing hole. Too, in ranching communities neighbors often swap out work, so youngsters are encouraged to participate in cattle gathers, drives and brandings, which are often as much social as work-related occasions.

Almost anyone who rides for pleasure or work wants to share his enthusiasm for horses with his children and grandchildren. All it takes is a well-broke horse and an adult who uses good judgment to make riding fun and safe for a kid. In fact, most any child who's ridden at all can do almost everything horseback that's discussed in this book, and tips for helping him along are found in Chapter 17.

As for cowboy-style entertainment, horses always have played the major roles. Ranch-cowboy competition dates back about 150 years, when area and regional ranch cowboys first held bronc-riding and roping contests, the precursors to modern rodeo events. In recent years, however, competitive events that highlight working-ranch-cowboy skills have again become popular among ranching communities and even with big-city spectators. That's why Chapter 18 includes an overview of the growing number of such events held nationwide.

Ranch kids are prone to ride off the beaten path.

JUST FOR KIDS

17

One of the best things an adult rider can do is watch a kid ride his horse. Although sometimes a kid doesn't always think about safety, he just naturally finds the middle of a saddle and, because he has fun, his horse does, too. So a grownup might learn more from a kid and what he does horseback than the kid actually learns from the adult.

The ideas for developing a broke, well-seasoned riding horse in this book aren't for adults only. The same riding techniques also can build a child's confidence in his skills and trust in his horse. In fact, the do-it-yourself exercises in this book are almost like games to most kids.

It's so important that a kid have fun when he rides. No matter if only one child in the family rides, or if riding is the entire family's favorite pastime, the experience should be a pleasure. Good horsemanship is important, but no more so than any rider, adult or child, enjoying a fun sport.

However, the primary issue for a young rider is safety. Although the safety examples described here usually relate to a ranch kid's experiences, the same principles can be applied to any riding program.

An Important Point

When a kid truly has fun with horses, he usually isn't receiving much instruction at the same time. Too often kids nowadays are forced into riding lessons, that put-down-your-heels-keep-your-chin-up stuff. Those kids sometimes try so hard to please their parents that they don't seem to enjoy riding at all. When that's the case, a child rides only as long as he's made to ride.

But when a child's allowed to enjoy the experience, he'll probably ride for life. He might get away from it as a college student or young married adult, but he'll usually come back to enjoy the sport with his own family. Unfortunately, so many kids now live in suburban areas, where riding space is limited. The focus is often more on arena riding, which usually leads to competitive events, where the kids often are pressured to do well.

On the other hand, a ranch kid usually rides across pastures, jumps ditches and pretends to be John Wayne or a cowboy. Maybe the kid's heels aren't all the way down, but he has fun and learns a natural seat in the saddle while he plays. He's so busy thinking about the fun he's having that his body finds a natural way to go with his horse's flow. It's really pretty to see. The kid doesn't force anything — it just happens.

One Approach

Most parents are safety-conscious when their children are involved, even those who want their children to enjoy riding horseback. Most avid riders also want their children to begin riding at as young an age as possible, so it's really important to introduce a child to riding on a solid, experienced, kid-broke horse. Such horses usually have some age and many miles on them.

At first the adult should saddle his and the child's horse, then lead the child's horse

207

A young rider might start out following…

… but before long she's leading the way.

long that the child becomes really tired, cold or hungry. Riding should be fun for children, not a miserable experience.

As a child begins to learn to ride the horse by himself in a pen, at first he might sometimes find it hard to quit looking down at the horse and to look where he's going. Like a colt in the pasture, kids horseback need to learn to focus and ride to something. Putting a rock or a piece of candy on a fencepost is a great way to teach a child to ride his horse straight to something. Otherwise, he and his horse wander everywhere.

It's also important to get a child riding horseback out of the arena as soon as possible.

DO IT YOURSELF

No matter a child's age, if he gazes down toward his saddle horn continually, then he has a problem getting where he wants to go. That's because he's not focused on where he's going, as he should be.

When you're trying to persuade a child to ride straight across the pen, scatter a few pieces of incentive candy on top of the fence posts. This gives a young rider something to focus on as he rides across the pen.

Another great thing for kids and adults to do is play tag horseback. Any kid, or even a grownup, who doesn't look ahead as often as he should or is a little hesitant to get moving on a horse, becomes far less timid when the competition in tag begins.

around for a relatively short, but pleasant ride. The two of them might check cattle or fences, or take a quiet ride through the neighborhood.

The main thing with a kid, especially one under 5, is not to ride too long. A half-hour or 45 minutes is long enough for most youngsters. A ski instructor once told me that adult skiers should leave their kids hungry for more, and that's true of adult riders, too. Nobody should ride his kid around for so

As with colts being worked in a round pen, kids get bored riding there, just as they seem to during long rides. When either of those things continues to happen, a child usually comes to dislike riding altogether.

The guideline for a kid 5 or younger: He should be on a lead rope whenever he's outside. Depending on the horse, he might be able to ride by himself with no problem in a round pen or arena.

The average parent realizes that he must turn loose and allow his child to ride by himself sometime, usually between the ages of 5 to 10. No one can say what age is best in every situation. At first, a child might be required to ride near the parent for a period of time, and shouldn't be turned loose on his own without some supervision. Such things are hard calls to make, especially if the parents began riding as adults.

The First Horse

A relatively safe way to introduce a child to horseback riding requires the parents to find one of those wonderful, old bomb-proof horses, that's a solid reliable performer. Good standards for selecting a broke horse have been described in the book's first section. The horse doesn't have to be really old; his suitability depends more on his personality. Some horses seem old and solid at 7; others never do. But the older a horse, the more experience he has and the safer he'll be — as a general rule.

A really young kid from 3 to 5 years old needs a really old horse that barely goes. However, when that child gets a little older and wants his horse to go faster and for longer periods of time, that type of riding can become cruel to the old horse that doesn't have the stamina for it. That seems unfair to those good, old horses; they shouldn't have to tolerate that. A really old horse is okay for a 3-year-old, but not for a 7-year-old. Then the kid becomes discouraged anyway because he wants more than the horse can give.

No parent should be afraid to spend good money for his child's first horse; it's better to spend it now than later for a high-dollar barrel or reining horse. Let the child learn to make his own horse later; that's a matter of learning horsemanship anyway and what 4-H and other youth horse programs are for.

It's best to think about getting a great horse for a child during the time frame when he's younger and his mind can be so influenced by having a good horse to ride. When a child really learns to love horses right then, it pays off when he's older, and he stays busy with a 4-H club or high school rodeo. Those are great horse programs and family programs, too, that help instill good horsemanship.

Although both mares and geldings can make great first horses, more of them seem to be geldings. Mares just seem a little bit cranky sometimes; maybe their rider-tolerance factor isn't quite as high.

Ponies aren't always the most satisfactory child's mount in the barn — from the adult perspective. A child might get along just fine with the pony, but can't provide any necessary additional training, and the parent's usually too large to ride and train the pony. Another possible safety issue concerns the child riding a pony around full-size horses. Kids don't always pay attention when they ride and sometimes allow their mounts to crowd other horses. That's not such a big deal with full-size horses; even if one kicks the other, he usually hits the other horse and not the child. But, if a full-size horse kicks at a pony, that increases the odds that the horse might hit the child sitting on the much smaller pony.

The greater the variety of horses a child can ride as he grows up, the better. A child's horsemanship skills really improve that way because the child learns how to use his own judgment and apply the same riding skills to many horses.

Horror Stories

So many people tell of being involved in a horse wreck or accident as a young child, and they've never conquered that fear. The person might want to ride, but the fear is so great that making the effort just isn't worth it, and the adult often seems to think he's let himself down by not rising to the challenge.

That's why it's so important that adults with kids who ride should be as careful as possible not to let a similar situation occur with their children. And that's not to say all the kids who have little trotaways and run-aways fall off and never get back on a horse again. But it's possible that could happen.

Horse Gear for Kids

A kid might ride his horse in a snaffle bit indefinitely, but that's a controversial topic in some industry circles. Typically, when a kid using a snaffle bit pulls on his horse, the horse learns how to pull back against the kid; as a result, the horse becomes stiff and unresponsive.

A shanked bit seems better for a child because it gives him more control of his horse than a snaffle bit does. Few kid horses have great headsets any-way. If the child's having fun and not worried about such things, and the horse is the old, broke kid's horse he ought to be, he might ride just fine in a snaffle, but not every parent is willing to take that risk.

A closed-loop rein also is good for children because a young kid's always drop-ping his rein. However, the loop should be long enough that the child can reach it without leaning forward all the time. If the rein length is normal for an adult, it won't work well for a child because his

A too-long stirrup leather that's not tucked out of the way can be poten-tially dangerous for a young rider.

A long stirrup leather can be tucked under the hobble strap to keep the leather from binding a child's foot in the stirrup.

arms are so much shorter. Most kids figure that out anyway and tie a piece of baling twine on the rein so they can reach it easily.

One thing that's risky: allowing a child to ride with only a halter on the horse. Like the snaffle bit, a halter simply doesn't allow a child enough control over his horse, and that's a safety concern.

Kid-size gear is usually easy to obtain. Some people borrow it, but it's also fairly inexpensive to buy. The important thing is that the saddle fits the horse and the child, too, so he doesn't bounce all over — another safety issue.

Stirrups must be small enough for a child's foot. It's far too easy for a child's tiny foot to go completely through a stirrup. That's dan-gerous should something startle the horse.

And although this seems very obvious, a child should never be allowed to ride horse-back in tennis shoes. A child needs to wear hard-soled cowboy boots with heels to pre-vent his feet from working through the stir-rups. Pull-on boots are better than lace-up boots because, should a child's foot hang up, his foot's more likely to slip free of the pull-on boot. Crepe-soled boots are fine for cow-boys walking in town, but the crepe sole often binds in a stirrup, unless it's a large, oversized winter stirrup that's sized for insulated boots.

Spurs are rarely suitable for a child to use. He's too busy learning to stay on a horse to worry about accidentally jabbing the horse in the side. And that happens because the kid's legs are so short. A little stick or bat is usually better for a child to use any-way because then he must consciously think about using it to make his horse go.

One of the worst things an adult can do is put his child on a saddle with a rope tied on it. It happens at brandings all the time at the end of the work day. The child wants to ride, but can't reach the stirrups. If he happens to come off and gets a leg hung in the rope — well, it's a terrible thought.

A helmet protects a rider's head, but a bicycle helmet won't do for horseback pro-tection. The helmet should ASTM/FEI-cer-tified to ensure that it meets high quality

The younger generation admires the old buckaroo traditions.

Tammy, Curt's wife, enjoys riding as much as her husband and children do.

standards for riding protection.

However, a helmet almost seems a bad thing when a rider wears one and feels like that's what makes him invincible. It doesn't. Horseback safety comes from a person knowing his boundaries, having a horse that's right for him at his level of expertise and riding in safe places.

Staging Success

When real ranch work ensues, a ranch kid just tags along and grows into the work as he

Playing follow-the-leader horseback is a great way for kids to improve their riding skills.

DO IT YOURSELF

The do-it-yourself tips provided throughout this book are great for almost any youngster to use, and he'll probably make games of seeing if he or a friend can ride between the poles or over the sacks first. A kid can relate easily to most of the do-it-yourself tips in the book because most are broken down step-by-step for the horse anyway. And kids especially seem to like the teeter-totter. It might not sound like the safest of obstacles, but it moves only a few inches from one end to the other.

A parent shouldn't drill his child on these do-it-yourself routines, however, but rather let the youngster watch him do the maneuvers. Before long the child can do them, and most kids seem to learn better that way. That's why it's important to let a young rider make his own mistakes and then figure out ways to solve his problems. Another real benefit: While a kid has fun playing with his horse at home, the child also prepares his horse to meet many of the challenges they'll encounter while riding with friends around the neighborhood or on an organized group trail ride.

A child can learn a lot about safety and good horsemanship, and have a great time doing it. Ultimately, however, it's a parent's responsibility to apply good judgment to any situation he sees his children riding into.

grows up. But sometimes a kid is yelled at so much around the cattle pens that he never wants to be around cattle work again.

That's not the way things should be. It's up to the adult to set up things for his child to succeed. He must give the child a riding job that seems important, whether it is or not, because when a youngster has a job at, for example, the branding pen, he feels like he's the most important cowboy in the world.

The adult should set up any situation for the child, just as he would for a young horse. The child should have the opportunity to make mistakes and learn from them, but without having too much pressure on him. A kid might need to ride at the back of the herd and bring up the calves or stragglers. Those cattle move so slowly that they shouldn't overload the child or his horse. It's all a matter of finding the right spot for a young person to ride.

Around the branding pen, for example, most ranch kids just hang around and play at first. But they must learn where to play or not play, and it's up to an adult to tell them. Again, this is a safety issue. It's dangerous for

Riding with a halter and throwing the rope from one side to the other — within the safety of a pen — builds confidence and riding skills.

The kids turned the tables, driving away the four-wheeler, rather than running from it.

parents to forget about their children at a branding; there's simply too much going on. It's the parent's responsibility to kick the child out of the branding pen, so he's out of harm's way, and out of the way of the flow of cattle, which interferes with the work.

Later, when a child's a little older, he might start working at the branding by wrestling small calves — provided his parents have selected the roper and the particular calf, which should be a small one. The roper should be smooth and handy, someone who won't get a child into trouble.

Helping his child wrestle the first calf, for a rancher, can be a real father-son — or father-daughter — experience. Wrestling calves seems safer for kids than to have them vaccinate calves; then it's just too easy for a kid to get poked or punched with the vaccines.

It's important to show and teach a kid the proper way to do ranch work, not just tell them. A kid learns such skills quickly and likes being part of what's going on, but he also needs to learn that using proper cow-handling techniques shows respect to the rancher and his cattle.

Our thanks to the Wild Bunch for participating in the photo shoot for this book.

THE WILD BUNCH

Briana Beich

Kyle Beto

Rial Pate

Marley Marsh

Julie Born

Mesa Pate

In some respects ranch-horse competition is similar to reined cow-horse events.

COWBOY COMPETITION

18

Modern rodeos, of course, began as ranch competitions more than a century ago and evolved into the sport as it's known today. Through the years competition among working ranch cowboys and their horses continued to exist although sometimes on a more regional scale. But in the mid-1980s interest in authentic, ranch-type events revived, thanks in part to a new-found curiosity about America's strong ranching tradition and the need to preserve that heritage for generations to come.

Now many organizations and associations showcase ranch-cowboy and ranch-horse skills. Big-loop competitions that feature fancy roping skills are gaining popularity nationwide, as are all types of ranch-roping, ranch-rodeo and working cow-horse activities.

These events have been patterned to fit the ranch horse — the most versatile horse in world. He's a jumping horse when necessary, a dressage horse in the corral, a gate horse in the cow pen, an endurance horse when making a big circle, a cutting horse when sorting cattle. He must do it all and remain calm and relaxed.

And a ranch horse also must last a long time. The reason most do, as much as anything, isn't so much that ranch horses are physically right, but that they're mentally right. That means the ranch horse can relax and do his work for a long, long time.

The Versatile Horse

All the horsemanship skills presented in this book lead to developing a horse that's calm, relaxed and responsive enough to do the things ranch-style competitions require. The great thing about the ranch-type competitions is that they all come down to a versatile horse, one that can be ridden on the trail all day, punch cows for a week or compete in town on the weekend. More and more, it seems, that's what the recreational rider wants, too.

In the past, California horsemen had such versatile horses because they took the time to train horses correctly and to allow the horses to mature. But in the late 20th century we moved away from that versatile mount as horse breeding and training became increasingly specialized to produce younger horses that performed well in one field of expertise, such as cutting, reining or roping. Sometimes it almost seems horsemanship had become so patterned and locked into place that only a particular type of horse could fit the training process.

However, now the spotlight's shifting back to the versatility of ranch-horse competitions, which require decisions and timing, not programs and patterns. And that makes better all-around horses and horsemen as a result. The recreational rider now wants to be able to ride anywhere, as he sees ranch cowboys do, and he wants to feel safe no matter what he does horseback. With the average American age creeping higher each year, it's possible that the popular horse for pleasure-riding adults in the future might be a jack-of-all-trades similar to a kid's 4-H horse that performs well at shows and also is a pleasure to ride on the trail.

Working ranch cowboy competition includes cowgirls, too. This one's trying to milk a wild cow with her teammates' help.

Ranch Rodeo

Throughout the past century working ranch cowboys continued to join ranch teams and pit their skills against those of neighboring cowboys from nearby ranches. Although ranch rodeo was popular in many regions of the country, few people outside the livestock industry were even aware ranch rodeo existed.

Team penning is often an event in working ranch competition.

The Working Ranch Cowboys Association changed all that. Organized in 1985, the WRCA now hosts the annual WRCA World Championship Ranch Rodeo in Amarillo, Texas, each year. The WRCA now sanctions many ranch rodeos nationwide, most considered qualifying events for the annual finals.

For the most part, ranch rodeo is a team sport with the exception of the bronc-riding phase of competition. No fancy bronc saddles are allowed; cowboys compete with the same gear they use at work. Although only one ranch cowboy rides for the brand in that event, his points count toward the team's total standings. In addition to bronc riding, WRCA ranch teams, which include both men and women, also compete in wild-cow milking, cattle doctoring, team branding and team penning. The most coveted awards, however, are those presented to the best working horse and to the top hand.

WRCA membership requirements define a working ranch as any outfit that has at least a 300-head cow-calf operation or runs a minimum of 500 yearlings for at least 6 months of the year. WRCA participants must be ranch owners, full-time ranch employees or day workers, who have drawn at least $1,500 cowboying for a qualifying ranch in the preceding year.

Ranch-Horse Competitions

In addition to seeing which ranch cowboy can best another in rough-stock competition, through the years ranch cowboys also have pitted their best bridle horses against one another. California's stock-horse classes have been held for many years, and a few special events for working cow-horse enthusiasts, such as the World's Greatest Horseman, have found a following among top horsemen and spectators alike.

National Reined Cow Horse Association events continue to grow in popularity, particularly the prestigious annual NRCHA Snaffle Bit Futurity. This organization also honors the vaquero tradition with classes for hackamore, two-rein and full-bridle horses, demonstrating their expertise in reining maneuvers and their cow savvy.

The seeds for the Ranch Horse Association of America were sewn when early WRCA-sanctioned events included ranch-horse classes similar to those at NRCHA events. At RHAA-sanctioned events, working cowboys display their horses' handle and maneuverability as each contestant completes his flat work, boxes a cow at one end of the arena, fences and circles the cow in each direction and ultimately ropes the cow. Although judges score the cow work, there's also a time limit within which these tasks must be performed.

Many breed organizations, such as the American Quarter Horse Association, also feature ranch-cowboy and ranch-horse skills. AQHA ranch-horse versatility classes evaluate entries in five categories. The ranch riding portion evaluates a horse's walk, trot and lope and the smoothness of his transitions between these gaits. Ranch trail is similar to any trail course and uses a minimum of six obstacles. In ranch cutting a single numbered cow is cut from the herd and penned at the far end of the arena. The working-ranch horse class is similar to the RHAA competition previously described in which both reined work and fence work are evaluated. Ranch conformation is a halter class for working horses, and an everyday halter, rather than a show halter, is used. In fact, in each phase of competition, these working horses are shown in working gear.

Big Loops and Ranch Ropings

Ranch roping contests in many forms have become popular, too, and the interest continues to grow. Big-loop contests require a cowboy to have much finesse with a rope and a 20-foot loop, even if the roping actually is a timed-event. Other California-style ropings have become popular because they're slow, judged events, where a roper might take four or five shots at a critter,

Ranch-horse competition usually requires the rider to demonstrate that his — or her — horse is rope-broke.

but the loop he uses is the important thing. That type of roping is an art form.

Ropers are scored on the difficulty of the loops they throw. A low-scoring loop is a regular overhand or heel shot; they're effective loops, but pretty normal. A houlihan scores a bit higher, but not a lot because it's a very practical loop and not that fancy a throw. Some of the Spanish- or Mexican-style throws and backhand shots are among the

Working ranch rodeo competition isn't for the faint of heart.

most difficult. Basically, the more time it takes to practice a loop and get it right, the more difficult the loop and the higher the score.

Ranch-roping competitions in the northern United States, Montana and Wyoming, for example, are designed to show off the lifestyle. These events showcase methods for working horses and cattle slow and easy, where people take pride in their livestock handling. At the Northern Range Ranch Ropings, for example, different values are placed on the loops, and horsemanship is the big thing.

In this team competition one cowboy necks a yearling, one team member heels him, and they lay down the animal so the third team member can dismount, put a rope on the front feet and then brand or mark the cattle. In a three go-round competition, the team member who headed the yearling in round one, for example, can't head

another steer, but must take a heel shot or handle the doctoring and branding chores. So the competition comes back to the versatility of horse and rider.

The greatest rule at some of these events: Competitors can't break out of a trot. Loping a horse means disqualification, so horsemanship and livestock-handling skills are the focus. Everybody's more into the art form than the speed.

However, some regional ranch-roping events seem about like a ranch gather. Friends come and cheer, and sometimes a dog runs out to head the cow. It's all fun, but even the more relaxed events still allow people to slow down and pay attention to their horsemanship, too.

No matter anyone's preference, there are many ways to enjoy a seasoned, broke ranch-horse in the competitive arena, just as there are outside the pen and beyond.

RANCH HORSE PREFERENCES

At the Ranch Horse Association of America's National Finals held in conjunction with the Western Heritage Classic in Abilene, Texas, several ranch horsemen and -women discussed qualities they prize in their ranch horses. Here's their short list in no particular order.

1. A quiet willingness to operate on a loose rein across the pasture and during competition.
2. The cow savvy to do the necessary ranch work and the ability to demonstrate that same cow savvy in the competitive arena.
3. A gentleness and unwillingness to buck.
4. Correct conformation to hold up to the ranch work.
5. A pretty head and big, soft eye.
6. A stout, balanced, structurally correct horse that's strong enough to hold cattle when doctoring cows outside.
7. A trainable mind.
8. An extra bit of try.
9. A good disposition.
10. A horse with good, sloping shoulders that cinches up big (is deep through the chest) even though he might not be that large a horse.

The same cowboys and cowgirls shared tips about preparing for ranch-horse competition. Here's their list.

1. Pay attention to the little things every day at home, so the horse will work well at the event.
2. Perform only one maneuver at the time; don't let all the phases of competition become overwhelming.
3. Ride to get the best out of the horse, not to beat the other cowboys.
4. Try to figure out what the top hands are doing, then do it.
5. Be able to read a cow.
6. The horse doesn't have to be fast in his maneuvers as long as he's correct in what he does.
7. Read the rules. Know them backward and forward.
8. When a pattern's required, study and get that pattern in mind.
9. Show what your horse can do, not what he can't do.
10. Compete with a winning attitude.

FRAN DEVEREUX SMITH

Western Horseman Managing Editor Fran Devereux Smith has a broad-based background in the equine industry. A lifelong horsewoman, she grew up trail riding and showing horses regionally — primarily in reining, western pleasure, horsemanship and barrel racing, with some experience in halter and showmanship. A high-school rodeo competitor, Fran also was a member of her intercollegiate rodeo team, winning a regional barrel-racing championship and qualifying for the College National Finals Rodeo in that event and goat-tying. Along the way, she was named Miss Rodeo Arkansas and also won a rodeo association year-end all-around title.

Fran later taught horsemanship to riders of all ages, served as a 4-H horse-project leader, earned a state Quarter Horse association reining championship, showed in hunt-seat classes and team-penned. She has ridden trails in 25 states, worked cattle along the way, driven a wagon team occasionally and served as an officer or board member for several equine organizations. Such varied horse-industry experience has been an asset in her work as an equine journalist.

Books Published by
WESTERN HORSEMAN®

ARABIAN LEGENDS by Marian K. Carpenter
280 pages and 319 photographs. Abu Farwa, *Aladdinn, *Ansata Ibn Halima, *Bask, Bay-Abi, Bay El Bey, Bint Sahara, Fadjur, Ferzon, Indraff, Khemosabi, *Morafic, *Muscat, *Naborr, *Padron, *Raffles, *Raseyn, *Sakr, Samtyr, *Sanacht, *Serafix, Skorage, *Witez II, Xenophonn.

BACON & BEANS by Stella Hughes
144 pages and 200-plus recipes. Try the best in western chow.

CALF ROPING by Roy Cooper
144 pages and 280 photographs. Complete coverage of roping and tying.

CUTTING by Leon Harrel
144 pages and 200 photographs. Complete guide to this popular sport.

FIRST HORSE by Fran Devereux Smith
176 pages, 160 black-and-white photos, numerous illustrations. Step-by-step information for the first-time horse owner and/or novice rider.

HELPFUL HINTS FOR HORSEMEN
128 pages and 325 photographs and illustrations. WH readers and editors provide tips on every facet of life with horses and offer solutions to common problems horse owners share. Chapters include: Equine Health Care; Saddles; Bits and Bridles; Gear; Knots; Trailers/Hauling Horses; Trail Riding/Backcountry Camping; Barn Equipment; Watering Systems; Pasture, Corral and Arena Equipment; Fencing and Gates; Odds and Ends.

IMPRINT TRAINING by Robert M. Miller, D.V.M.
144 pages and 250 photographs. Learn to "program" newborn foals.

LEGENDS 1 by Diane Ciarloni
168 pages and 214 photographs. Barbra B, Bert, Chicaro Bill, Cowboy P-12, Depth Charge (TB), Doc Bar, Go Man Go, Hard Twist, Hollywood Gold, Joe Hancock, Joe Reed P-3, Joe Reed II, King P-234, King Fritz, Leo, Peppy, Plaudit, Poco Bueno, Poco Tivio, Queenie, Quick M Silver, Shue Fly, Star Duster, Three Bars (TB), Top Deck (TB) and Wimpy P-1.

LEGENDS 2 by Jim Goodhue, Frank Holmes, Phil Livingston, Diane Ciarloni
192 pages and 224 photographs. Clabber, Driftwood, Easy Jet, Grey Badger II, Jessie James, Jet Deck, Joe Bailey P-4 (Gonzales), Joe Bailey (Weatherford), King's Pistol, Lena's Bar, Lightning Bar, Lucky Blanton, Midnight, Midnight Jr, Moon Deck, My Texas Dandy, Oklahoma Star, Oklahoma Star Jr., Peter McCue, Rocket Bar (TB), Skipper W, Sugar Bars and Traveler.

LEGENDS 3 by Jim Goodhue, Frank Holmes, Diane Ciarloni, Kim Guenther, Larry Thornton, Betsy Lynch
208 pages and 196 photographs. Flying Bob, Hollywood Jac 86, Jackstraw (TB), Maddon's Bright Eyes, Mr Gun Smoke, Old Sorrel, Piggin String (TB), Poco Lena, Poco Pine, Poco Dell, Question Mark, Quo Vadis, Royal King, Showdown, Steel Dust and Two Eyed Jack.

LEGENDS 4
216 pages and 216 photographs. Several authors chronicle the great Quarter Horses Zantanon, Ed Echols, Zan Parr Bar, Blondy's Dude, Diamonds Sparkle, Woven Web/Miss Princess, Miss Bank, Rebel Cause, Tonto Bars Hank, Harlan, Lady Bug's Moon, Dash For Cash, Vandy, Impressive, Fillinic, Zippo Pine Bar and Doc O' Lena.

LEGENDS 5 by Frank Holmes, Ty Wyant, Alan Gold, Sally Harrison
248 pages, including about 300 photographs. The stories of Little Joe, Joe Moore, Monita, Bill Cody, Joe Cody, Topsail Cody, Pretty Buck, Pat Star Jr., Skipa Star, Hank H, Chubby, Bartender, Leo San, Custus Rastus (TB), Jaguar, Jackie Bee, Chicado V and Mr Bar None.

LEGENDS 6 by Frank Holmes, Patricia Campbell, Sally Harrison, GloryAnn Kurtz, Cheryl Magoteaux, Heidi Nyland, Bev Pechan, Juli S. Thorson
236 pages, including about 270 photographs. The stories of Paul A, Croton Oil, Okie Leo Flit Bar, Billietta, Coy's Bonanza, Major Bonanza, Doc Quixote, Doc's Prescription, Jewels Leo Bar, Colonel Freckles, Freckles Playboy, Peppy San, Mr San Peppy, Great Pine, The Invester, Speedy Glow, Conclusive, Dynamic Deluxe and Caseys Charm

NATURAL HORSE-MAN-SHIP by Pat Parelli
224 pages and 275 photographs. Parelli's six keys to a natural horse-human relationship.

PROBLEM-SOLVING, Volume 1 by Marty Marten
248 pages and over 250 photos and illustrations. Develop a willing partnership between horse and human — trailer-loading, hard-to-catch, barn-sour, spooking, water-crossing, herd-bound and pull-back problems.

PROBLEM-SOLVING, Volume 2 by Marty Marten
A continuation of Volume 1. Ten chapters with illustrations and photos.

RAISE YOUR HAND IF YOU LOVE HORSES by Pat Parelli w. Kathy Swan
224 pages and over 200 black and white and color photos. The autobiography of the world's foremost proponent of natural horsemanship. Chapters contain hundreds of Pat Parelli stories, from the clinician's earliest remembrances to the fabulous experiences and opportunities he has enjoyed in the last decade. As a bonus, there are anecdotes in which Pat's friends tell stories about him.

RANCH HORSEMANSHIP by Curt Pate w. Fran Devereux Smith
220 pages and over 250 full color photos and illustrations. Learn how almost any rider at almost any level of expertise can adapt ranch-horse-training techniques to help his mount become a safer more enjoyable ride. Curt's ideas help prepare rider and horse for whatever they might encounter in the round pen, arena, pasture and beyond.

REINING, Completely Revised by Al Dunning
216 pages and over 300 photographs. Complete how-to training for this exciting event.

RIDE SMART, by Craig Cameron w. Kathy Swan
224 pages and over 250 black and white and color photos. Under one title, Craig Cameron combines a look at horses as a species and how to develop a positive, partnering relationship with them, along with good, solid horsemanship skills that suit both novice and experienced riders. Topics include ground-handling techniques, hobble-breaking methods, colt-starting, high performance maneuvers and trailer-loading. Interesting sidebars, such as trouble-shooting tips and personal anecdotes about Cameron's life, complement the main text.

RODEO LEGENDS by Gavin Ehringer
Photos and life stories fill 216 pages. Included are: Joe Alexander, Jake Barnes & Clay O'Brien Cooper, Joe Beaver, Leo Camarillo, Roy Cooper, Tom Ferguson, Bruce Ford, Marvin Garrett, Don Gay, Tuff Hedeman, Charmayne James, Bill Linderman, Larry Mahan, Ty Murray, Dean Oliver, Jim Shoulders, Casey Tibbs, Harry Tompkins and Fred Whitfield.

ROOFS AND RAILS by Gavin Ehringer
144 pages and 128 black-and-white photographs plus drawings, charts and floor plans. How to plan and build your ideal horse facility.

STARTING COLTS by Mike Kevil
168 pages and 400 photographs. Step-by-step process in starting colts.

THE HANK WIESCAMP STORY by Frank Holmes
208 pages and over 260 photographs. The biography of the legendary breeder of Quarter Horses, Appaloosas and Paints.

TEAM PENNING by Phil Livingston
144 pages and 200 photographs. How to compete in this popular family sport.

TEAM ROPING WITH JAKE AND CLAY by Fran Devereux Smith
224 pages and over 200 photographs and illustrations. Learn about fast times from champions Jake Barnes and Clay O'Brien Cooper. Solid information about handling a rope, roping dummies and heading and heeling for practice and in competition. Also sound advice about rope horses, roping steers, gear and horsemanship.

WELL-SHOD by Don Baskins
160 pages, 300 black-and-white photos and illustrations. A horse-shoeing guide for owners and farriers. Easy-to-read, step-by-step how to trim and shoe a horse for a variety of uses. Special attention is paid to corrective shoeing for horses with various foot and leg problems.

WESTERN TRAINING by Jack Brainard
With Peter Phinny. 136 pages. Stresses the foundation for western training.

WIN WITH BOB AVILA by Juli S. Thorson
Hardbound, 128 full-color pages. Learn the traits that separate horse-world achievers from also-rans. World champion horseman Bob Avila shares his philosophies on succeeding as a competitor, breeder and trainer.

Western Horseman, established in 1936, is the world's leading horse publication. For subscription information: 800-877-5278.
To order other Western Horseman books: 800-874-6774 • Western Horseman, Box 7980, Colorado Springs, CO 80933-7980.
Web site: **www.westernhorseman.com.**